DEALING
WITH DARWIN

DEALING WITH DARWIN

HOW GREAT COMPANIES INNOVATE AT EVERY PHASE OF THEIR EVOLUTION

GEOFFREY A. MOORE

CAPSTONE

Published in the UK by   Capstone (A Wiley Company) The Atrium, Southern Gate, Chichester,
West Sussex PO19 8SQ, England

Telephone   (+44) 1243 779777

Copyright © 2006   Geoffrey A. Moore

Published by arrangement with Portfolio: a member of Penguin Group (USA) Inc.

Email (for orders and customer service enquiries): cs-books@wiley.co.uk
Visit our Home Page on www.wiley.com

Other Wiley Editorial Offices

John Wiley & Sons Inc., 111 River Street, Hoboken, NJ 07030, USA

Jossey-Bass, 989 Market Street, San Francisco, CA 94103-1741, USA

Wiley-VCH Verlag GmbH, Boschstr. 12, D-69469 Weinheim, Germany

John Wiley & Sons Australia Ltd, 42 McDougall Street, Milton, Queensland 4064, Australia

John Wiley & Sons (Asia) Pte Ltd, 2 Clementi Loop #02-01, Jin Xing Distripark, Singapore 129809

John Wiley & Sons Canada Ltd, 22 Worcester Road, Etobicoke, Ontario, Canada M9W 1L1

Wiley also publishes its books in a variety of electronic formats. Some content that appears in print
may not be available in electronic books.

A catalogue record for this book is available from the British Library

ISBN-10 1-84112-717-5
ISBN-13 978-1-84112-717-0

Typeset in 10.75 pt on 15.75pt New Baskerville
Printed and bound in Great Britain by TJ International Ltd, Padstow, Cornwall
This book is printed on acid-free paper responsibly manufactured from sustainable forestry
in which at least two trees are planted for each one used for paper production.

To Marie

Always.

ACKNOWLEDGMENTS

Writing any book is inevitably a journey, but I have to say this one took a more roundabout path to its destination than I had imagined. I remember vividly circulating the first draft to a long list of colleagues, fully expecting a chorus of accolades (we authors lack not for fantasy or hubris). Imagine my chagrin when not a few came back with gentle but unmistakable guidance that I had spread myself all over the map writing a tome that was impossible to follow. That trip to the woodshed was followed by one back to the drawing board, out of which came the text you are about to read. I am very proud of this book, and thus I am deeply grateful to the following people who helped me find it amid the flotsam and jetsam of that first effort:

- My first vote of thanks goes to my fellow partners at TCG Advisors—Philip Lay, Lo-Ping Yeh, Tom Kosnik, and John Metcalfe—whose contribution to these ideas is so intertwined with my own as to be inextricable. Consulting is a wonderful profession for an author, for clients give you instant feedback on the viability of your ideas. Fellow consultants are then there to help you sort out the good bits from the bad, patch things up, and trot them out again. I have been blessed to have some of the best as colleagues.

- In proximity to this group are my colleagues at Mohr Davidow Ventures, especially my fellow venture partners, Donna Novitsky and Randy Strahan. Both have made wonderfully pragmatic sounding boards for ideas that were anything from formative to just half baked.

- I owe a similar debt of gratitude to my office-sharing companions at The Chasm Group and The Chasm Institute, particularly to Paul Wiefels and Michael Eckhardt, both of whom gave me detailed critiques of the first draft that were extremely helpful.

- But there were others who waded in deep as well. Of these I would like to particularly acknowledge Bill Meade, who meticulously and thoroughly critiqued the entire manuscript; Kevin Kennedy, who forthrightly but considerately communicated to me the incomprehensibility of the first draft; Avery Gavigan, who gave superb advice on ideas and examples from the consumer sector; and Mark Deck, Patrick Gordon, John Ciacchella, and Francis Hawkings, who gave great advice from a consulting perspective.

- Finally, this entire line of thinking got its start in an article opportunity provided by Tom Stewart and Julia Kirby at *The Harvard Business Review,* "Darwin and the Demon." That stimulus and their encouragement were the true seed of this book.

So much for the writing. Then there is the story. And here I owe an extraordinary debt to John Chambers and the entire executive team at Cisco who made themselves accessible to me time and again and shared their innermost thoughts on more than a few volatile subjects. The Cisco case study is for me a highlight of the book that follows because it allowed me to ground a great deal of theory in a real-world context.

After the story comes the editing. Here I have enjoyed the support of a terrific tandem, Jim Levine and Adrian Zackheim, my literary agent and publisher, respectively. When I was lost in the woods between the first and second drafts, it was they who came and found me and helped show the way out. This is our fifth book together, albeit our first at Portfolio, and I am delighted to have their support.

Of course, books don't happen in a vacuum. They have to make their way through a work life littered with other commitments. Here I have the inestimable assistance of one of the world's great personal assistants, Pat Granger. Pat and I have been working together for more than five years, and it is simply a joy to have her support. And when we have needed to reach out for some extra help, Rita Gray, the other half of the administrative team, has been generous with her support as well.

Finally, work itself is but a part of a larger life, in my case one shaped by my family, my children, Margaret, Michael, and Anna (along with some increasingly significant others, Daniel and Dave), and most of all, Marie. We have been married thirty-seven years, and each one has seen her role deepen in my life. When I write a book, my head goes on an extended walkabout, and I make poor company as a life companion. That she is there for me nonetheless is more important and wonderful than I could possibly express.

CONTENTS

PREFACE: WHAT THIS BOOK IS ABOUT AND HOW IT CAME TO BE

You have read the headlines. You know about the dismal economic performance in the airline industry. You have seen the recurrent layoffs in the automotive industry. You have read about how the computer industry is maturing into a slower growth sector. You have heard about how radically escalating R&D costs in the pharmaceutical industry are producing fewer and fewer drugs. You may not have learned that in 2003, when the Indian consulting firm Infosys hired ten thousand new professionals, they chose them from a pool of *1.2 million qualified applicants*. But you do know that business is becoming increasingly competitive; that globalization, deregulation, and commoditization are taking their toll everywhere you look; and that your company is under increasing pressure to innovate.

So what do you call all this pressure you are under? We call it dealing with Darwin. That's because free-market economies operate by the same rules as organic systems in nature:

- Competition for the scarce resources of customer purchases creates hunger that stimulates innovation.

- Customer preferences for one innovation over another create a form of natural selection that leads to survival-of-the-fittest outcomes.

- Each new generation restarts the competition from a higher standard of competence than the prior generation.

- Thus over time successful companies must evolve their competence or become marginalized.

Keeping up with this continual raising of the bar is an unending challenge. Successful companies share a proud heritage of past accomplishments from which their current franchises were born, legacies that are now theirs to continue. They bring to this task a suite of core competences with proven capability to create competitive advantage. There is every reason to be optimistic. But each new day also carries with it odd currents and disturbing reports of marketplace setbacks. There are signals that the old maneuvers no longer work quite as well as they used to, that the competition has learned to neutralize some of your moves, that you must evolve.

Dealing with Darwin is about leading your enterprise's evolution. It is about creating competitive advantage in an increasingly commoditizing world. To lead that effort, you must continually reappraise what role your company is playing in the market ecosystem, how the landscape of competition is changing, where your competitive advantage has come from in the past and where it is likely to come from in the future, what kinds of differentiation will be most rewarded, and what kinds of innovation are most required. That is the outward-facing portion of our story. At the same time, you need to take a fresh look at your internal dynamics, at what happens when core competences cease to differentiate, how resources must be shifted to new areas, how deeply threatening such changes can be, how a kind of protective inertia emerges as the enemy of destabilizing innovations, and what kinds of management responses can best deal with this inertia and redirect its energy toward innovation. That is the inward-facing portion of our story.

In sum, then, this is a book about innovation and inertia. It seeks to address the fundamental question that Darwinism poses: How can we innovate forever? Because that is precisely what natural selection forces us to do. Evolution requires us to continually refresh our competitive advantage, sometimes in dribs in drabs, sometimes in major cataclysms, but always with some part of our business portfolio at risk and in play. To innovate forever, in other words, is not an aspiration; it is a design specification. It is not a strategy; it is a requirement.

Innovation comes in many forms, far more than management teams usually acknowledge. In the chapters that follow, we will identify more than a dozen innovation types and explore where, when, and how each may be used to meet the Darwinian imperative. For just as nature's ecosystems reward different strategies for living in different niches, so markets reward different types of innovation in different segments. The challenge for management teams is to choose the type of innovation appropriate to their situation and to exploit it deeply enough to create definitive separation from their direct competitors. How to do so successfully is the focus of the central section of this book.

The longer one has been at this exercise in continual renewal, the more one develops a legacy of past achievements. This should encourage us, but occasionally it instead gives rise to anxieties: What if we have lost our ability to innovate? What if we are not worthy successors to our forbearers? Can our people still compete? Do we really get it? And even if we do, can we still get it to market? Can we make it fast enough, cheap enough, and bold enough? Or will the planners and the analyzers and the consultants and the advisers all swarm around the innovation with their unending litany of questions and comments and prevent it from seeing the light of day? These are thoughts that truly do keep management teams up at night.

But let's step back a minute and analyze our anxiety. How is it possible that innovation could be a significant challenge in any human enterprise? We are the most innovative beings ever to grace this planet. We love to innovate, as any parent, spurred by an odd moment of silence to investigate what the children are up to, can readily testify. We share our new ideas, we build upon the ideas of others, we incorporate them into our products and processes, we pass them on to future generations—and still, every year more and more keep coming, tumbling out one after another, endlessly jostling for our individual and collective attention. How in the world could any corporation have a problem with innovation?

It turns out there are a myriad of answers to this question. Some corporations get stuck on a particular type of innovation, for example, and fail to adapt to market changes that diminish its impact. Others get anxious about growth and fund too many innovations, creating an internal traffic jam of sorts, with frustrations and tempers to match. Still others innovate injudiciously, squandering the scarce resources of time, talent, and management attention on initiatives that do not further competitive advantage. And finally, all corporations striking out in a new direction are impeded by the force of inertia. Indeed, the more successful their past innovations have been, the stronger the resistance to any subsequent innovation changing the course.

All of which leads us to a fundamental premise of this book: Innovation and inertia are so deeply intertwined that both must be engaged concurrently for any progress to occur. This is not the common practice. Most companies tackle the two in series, not in parallel: Invest. Downsize. Invest. Downsize. This rhythm of binge and purge is often masked by the oscillation of business cycles, but the two should not be confused. Although business is inherently cyclical, the need for innovation and the resistance of inertia are perennial, and every phase of the cycle creates the opportunity to address the pair in tandem.

At the heart of our effort to understand innovation and inertia as a single system is a framework called core/context analysis. *Core* is defined as any aspect of a company's operations that creates differentiation leading to customer preference during a purchase decision. It is innovation in service to competitive advantage. *Context*, by contrast, represents everything else, all other work performed by the enterprise. The work is extremely important and can be highly valued, but it does *not* differentiate you from your competition. It does, however, play host to the forces of inertia.

The formula for tackling innovation and inertia in tandem is simple: Extract resources from context to repurpose for core. This is offered not as an occasional prescription but rather as the very fabric of day-to-day business operations. It is in effect the formula that fulfills the innovate forever specification. Its intent is to bind investment to frugality, strategy to execution, and long-term value creation to short-term financial return. It decries the notion that one line of business can be managed as an innovationless cash cow while some other line is treated as an inertia-free rising star. Every business at every stage of its life cycle can and should attend to both ends of its innovation-inertia spectrum simultaneously. By deconstructing legacy concurrently with developing new futures, management not only clears the path for innovation but also recoups the resources with which to fund it.

The idea of extracting resources from context to repurpose for core is uncomplicated, logical, rewarding—and more than a little challenging to execute. And that brings us to another dimension of this book, an extended case study of a company that is deeply engaged in just such an effort.

The company is Cisco Systems, the market leader for Internet-enabling network equipment. During its rise to prominence in the 1990s, the company innovated dramatically not only in its products but also in its business practices. Indeed, the two became tightly linked, for Cisco's formula was to use its products to create productivity results that were astounding. The company in essence became its own best advertisement, and management teams from around the world traveled to San Jose to learn more about its best practices.

When the tech bubble burst, many assumed that Cisco's best practices had been exposed as simply passing fads. Subsequent results, however, proved otherwise. Three years into the worst recession the technology sector had ever known, Cisco was generating $1 billion of free cash flow—per quarter! Its market cap, which had been four times the sum of its ten closest competitors during the bubble, was now *ten times* that sum. Clearly there was merit and stay-ing power to Cisco's ways, and not surprisingly, the company re-mains a favorite target for Fortune 500 benchmarking.

That's the good news. The bad news is that investors already have priced all that performance into Cisco's stock, and now they are asking once again, as they are wont to do, what have you done for me lately? This calls for a new generation of best practices. At the same time, some of the older best practices, ones optimized to take advantage of hypergrowth markets, are not presently called for. Cisco, in other words, is being asked to evolve. It must innovate again, but this time it must concurrently deal with the burden of legacy. That is the essence of the dealing-with-Darwin challenge.

Remarkably, it is one that is being chronicled while in progress, by invitation of the CEO. In the fall of 2002, John Chambers ap-proached me about writing a book about Cisco. John felt—rightly, in my view—that if companies really understood the power of network-enabled virtual organization, they would become bigger and better customers for Cisco's offerings. Since Cisco is one of the leading practitioners of this model—and since he couldn't very well offer up someone else's company for study—he wondered if I might be interested in the task.

Every bone in my body wanted to say yes to this invitation. I had known the company since 1996, was on friendly terms with much of the management team, and had huge respect both for its culture and its accomplishments. At the same time, however, I couldn't quite see how this was a book I would feel comfortable writing. It seemed as if it called more for a journalist than a management author. More-over, there were a number of books coming out about the company at that time, and I thought some of them might fill the bill. John was adamant, however, that they would not, that what was wanted *was* a book about management ideas, not a lionizing puff piece or a dish-and-tell corporate saga. And in order to ensure that I really under-stood Cisco's ways, we agreed I would participate in a series of key projects, working closely with the executives involved, attending the key meetings where tough issues got exposed and critiqued, leveraging my consulting expertise to add value wherever I could.

Dealing with Darwin is an outcome of that collaboration. It is not a book *about* Cisco. It is a book about how to innovate forever in which the example of Cisco provides a recurrent case study that interleaves with each of the chapters. The chapters themselves are filled with examples from other companies—more than one hundred of them—and I specifically banished Cisco from these pages in order to better balance the book. You do not, in other words, have to be an aficionado of the networking sector to engage with the pages that follow.

I must confess, however, that the majority of the cited examples do come from the high-tech sector. This is simply a reflection of my twenty years of consulting experience in technology-enabled markets. I first wrote about these challenges fifteen years ago in a book called *Crossing the Chasm,* which focused on the challenges of gaining mainstream adoption for disruptive technologies. It was subsequently followed by *Inside the Tornado,* which dealt with the opposite problem of how to deal with the market share battles that ensue from explosive adoption of a new technology. That in turn led to *The Gorilla Game,* a book that reframed the implications of the tornado in terms of its impact on equity investing. And most recently it led to *Living on the Fault Line,* which looked at the challenges of managing businesses on the other end of all these forces where the goal is not to disrupt but rather to avoid being disrupted.

It is certainly fair to say, then, that the technology sector is at the epicenter of all my work. But with each book, the scope has widened to take in more and more companies, in part because the world is becoming increasingly technology enabled, and in part because the technology sector is becoming more like the rest of the economy. No longer does anyone think technology companies are exempt from the laws of gravity. No longer are words like *consolidation, commoditization, legacy,* and *inertia* inapplicable to the sector. The sector is coming of age.

As it does so, it is realizing that its whole approach to innovation has to evolve. For thirty years the sector has ridden wave after wave of semiconductor-technology-enabled price/performance improvements provided by the natural unfolding of Moore's law. But that law is breaking down, if not physically, at least economically, and it is no longer reasonable to forecast the recurrent massive churn in computing infrastructures that drove so much spending in the past three decades. That means that technology innovation must give way to other sources of competitive advantage, and the sector is struggling to discover just what those other sources ought to be. As it does so, it takes on more and more of the look of other sectors. Indeed, technology executives are looking to these other sectors for guidance as they begin to try out the various strategies and tactics other industries adopted once they had come to the end of their expansionist eras.

Meanwhile, as technology companies are becoming more like established enterprises in other sectors, so those enterprises are becoming more like technology companies. We saw it first in the financial sector, where computing has become the factory that manufactures its products and services. Then it moved to health care, as pharmaceutical research has become increasingly focused on the genome, which can neither be decoded nor manipulated without massive computing help. Now we see it in retail, as e-tailing migrates from being a novel business model to an inherent part of every major retailer's portfolio of options. And we are seeing it in media, as content becomes digitized, and the Internet is transformed from a communications channel to a media property in its own right. And we are seeing it in the automotive industry, where more and more of the differentiating features of a new car come from semiconductor-enabled electronics, be it the entertainment system, automatic climate control, in-car navigation, dashboard displays, or mechanical controls.

All of us, then, are exposed to the full range of innovation types from which competitive advantage can be created, from the disruptive innovations that birth new categories to the sustaining innovations that maintain them and the renewal innovations that reinvent them. All of us are living under Darwin's design requirement, perpetually forced to come up with new moves to win the next round of marketplace competition. Is it any surprise then that we all have a lot to learn from each other? So whether we are Cisco or SYSCO, Sun or Sunoco, the Oracle of Redwood Shores or the oracle of Omaha, SAP or ADP, we would all like some help dealing with the pressure to reinvent ourselves all the time.

That is the purpose of the book that follows. It is divided into three sections. The first, Foundational Models, presents a set of three frameworks that cast new light on the domain of innovation. The first of these frameworks focuses on the economics of innovation, specifically on the need to create sufficient separation between our offers and the competition's to win our targeted revenue at our targeted price margin. The second focuses on the category dynamics that surround innovation, setting the groundwork for understanding why different types of innovation are more effective at different points in the maturity of a category. And the third focuses on business architecture, specifically the contrast between high-volume and high-complexity business models, and how innovation plays out very differently in these two environments.

From these beginnings we then turn to the first of our two primary topics, Managing Innovation. The chapters in this section provide detailed examinations of some fourteen different types of innovation, providing more than one hundred examples of how companies have used one type or another to create definitive separation from their competition and to sustain it over a prolonged interval. They include a catalog of opportunities from which you can select and develop the most promising type for your situation, and the last chapter in this sequence provides a methodology for leading your organization through that process.

But it is one thing to see the promised land of competitive differentiation and another to lead your people to it. Many aren't sure they want to go, and some actively try to hold the rest back. That brings us to the third and final section of this book, Managing Inertia. It is about the twin arts of extracting resources from context and repurposing them for core. It teaches the kind of recycling behavior that all ecosystems reward. It is nowhere near as novel to implement as one might think. But it will require the voluntary, indeed the enthusiastic, cooperation of all parties in the equation, and securing that takes time, intelligence, empathy, and patience. The frameworks in this section provide a vocabulary for conducting the dialogues that enable this outcome.

And I do believe the time has come for those dialogues. The world economy is undertaking another of its major migrations, the sort of thing it seems to do every century or so, where it transplants the center of economic advantage to a new geography. In the past five centuries we have seen it migrate from the bankers of Italy to the traders of the Netherlands, from thence to the imperial forces of France, Germany, and England, and then in the twentieth century across the Atlantic Ocean to the United States. Now we are seeing this migrant cross the Pacific Ocean, and there are few economists who do not believe that Asia, led by China and India, will be the center of economic power in the twenty-first century.

Obviously, any such migration has huge implications for competitive advantage strategy. It is a rare business plan indeed that will not have to rewrite itself from the ground up. This is not to say that you have to get it all done by next Monday—evolution proceeds more gradually than that—but it does call for you to step back and reflect. And the sooner you start, the sooner you will be able to extract yourself from those commitments that make you vulnerable and establish those commitments that will strengthen your new position.

With that thought in mind, let us turn to the task at hand.

PART ONE

FOUNDATIONAL MODELS

Innovation and inertia are two forces that established enterprises have struggled with since barter was the only form of trade. These struggles are rooted in a fog of misunderstanding, and the purpose of this section is to dispel this mist so we can get on with the business of managing our enterprises.

The specific myths that we need to dispel are as follows:

1. Innovation in and of itself is valuable.

2. Innovation becomes less necessary and less possible as categories mature.

3. The essence of innovation is the same in any company.

What we will see by the end of chapter 1 is that innovation is valuable only if it helps us achieve economic advantage. Its greatest value is when it differentiates us from our competitors sufficiently that customers prefer our offers to theirs and will pay a premium to support that preference. It also has value when it helps neutralize our rivals' competitive advantages over us and when it helps us improve our own productivity and thus profitability. But we should realize there is a lot of innovation going on today in our company that meets none of these criteria, that is in fact creating waste. Managing innovation successfully requires us to redirect that energy into economically rewarding outcomes.

In chapter 2 we will see innovation through a different lens, looking at how, as categories mature, customers reward different forms of innovation. There is no time, however, when the market rewards ceasing to innovate. Even at the very end of a category's life cycle, there are still opportunities to create superior economic returns from innovation if it is of the appropriate type. Success does, however, require aligning the type of innovation selected with the category's prevailing dynamics, and the purpose of this chapter is to set up that alignment.

Finally, there is another form of alignment that is also required between the tactics of innovation and the business architecture of the firm deploying it. In chapter 3 we show that each of the two primary architectures of business, the volume-operations model that underlies consumer transactions and the complex-systems model that underlies enterprise commerce, has a distinctive approach to innovation that is contraindicated in the other architecture. Professionals whose careers lead them to switch between these two venues must rethink and revalue their experiences in the context of the situation they are currently in. Few rules of thumb work the same, or indeed at all, in both environments.

Once we have registered these insights, we will then move on to the primary focus of the book, managing innovation and overcoming inertia in established enterprises.

CHAPTER ONE

THE ECONOMICS
OF INNOVATION

The economic argument in favor of innovation focuses on pricing power. Without innovation, offerings become more and more like each other. They commoditize. As they do so, customers are able to play off one vendor against the next to get a lower price. Over time, the market stabilizes at prices at or below cost, creating returns for investors below the cost of capital, causing investment to flee the marketplace. By contrast, when innovation is applied, offers become more and more differentiated from one another, leading to different ones becoming the preferred choice for different market segments, giving those vendors pricing power within those segments. In this scenario the market stabilizes at prices well above cost, creating returns above the cost of capital, attracting more investment into the marketplace.

The fundamental principle that drives this argument is that when innovation creates differentiation, it creates attractive economic returns. This is not, however, the only possible outcome from innovation, so we need to put it in context. Consider the diagram on the following page.

The pie chart defines the possible returns from all innovation efforts in an enterprise: research projects, development programs, cross-functional initiatives, and the like. In addition to differentiation, there are three other possible outcomes, two of which are desired, one not. Although every organization would have a different

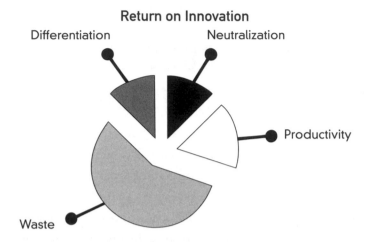

pie-chart allocation across these four categories, I have drawn this chart to be as provocative as possible.

The first of the alternative desired outcomes is neutralization. Its goal is to eliminate differentiation by catching up either to a competitor's superior performance or to a market standard one has fallen short of. When sport-utility vehicles (SUVs) first came out, Ford and a few others achieved differentiation with their entries. When every other car manufacturer came out with one, the goal was neutralization. Netscape achieved differentiation with the Internet browser; then Microsoft achieved neutralization. Citibank achieved differentiation with ATM machines in the 1970s; then all other banks achieved neutralization.

Neutralizing is an important adaptation to changing competitive dynamics, and it does call for innovation. Its economics are different, however, from those of differentiation. It does not create as great a positive return, in part because its function is to eliminate a negative return. The goals of innovation projects in service to neutralization, therefore, should be set differently. Here we are seeking good enough, not best in class, for two reasons: The first is that best in class, when it is not first to market, does not earn rewards commensurate with the investment required. The second is that time to market for neutralization has more impact than feature/function comparisons. The goal is to slow the other team down; and the shorter their period of market exclusivity, the less momentum they can build.

In addition to differentiation and neutralization, a third goal of innovation is productivity improvement. Here the intent is not to affect market outcomes but rather to achieve them at a lower cost. To be sure, productivity improvements can create differentiation if they are radical enough, and they can also be part of a neutralization effort to get your company up to a new par. But the majority of them are simply designed to cost-reduce a set of existing processes in order to either invest the savings elsewhere or increase profits.

Productivity improvement is essential to evolutionary adaptation because it frees resources that other forms of innovation can use. It requires significant innovation focused largely on reengineering existing processes based on either a better understanding of their dynamics or a better set of tools. The focus is on resource reclamation to ensure that the project pays for itself, and this is normally accomplished by reducing budget and head count. One place where many companies need to improve is in repurposing the resources that are freed up. Too often management resorts to layoffs and write-offs, disrupting both the workforce and the hosting social environment and sowing seeds of distrust and misalignment. This is a highly expensive and inefficient approach, and finding sounder alternatives is key to sustaining innovative performance—a topic we will discuss at length later in this book.

Differentiation, neutralization, productivity improvement—what's left? Waste. Wasted innovation falls into a number of classes. The first simply comprises those attempts at any of the other three goals that don't succeed. This is just part of business. Nothing is guaranteed, everything is a bet, and some bets lose. If a lot of bets lose, you probably ought to look into your betting process or change the bettors, but for the most part you just have to price such risks into your overall plan.

The other forms of waste are more pernicious. Neutralization efforts that go beyond the good-enough goal, often for reasons of pride, do not generate any additional economic returns—indeed, their returns are lower because you overspent the market requirement. Productivity efforts that go beyond cost-reduction or cycle-time improvement and branch into nice-to-have enhancements also represent a waste of resources. But the worst form of waste occurs when an innovation project actually succeeds in meeting its specified targets but fails to achieve competitive separation in the marketplace because it *did not go far enough.*

This is a horrible outcome. In effect, you have spent the resources for differentiation but have achieved the outcomes of neutralization. That means you get no net gain in pricing power, which means you are not getting the fundamental economic return that justifies innovation in the first place. You are sliding down a hazardous commoditization curve, and if you do not do something drastic in fairly short order, you will find yourself stuck at the bottom of the hill, with neither the energy nor the funds to get yourself back to the top.

This has been the fate of the Chevrolet division of General Motors and the personal computing division of HP, not to mention a whole host of airlines and telecommunications service providers. It is not that these companies do not innovate. It is that their offers do not achieve separation—and here is the kicker—*they were never designed to!*

Picture in your mind a Chevrolet sedan from the past ten years. Just try. Nothing? That's my point. Now can you picture a Corvette, a Chrysler PT Cruiser, a Cadillac Seville, a Hummer, a Mini Cooper? Of course you can. That's the other half of my point. Innovation for differentiation must be bold enough that, if it wins, it achieves separation. That's why Chrysler's failures are more memorable than Chevrolet's successes—the Viper and the Prowler, for two.

So why does this happen? How does innovation in service to differentiation get chartered in a way that, even if it wins, it loses? Sadly, all too easily. There are two deep-seated causes for innovation underperformance, and we are going to have to deal with both of them directly if we are to get out of the woods. The first is risk-reduction mentality and the second is lack of corporate alignment.

THE ENEMIES OF DIFFERENTIATION

Risk-reduction mentality encourages people to shun bold actions that jeopardize existing assets and relationships. It is based on staying close to norms, thereby leveraging the experience of the herd. As such, it is actually a positive evolutionary response to situations that do not reward differentiation. We call these situations context.

Risk reduction is the sensible strategy for managing context. There are penalties for failing to execute context properly but no reward for performing it brilliantly. So there is no upside to warrant taking risk and more than sufficient reasons to discourage it. Risk-averse behavior is the perfect tool for addressing such challenges.

But it is a horrible tool to deal with core. *Core* is the word we use to describe innovation that creates differentiation. To succeed with core, you most take your value proposition to such an extreme that competitors either cannot or will not follow. That's what creates the separation you seek. By definition you are separating from the herd, making the choices the herd will not—indeed should not—make. These are risk-bearing decisions, and you may well fail. But this time there is an upside to play for, the gain in pricing power that counteracts commoditization. So risk-averse behavior here is a losing strategy. All it does is increase the probability that the innovation will go to waste.

All would be well if we would just recognize this distinction and put our risk-reduction mind-set on hold when dealing with innovation issues. But this is not easily done, particularly if managing context is the bulk of your focus. Moreover, risk reduction is often a form of camouflage used by underperforming and disaffected employees who seek to avoid accountability or act out their frustrations in minor acts of passive-aggressive terrorism, pulling down anything that ventures to soar up. This creates huge frustration among leaders who cannot understand why everyone does not collaborate for the greater good.

That lack of collaboration, however, is often caused by those very same leaders' falling prey to the other enemy of innovation: lack of corporate alignment. To achieve breakaway differentiation requires a highly coordinated effort across the entire enterprise. It may well begin in a skunk works with a tiger team, but that is only the beginning. At the end of the day, every function in the corporation has to realign its priorities in order to amplify the innovation to breakaway status. Anything less is simply too easy for competitors to neutralize.

Thus PC vendors were able to neutralize Gateway but not Dell. Grocery retailers were able to neutralize Pack 'n Save but not Wal-Mart. Luxury hotels can catch up to the Ritz-Carlton but not the Four Seasons. Search engines can take on Ask Jeeves but not Google. Why? Because each of the breakaway companies is totally aligned end to end around a single defining value proposition.

Why is there not more of this alignment? The answer is that in most corporations innovation is a highly decentralized activity that proceeds on multiple fronts in multiple directions. This is actually good strategy, for it gives the corporation a portfolio of options from which to draw. The failure—and this is a failure of leadership, not of the rank and file—lies in the failure to prioritize one line of innovation above all others. We shrink from putting all our eggs in one basket. We hedge our bets. We would not do so if we had paid more attention in math class when the teacher was explaining vector addition. You remember vectors—those arrows that show the direction and magnitude of a given force. Remember what happens when you add them?

If management does not take a position on innovation strategy, the company's innovations will continue to bubble up, but they will not be aligned. If all are brought to market—and that is the default option in this scenario—none will achieve breakaway status.

This, in my view, is the pit into which HP has fallen. There was

Innovation Strategy

Remember Your Vector Math!

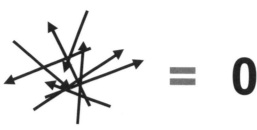

= 0

**Multiple innovation initiatives
Bubble-up management**

a time when each separate unit could innovate independently because each served a slightly different technical segment. That was the HP way. But once the company's markets converged into larger enterprise and consumer segments, its invention-focused strategy created waste, not differentiation. That is why it has been unable to catch and surpass Dell and IBM. It is not a rank-and-file problem. It is a leadership issue. Specifically, it is an issue of prioritizing and focusing, two favorite words of all consultants. They are so easy for us to say and so hard for you to do. Why is that?

Well, let's conduct a simple thought experiment based on the following pictures:

Core and Context

Jeff Gross, Getty Images

Core   **Context**

Say Tiger Woods comes to you for advice. He wants to know how much time he should allocate to core versus context. What would you tell him? If you are like most people, you would say, "Spend all your time on core and hire other people to worry about the context." But then he says, "You know, 90 percent of my revenue comes from context, not core. Are you sure I should not be spending more time there?" "No!" we say back confidently. "Use the revenue from context to buy more time to focus on your core! That's what will pay off in the end."

But that is not what we do ourselves. We allocate our time proportionately to revenue production, not competitive advantage achievement. We do precisely what we tell Tiger not to do. We urge him to trust that revenue will flow from competitive advantage focus, that he does not need to manage that himself. We need to take the same advice.

Focus and prioritization. Those are the issues when it comes to innovation for differentiation. If we do not break away from the herd, we have wasted our budget. In order to break away, we must overcome risk-reduction mentality and lack of corporate alignment. Neither is a natural act.

To take the next step we need a framework, one in which we can properly characterize the innovation options we have on our plate, surface the legitimate risk-reduction issues, call attention to the need for bold action to gain separation, and support achieving the corporate alignment necessary to breakaway differentiation. We call that framework the innovation types model, and it is the subject of the next chapter.

CHAPTER TWO

INNOVATION AND CATEGORY MATURITY

E conomic outcomes occur within categories. That is how customers sort out what they want to buy, what aisle to find it on in a grocery story, what price they expect to pay for it, what benefits they intend to gain. It is how investors allocate their portfolios, choosing first which sectors to invest in, then how much per sector, and only then which actual companies' stock they want to own. If you are going to be successful with innovation, you have to understand that different categories reward different types of innovation at different points in time.

Specifically, like most things under the sun, categories have a beginning, a middle, and an end. The economic dynamics of these phases are very different from one another, and it is important to locate where your category is in its life cycle before you set your innovation strategy. The purpose of this chapter is to provide a straightforward framework to assist in the process. It is called the category-maturity life cycle.

The model comprises five phases, labeled A through E. The first phase covers the coming into being of a new category and is rather complex in its own right, earning its own submodel called the technology-adoption life cycle. This arena has been the focus of several earlier books, most notably *Crossing the Chasm* and *Inside the Tornado*. If you are familiar with them, feel free to skim the next few pages; but if not, what follows is a recap of the key ideas involved.

The Category-Maturity Life Cycle

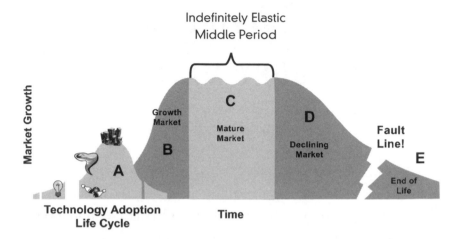

The roots of the technology-adoption life cycle lie in the different responses that people and organizations can make whenever a disruptive innovation is introduced into their midst. Essentially these are five, as illustrated by the following diagram:

Underlying Drivers in Growth Markets
Technology-Adoption Strategies

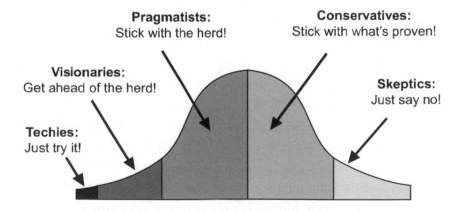

The five responses—Just try it, Get ahead of the herd, Stick with the herd, Stick with what's proven, and Just say no—represent the universe of alternative reactions, and the area of the total curve they occupy is proportional to their frequency of occurrence. Most people find themselves drawn to one of the five more than the others, and to the degree this is true, they can accurately categorize themselves with the labels in the diagram. But every category represents a new choice, and people can be late adopters in some and early adopters in others.

In the actual development of any specific market, individual choices are masked in the statistics of the group, and what we see are these five strategies interacting to create a pattern described by the technology-adoption life cycle, as follows:

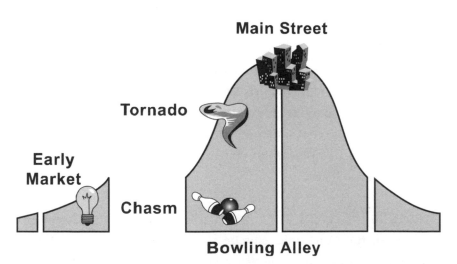

Technology-Adoption Life Cycle

Main Street

Tornado

Early Market

Chasm

Bowling Alley

Each of the icons represents a different stage in the unfolding of the model, and each stage represents in some sense a rebellion against and a repudiation of the prior stage. Here's how it plays out:

EARLY MARKET. When a disruptive innovation is first introduced, it initially attracts the attention of technology enthusiasts (who see it as cool) and visionaries (who see it as potentially disruptive). The latter fund projects to see if they can exploit the disruptive capabilities with a view toward gaining a dramatic competitive advantage over their peers. Pragmatic buyers are curious about these efforts but are far too cautious to actually participate in them. They are on the other side of the chasm. When these early adopting projects bear fruit, the press, fascinated, writes glowing articles describing the technology as the next big thing. A new category is named—digital marketplaces or genomic medicine, for example—but in truth it is not yet clear if it will be for real or just a flash in the pan.

THE CHASM. The chasm represents a betwixt-and-between state. Having now been in the marketplace for some time, the offer has lost its novelty, and visionaries no longer see it as a source of dramatic competitive advantage. They pursue their search for disruptive opportunities elsewhere. At the same time, there has not been the kind of widespread adoption necessary to convince pragmatists that it would be safe to purchase. Pragmatists with their stick-to-the-herd strategy need to see other pragmatists buying before they buy. As a result, the market is stalled. In 2005, examples of technologies seeking to pass through the chasm include grid computing and hydrogen fuel cells. Some artifacts, like gyro-balanced motor scooters, seem destined never to leave.

CROSSING THE CHASM. The only reliable way to exit the chasm is to target on the other side a niche market made up of pragmatists united by a common problem for which there is no known solution. Such "pragmatists in pain" are motivated to help the new technology cross the chasm if, and only if, it is packaged as a complete solution to their problem, what we learned first from Ted Levitt and then from Bill Davidow to call a whole product. Products that have crossed the chasm in recent years include RFID sensors (in the transportation and logistics market), DNA testing (in criminology), and online banking (for bill paying).

BOWLING ALLEY. In this phase of category maturity, the technology has gained acceptance among pragmatists in multiple-niche markets where it enables genuine solutions to uncommon problems. Wherever one niche adopts, adjacent niches become more susceptible—hence the bowling-pin metaphor. Within adopting niches, the new paradigm builds a loyal following among customers and value-chain partners who see a market in the making. Outside these niches it is becoming more widely known and accepted—but not yet adopted—by the general public. In 2005, voice-over IP, video conferencing, and applications using the Global Positioning System are in the bowling alley.

TORNADO. The technology has proved its usefulness in niche markets, and in the process, a killer app has emerged, something that makes it both broadly applicable and highly attractive to a mass market. Overnight it becomes perceived as necessary and standard. All the pragmatists who were hanging back from committing rush into the market to make sure they aren't left behind. Competition to capture this influx of new customers is fierce. Revenues grow at double- or even triple-digit rates, with investors bidding up the stock of every company that can participate in the category. In 2005, wireless LANs, flat-panel displays, and digital cameras are all inside the tornado.

MAIN STREET. The initial surge of hypergrowth subsides, leaving behind a market-share pecking order that is likely to persist for a long time to come. Customers have selected their vendor of choice and are now focused on deploying the technology more broadly. At the same time, they expect to see systematic improvements in the offerings and reward each with an uptick in purchasing. In 2005, laptop computers, cell phones, and Web sites are all on Main Street.

The technology-adoption life cycle comes to an end once the marketplace has completely assimilated the disruption that triggered it. In the case of automobiles, this happened sometime between the First and Second World Wars; in the case of television sets, in the 1960s; in the case of cell phones, in the past decade. Until this end is reached, the influence of technology-adoption forces is so dominant that it suppresses other dynamics.

Once assimilation has occurred, on the other hand, a new set of dynamics emerge, as noted by the remaining stages in The Category-Maturity Life Cycle chart on page 14:

PHASE B. GROWTH MARKETS. Even though the technology has been thoroughly assimilated, the offerings it has spawned remain in high demand for a while longer. Markets grow at double-digit rates; profit margins are healthy. In evolutionary terms, think of the population of a new species expanding to consume an untapped field of nutrients, a time when the condition of scarcity does not yet obtain. This is an exceedingly pleasant time to be a manager because you are presiding over what is essentially category growth generating superior economic returns while entailing little company-specific risk. In 2005, broadband networks, e-tailing, and information storage systems are all growth markets.

PHASE C. MATURE MARKETS. Category growth has flattened, and commoditization is under way. In Darwinian terms, we have reached the boundaries of our niche and are experiencing the condition of scarcity for the first time. Growth cannot be achieved by simply riding the wave of category expansion. Instead, it must come from increasing the yield from our current customer base or growing it at the expense of some other competitor. A round of natural selection ensues with a wave of consolidation thinning out the bottom of the pecking order. Market leaders create top-line growth both organically and through acquisitions. Customers now take the category for granted, and the press no longer writes about it. On the plus side, however, as long as there are no obsoleting technologies on the horizon, category risk is virtually nil. Markets can continue in this state indefinitely, experiencing round after round of renewal, renovation, and natural selection within category, subject to the continued absence of viable disruptive alternatives. In 2005, personal computers, ink-jet printers, and relational databases are all mature markets.

PHASE D. DECLINING MARKETS. The category has become thoroughly boxed in, opportunities to innovate are increasingly harder to find, and even the market dominators are finding it challenging to create attractive returns. Investors are restive about lack of growth, stagnant margins, and weak returns on capital. Next-generation technologies are on the horizon, although none has yet gone through its tornado phase. The market is ripe for some form of disruption, through either an obsoleting technology or a radically innovative business model. In 2005, mainframe computers, airline transportation, and voice telephony are all declining markets.

PHASE E. END OF LIFE. A disruptive technology has emerged, crossed the chasm, and entered the tornado. As a consequence, the incumbent technology has been rendered obsolete. The only customers left are conservatives and laggards. Although the category still has a long tail, its future prospects have been permanently curtailed, and investors in public markets flee. This is a classic time to take a company private to harvest the remaining economic value in the category, brand, distribution channel, and customer relationships. In 2005, film photography and consumer long distance have crossed over the fault line to their end-of-life phases.

In summary, if we step back from the model and look at it as a whole, we see a wide variety of market dynamics unfolding over the course of a given category's life cycle. Each locale in the landscape encourages or constrains competition in its own way, thereby privileging certain kinds of tactics while marginalizing others. It is for this reason that different innovation types come into prominence at different points of the life cycle.

In the coming section on managing innovation, we are going to overlay onto the category-maturity life cycle a series of innovation types. Each one will be situated in that phase of maturity where it can have the most influence. This will provide a key context for choosing which type of innovation will give your company the best chance to create definitive separation from your competitors in the battle for customer preference.

For now, let us introduce our case study company, Cisco, to illustrate how the category-maturity life cycle helps sort out a major enterprise's product portfolio.

CISCO'S PRODUCT PORTFOLIO

Cisco Systems is a network equipment company with more than $20 billion in revenues in 2005. Its products provide the backbone for the Internet and the World Wide Web, and it is the undisputed market leader in this sector. Although Internet infrastructure is relatively new, the pace of change in the technology sector is so rapid that the company has offerings in virtually every phase of the category-maturity life cycle. As such, it makes a good case example for demonstrating the use of the category-maturity life cycle model.

For readers unfamiliar with the technology sector, however, there is a second dimension of novelty to this exercise, and that is the introduction of a number of new product and market terms specific to Cisco's industry. In this chapter I will do my best to provide enough background to make them meaningful without boring you to tears. For those already familiar with this material, skimming is not only permitted but encouraged.

Life cycles unfold over time from left to right, but they are actually easier to understand if you read them right to left, beginning

Cisco Systems and
the Category-Maturity Life Cycle

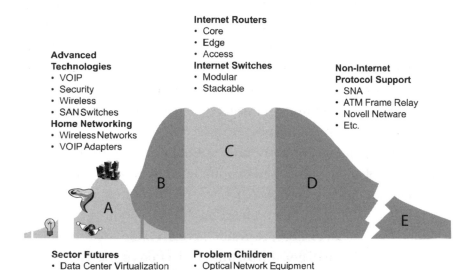

Internet Routers
- Core
- Edge
- Access

Advanced Technologies
- VOIP
- Security
- Wireless
- SAN Switches

Home Networking
- Wireless Networks
- VOIP Adapters

Internet Switches
- Modular
- Stackable

Non-Internet Protocol Support
- SNA
- ATM Frame Relay
- Novell Netware
- Etc.

Sector Futures
- Data Center Virtualization
- Service Provider Triple Play
- The Networked Home

Problem Children
- Optical Network Equipment
- Service Provider Access

with the most mature offers and ending with the most futuristic. That is what we are going to do here.

Cisco's business began in the 1980s with routing network traffic between incompatible proprietary networks, initially on Stanford University's campus between DEC and HP computers. It built up its initial market position by providing widespread support for as many different proprietary protocols as possible, including those from IBM and Novell, the leaders in wide area and local area networking, respectively. In the 1990s, however, one standard emerged to displace this Tower of Babel, the Internet protocol, or IP for short, and today virtually all network development is based upon IP. Nonetheless, legacy systems dependent upon prior generations of proprietary protocols will persist for decades.

This explains Cisco's ongoing commitment to a set of products in declining markets. It is not important to understand the specifics of these products, only to understand that they continue to provide mission-critical services in enterprise and telecommunications networks. Although they offer no opportunity for growth, customers assign a high value to their availability, reliability, and adaptability; and the products garner premium pricing. The company has no interest in renewing these categories, but there is also no urgency to jettison them either. So the current innovation strategy is to continue to harvest indefinitely, exiting only if a more strategic opportunity for the resources involved arises.

Such a strategic opportunity would likely come from the two mainstays of its current network equipment business: IP routers and IP switches. Routers and switches are relatively new concepts to most people, but their functions are easily understood. A router is a device that manages network traffic across a wide area, handling the long hauls, analogous to air travel between cities. The router category is segmented into core routers, the very long backbones that carry the traffic between distant places (think intercontinental airlines and 747s); edge routers, the intermediaries that manage it within a given region (regional airlines with short-haul planes); and access routers, the interfaces that get local traffic onto and off of the Internet (think airport-to-city shuttles and limos).

By contrast, a switch handles network traffic in a local area, getting it to the specific address it is intended for, analogous to subway, bus, taxi, and automobile travel within cities. The switch category is segmented into modular switches, which can be expanded via modules to provide advanced services (think of adding a club car to a commuter train), and stackable switches, which are optimized for base functionality (commuters in economy cars).

Routers and switches are the bread and butter of Cisco's business, contributing some 85 percent of 2005 revenues. The markets are quite healthy, growing overall between 8 percent and 15 percent depending on year, geography, and vertical sector. They are no longer hypergrowth markets, however, and the company has changed its strategy from one of pure product innovation to one of integration innovation complemented with line-extension innovation. Later in this book we will dig into the specifics of this shift from growth-market to mature-market innovation and what it has entailed.

Product innovation per se is certainly not passé at Cisco, but increasingly it is focused on advanced network technologies. The four that claim the most management attention at present are security, wireless, voice-over IP (VOIP), and storage area network (SAN) switches. Each of these markets is growing at the kind of high double-digit rates that reward the expense and risk of R&D-led innovation. At the same time, because they are hosted by and embedded in switches and routers, they also reinforce the company's mature-market value proposition of integration and line-extension innovation. In particular:

- Cisco's security offerings are the company's fastest growing product line, definitely inside the tornado. They began as appliance products and are migrating into switches and routers as Cisco pursues an innovation strategy called self-defending networks. In a world in which the value of digital assets is skyrocketing, attracting the attention of criminals and terrorists, this market can be expected to grow dramatically for the indefinite future. And because the attackers are focusing on both application and product innovation, so too must the defenders.

- Wireless networking is also inside the tornado, redefining the way we attach our laptops and personal digital assistants (PDAs) to the larger world of information services. Competition is fierce, and Cisco's initial offering was overkill for the market, allowing other companies to gain the early lead. It has fought back to regain the lead, including acquiring the company Airespace to fill a key gap in its product line. This is an example of acquisition innovation used not to renew a category but to reposition a company within it.

- VOIP is positioned further forward in the technology-adoption life cycle. It has crossed the chasm in business markets, specifically to manage voice traffic among branch-oriented businesses and to and from offshore call centers, and it is getting good early market traction among consumers with the rise of companies like Skype and Vonage. This is a time for additional product innovation, in expectation that all voice traffic will eventually become VOIP.

- Finally, SAN switches represent a relatively new foray for Cisco into the data center itself, helping to switch traffic back and forth between various computers and the data storage devices that serve them. While SANs are further along in their adoption than VOIP, they are based on a first-generation network protocol called Fibre Channel. Cisco expects this to be eventually displaced by IP protocol, which will greatly enhance its position in the category. For now it plays a relatively modest role, supplying the current generation of switches to flesh out the total storage offerings from partners like EMC.

Ultimately, fast growth in the consumer market for networking products led to another key acquisition, Linksys, the market leader in consumer applications of wireless routers and VOIP phone adapters. Because businesses are looking for the full-feature set from both these technologies, they are slower to adopt than consumers for whom a single-value proposition—cordless network support or free phone calls over the Internet—is quite sufficient. As a result, these market segments are being led from the consumer side, an increasingly frequent occurrence as digitized content takes a greater and greater share of our entertainment dollars. Cisco had no way to participate in consumer markets because its cost structure and business practices are optimized to serve enterprise customers. Acquiring Linksys filled this gap. At the same time, it exposed the company to the challenges of managing two very different business architectures in tandem, something we will discuss at length in the next chapter.

If we look further into the future, to the very front end of the technology-adoption life cycle and even into the white space to the left of that, there are three technology-enabled markets looming that are driving major ongoing investment at Cisco. They are Data Center Virtualization, Network Convergence, and The Networked Home. Each of these represents what amounts to a new universe of opportunity for Cisco, potentially as large or larger than the space it currently occupies. To be more specific:

- *Data Center Virtualization* makes every device in the data center able to share work with every other device, depending on specialization and current workload. This is made possible by interconnecting all devices via a single grid—in effect, a very high-speed high-traffic network confined to a single room (at least initially). It is a massive technical problem, requiring a whole new generation of switches with unprecedented performance capabilities. Whether those switches will come from a network equipment provider, a computer systems provider, or some other source remains to be seen, but it seems reasonable to assume a combination of some of each, and that alone opens up a market opportunity in the tens of billions of dollars for Cisco.

- *Network Convergence* is being driven by the competition between traditional telephone services companies, wireless operators, cable companies, and next-generation service providers, all focused on serving up digital content to consumers and corporations. At present its focus is the triple play: voice, data, and video. Today, although convergence is well under way, each of these networks is still largely separate from the other three. But all four are committed to an IP future, leading to what Cisco calls the network of networks. The implication of this transition is that Cisco, which has played relatively modestly in the voice and video markets historically, has enormous opportunity to take market share.

- *The Networked Home* is further out in the future, the natural outgrowth of the increasing digitization of consumer content, both commercial and personal. At present flat-panel video displays and iPods are garnering all the press, but in the future, as songs, movies, snapshots, family videos, and video telephony become part of our standard home entertainment package, we are going to want to access them independently from multiple rooms in our homes. And as we make those network investments, we will discover they can also support advanced management of a host of more mundane functions like security, air-conditioning, lighting, pool heating, garden watering, and the like. This is the future upon which the Linksys division of Cisco seeks to capitalize.

We cannot leave this survey of Cisco's business relative to the category-maturity life cycle without looking into a couple of problem children in the portfolio. Both dwell in the telecommunications service-provider sector. Raked by the forces of deregulation, service providers have been consolidating for some time and will continue to do so for the foreseeable future. This increases their buying power over network equipment providers, of whom there are more now than there will be in the future. To date, however, the pending consolidation has not come, which makes for the kind of brutal competition and profitless prosperity that characterized the computer industry before the emergence of Dell.

Cisco cannot ignore this sector by any means, since today it accounts for a quarter of its revenues, and one can only assume this will increase in the future as more and more network traffic migrates to an on-demand utility-provided model. But which vendors will supply these operations, and which business model will best thrive, remain to be seen.

In the short term, two areas represent the most severe challenges. The first is optical network equipment, which is absolutely essential to handle the volume of traffic that current and future scenarios demand, but it is also an overbuilt sector where Cisco does not have dominant market share and where it has been unable to differentiate its products. Couple that with the extraordinary complexity of optical R&D and you have a sinkhole for investment. The company has therefore adopted a surgical approach to the category, focusing on integrating optical interfaces into its routers and switches and awaiting further developments as the expected industry consolidation plays out.

The second area of challenge is service-provider access equipment, the devices that aggregate individual consumer and business lines to connect them to the network at large. This is an area where rivals Alcatel and Juniper Networks have made strong moves. Access is fundamental to the architecture of any end-to-end network, hence the desire to bring it into the Cisco fold. But the technology at present is so mature, and Cisco's position in the market is so marginal, that a direct assault makes no sense. At present it is playing at the margin in specialized subsegments, focusing on cable companies and on integrating public and private wireless data access points into the overall network.

The reason these challenges are so serious is that telecommunications service providers look to their vendors to provide end-to-end network solutions, and Cisco is missing key pieces of the total package. Moreover, it has no inclination to build up the specialized services expertise that traditional sector vendors like Lucent, Nortel, and Ericsson have developed over the years. It needs to partner with these companies for the services side, but its competing product portfolio precludes such alliances. Meanwhile, the entire sector is undertaking a once-in-a-lifetime conversion to IP network infrastructure. Vendor commitments made now will have huge switching costs, locking in the winners and locking out everyone else. Finding the precise angle of attack is still a work in progress for the Cisco executive team.

In summary, Cisco has offerings all along the category-maturity life cycle and therefore has occasion to consider virtually every innovation type we will be delving into. The company knows, however, that taking a smorgasbord approach to innovation types reduces rather than increases differentiation. As a result, it has chosen to focus primarily on product innovation in growth markets and integration innovation in mature markets. How it made those choices will be the subject of future installments in this ongoing case study of its business practices.

CHAPTER THREE

INNOVATION AND BUSINESS ARCHITECTURE

The purpose of this book is to analyze and discuss the best practices for innovation in established enterprises. We have already seen that one criterion for innovation is that it be focused on creating definitive competitive advantage. We have also seen that it must align with the current market dynamics of the category of offer in question. Here we want to make one final point: It must also fit the type of enterprise that plays host to it.

There is a fundamental division that separates the world of commerce into two independent yet interacting realms. It is defined by a pair of contrasting business architectures we call complex systems and volume operations. These two architectures create a divide across which best practices in innovation must not be shared.

Complex-systems architecture specializes in tackling complex problems and coming up with individualized solutions with a high proportion of consultative services. It underlies the way business is conducted at companies that have large public or private enterprises as their primary customers. This includes IBM, Cisco, and SAP; Goldman Sachs, Swiss Re, and the World Bank; Boeing, Tektronix, and Honeywell; Bechtel, Accenture, and IDEO; Apache, Halliburton, and Burlington.

Volume-operations architecture, by contrast, specializes in serving volume markets through standardized products and transactions. Although it has many applications for enterprise customers, its roots are in consumer-oriented businesses, including those at

Complex Systems Versus Volume Operations

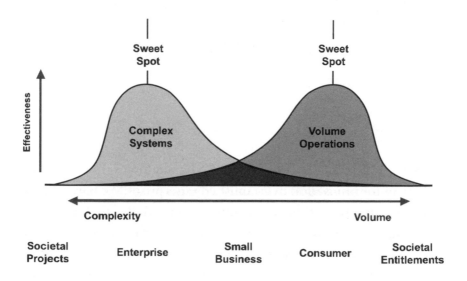

Nestlé, Procter & Gamble, and Nike; Kodak, Apple, and Sony; Microsoft, Adobe, and Electronic Arts; Hertz, Hilton, and United Airlines; eBay, Google, and Amazon.

As the diagram above indicates, each model has a sweet spot where it is optimally effective and from which it degrades to either side. In the case of the complex-systems model, it can be overloaded with such complexity that it breaks, as we often see in civil engineering and military projects that go massively over budget. On the other hand, if it does not have sufficient complexity to resolve, its cost structure becomes increasingly burdensome, as we often see when complex-systems companies seek to go down market to serve small business customers.

Comparably, the volume-operations model can be overtaxed with too much volume, as we often see when health-care or education systems struggle to provide basic services. On the other hand, if it is asked to manage too many exception conditions over too little volume, its systems become ineffective, as sometimes occurs when volume-operations companies seek to go up market to serve medium to large business customers.

In their pure forms, these two models are polar opposites in virtually every dimension of business. That is, they propose diametrically contrasting strategies and techniques for how offerings should be researched, designed, sourced, manufactured, marketed, sold, and serviced. What is a best practice in one domain can be expected to be a worst practice in the other.

And that brings us to the key thesis of this chapter: Sustainable competitive advantage is built atop one or the other of these two architectures—it is not built atop a compromise between the two. This is a deliberately provocative statement, not least of all because there are genuine gray areas between the two models where markets do reward a kind of hybrid performance. Nonetheless, this chapter will do its best to convince you of its validity.

To the degree that it is found to be true and valid, it has an important implication for innovation strategy. It implies that there will be not one but two bodies of knowledge in play: one for complex-systems enterprises, the other for volume operations. Although each of many innovation types reviewed in the prior chapter can and does play a role in both camps, some are more effective in one than in the other, and all play out differently depending on the hosting paradigm. That is why exchanges of best practices should be confined to companies sharing the same architecture and not be conducted across an architectural divide.

Simple and straightforward as this idea might seem, it is actually contravened with surprising frequency. Executives in a particular function—say engineering, or marketing, or sales—often assume that their professional experience transcends this division. If they have worked in both environments, as many have, they feel free to use any tool from their past experience to meet a present problem. Our experience is that this is a bad practice, that tools must be selected to fit with the prevailing architecture of the current enterprise, and that innovation, in particular, must be tuned to that architecture's peculiar properties. To see why this is the case, let us examine each of the two architectures in detail.

THE TWO ARCHITECTURES

The distinction between the complex-systems and volume-operations engines is at root one of contrasting economic formulas. In the complex-systems model, vendors seek to grow their customer base from tens to hundreds to perhaps thousands of customers, with no more than a handful of transactions per customer per year (indeed in some years there may be none), but at an average price per transaction in the hundreds of thousands or millions of dollars. In this model, a thousand customers paying a million dollars each per year generate a billion dollars in revenue. Such enterprises organize around the following model:

Complex-Systems Model

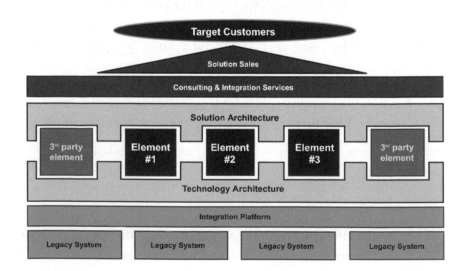

Here's how the model works:

- The entirety of the complex-systems model is organized around the target customer. Because its economics depend upon a relatively small number of customers making relatively large purchase commitments, qualified customers are the scarcest resource in the system, and in negotiations with the vendor they typically have the greater power.

- This leads the vendor to organize its business around an elaborate system of courtship led by a solution sales organization charged to align with the customer's interests and concerns. Its job is to ferret out customer needs and wants that will motivate a purchase.

- The vendor supplements this high-touch customer interface with a consulting and integration services capability to bridge between the customer's specific business requirements and the generic capabilities of its own offerings. Its job is to translate the identified needs and wants into a proposed solution, taking the form of a complex system.

- The complex system itself is a kind of sandwich in which two subarchitectures surround a set of multiple disparate elements. These elements are modules that can be used across solutions to provide the system's enabling capabilities and often are supplied by volume-operations subcontractors.

- What unifies these offers on the market-facing side is a solution architecture consisting of application-specific templates that align the generic offering to a given market segment's needs. Characteristically, they embody business processes peculiar to a given vertical market segment and reflect domain expertise unique to that industry.

- What unifies offers on the systems-facing side is a technology architecture made up of common facilities, protocols, and interfaces. Such an architecture enables disparate modular elements to be swapped in and out to create different solution sets without having to reconstruct the entire sandwich from scratch each time.

- Finally, the entire edifice is buffered from the rest of the customer's systems environment by an integration platform that permits the offering to be flexible above this layer while keeping a constant interface below it. This is critical because all complex systems must be able to integrate into the customer's legacy systems in a nonintrusive, readily maintainable manner.

The complex-systems model is exemplified in the operations of companies such as IBM, Boeing, Goldman Sachs, Halliburton, and Accenture. To be sure, what each firm will mean by *technology architecture* will be different, and each will populate its solutions with elements unique to its sector. But at the end of the day, this is how they all have organized their resources. And in so doing, they stand in direct contrast to the volume-operations model.

In the volume-operations model, vendors seek to acquire customer bases of hundreds of thousands to millions of consumers, with scores of transactions per consumer per year, at an average price of a few dollars per transaction. Here it takes eight million customers, each spending around ten dollars per month, to generate a billion dollars in revenue. It is a completely different economic formula, one developed around systematizing transactions in contrast to the complex-systems business that is based on cultivating relationships.

The dynamics of this transactional model lead to a very different organizational focus:

In the volume-operations model, the customer as an individual is not the scarce element in the system and hence is not its focal point. Instead, the scarce element is a means of production that can generate differentiated offers in high volume at low cost. This leads

Volume-Operations Model

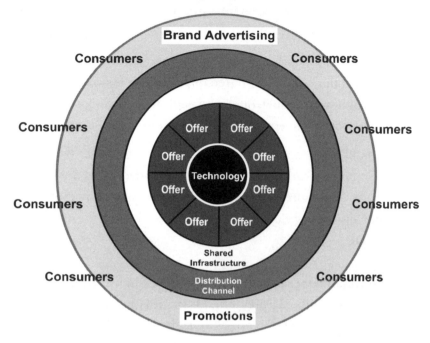

the volume-operations vendor to organize its business concentrically around an offer-generation capability, as follows:

- At the center of the volume operation is an offer-enabling technology. This can be anything from a stock trading platform to a telephone network to a software development organization to a food processing plant. Whatever it is, it will be optimized for producing mass-customized offerings that leverage the economics of scale while retaining the ability to differentiate at the surface.

- The goal is to generate both a volume and a variety of offers, be they financial instruments, software titles, or breakfast cereals. These are optimized to meet the three basic values of retail markets: price, availability, and selection.

- To keep costs as low as possible, the model exploits economies of scale through shared infrastructure for sourcing, manufacturing, logistics, and customer service.

- Additionally, both the scale of the model and the price points of the offer demand a shared distribution channel specializing in high-volume low-touch transactions, an activity that does not really *sell* to consumers but rather enables them to *buy*.

- Finally, these consumers are attracted to the offer by a variety of communications enabled by brand advertising and promotions. The more sophisticated of these may be personalized, but unlike the complex systems model, they are never personal.

The volume-operations model describes how business is done at Verizon, Dell, Nike, Disney, and Hertz. It is a world where brand promises must be linked to enabling systems to deliver competitive differentiation. It could not be more different from the business-to-business world of complex systems if it tried.

HOW THE TWO MODELS EVOLVED

The complex-systems model evolved in response to the challenges of introducing a new category of offering into a new marketplace. Under these conditions, many of the components of a complete offering are either unavailable or improperly positioned. As a result, the sponsoring vendor must take on the orchestration responsibilities for which the complex-systems organization has been designed. First it must seek out the customer, then it must uncover the compelling reason to buy, then it must imagine and design the complex system that fulfills that reason to buy, then it must recruit the partners and allies needed to complete it, and finally it must actually sell the entire solution and serve as a prime contractor for delivering it.

Much of the infrastructure for all this heavy lifting has to be built into the organization in advance, so both the price of the deal and its gross margins must be high enough to offset the capital required and the risk taken.

By contrast, as marketplaces mature over time, many of these constraints on commerce relax. In established categories, qualified prospects already exist, and buying motives have already been established. Moreover, a basic solution architecture has evolved and is embodied in many of the products in the market. As a result, there is much less need for partnering and integration assistance. This, in turn, reduces the pressures on the distribution channel and frees the sponsoring vendor from investing in a lot of support infrastructure. The net impact of all of the above is that gross margins need no longer be high, so prices can come down dramatically.

Under these conditions, a complex-systems business model becomes increasingly uncompetitive, and the market turns to the volume-operations model for lower costs and simpler deployments. In doing so, it agrees to accept certain limitations. Customers acquiesce to being lumped into segments for which a common solution can be created, and they expect that solution to be increasingly standardized, although they will still assign a premium to mass-customized offerings that speak to their preferences.

Not all customers are willing to do this, of course, so there is still complex-systems business to be done. But for those who can live within its limitations, the volume-operations model delivers reliable goods at a lower price and with lower cost of ownership. These attributes attract an increasing volume of customers, which leads to higher volumes of goods, which allow prices to be driven down even further as a self-reinforcing cycle of commoditization unfolds. This in turn forces complex-systems vendors to differentiate more and more on the complexity of the problems they solve, causing further bifurcation between the two strategies. Thus *what began as a spectrum ends up dividing into a polarity* because the ground in the middle becomes increasingly challenging to occupy.

The result is the evolution of two independent ecosystems. Each one supports an end-to-end value chain linking together all the functions necessary to make a market. But how those functions play out is radically different, so much so as to make switching between them or combining elements from each extremely challenging.

To see how challenging, let us look closely at how each business architecture responds to the demands of a simple value chain.

Simple Value Chain

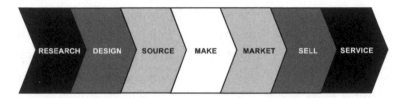

This is about as simple a value chain model as one can imagine. Yet even at this most basic level, there are stark contrasts as these functions play out across the two architectures:

VALUE CHAIN ELEMENT	COMPLEX SYSTEMS	VOLUME OPERATIONS
Research	Qualitative Scenarios	Quantitative Analytics
Design	Integration of Modules	Modules That Integrate
Source	At the Margin	At the Mean
Manufacture	Adaptive Methodologies	Deterministic Processes
Market	Value Chain Orchestration	Branding and Promotion
Sell	High-Touch Persuasion	Low-Touch Distribution
Service	Open-ended Consultations	Close-ended Transactions

Begin with Research. In the complex-systems model, market research has a *qualitative* bias because each customer constitutes a market reality unto itself. For example, the commercial airline businesses at Airbus and Boeing have perhaps two hundred or so primary customers worldwide to consider. Statistically averaging insights across such a modest customer population makes no sense. Instead, you want to delve deeply into the specific circumstances of each account, seeking out unique patterns, not mathematical correlations. This is where war stories and hypothetical scenarios, even just the occasional apt metaphor, can prove so insightful.

By contrast, the volume-operations model is all about the uniformity and scalability of transactions. A Palm or an HP needs to sell around one million units of a handheld device to repay the investment in R&D and marketing. Here *quantitative* analytics are critical, and teams must guard *against* the compelling war story or apt metaphor. Too often what appeals to a development or marketing team is not representative of what appeals to the target market at large, and the risk of getting this wrong at scale is frightening. Thus even the best intuitive insights must be tested in thoughtfully designed, statistically valid experiments, and this is the core focus of volume-operations market research efforts.

Move to Design. The essence of complex systems is that they tackle complexity. Think of a financial portfolio or a computer data center. No two customer implementations are ever exactly the same. There is no standard approach that fits all. Instead, complex-systems vendors must yoke disparate subsystems into a unique design. This is what we mean by an *integration of modules*.

By contrast, the goal of volume-operations models is to produce atomic output that can be integrated into larger systems without modification. In this world, *build-to-order* really means *configure-to-order* or *assemble-to-order*, where all the components are standard, and all the possible permutations have been worked out in advance. This is what we mean by *modules that integrate*. Think of clothing sold at the Gap or entertainment systems at Best Buy. The more modular, the more they can be mass customized to meet the preferences of specific customers, but at no time are they genuinely custom.

Turn to Source. In a complex-systems solution, sourcing focuses on securing the scarcest elements as opposed to getting the lowest price for the high-volume components. That is because the primary escalator of total system cost is not inventory pricing but missing schedule. That schedule is gated by system testing, and testing cannot be completed until the last component is installed. Expediting is a virtue in this system.

By contrast, in a volume-operations offer, price and inventory management of the most common elements are the biggest concern. Here the primary cost escalators are paying the wrong price, buying too much and getting stuck with inventory, or buying too little and being unable to meet demand. Controlling these variables is accomplished by installing sophisticated processes and systems and sticking to them rigorously. Expediting is a vice in this model.

Look at Manufacture. In complex systems there are no truly repeatable processes. No two pieces of heavy equipment and no two projects are ever exactly alike. Continuity, predictability, and reliability derive instead from consistent methodologies that adapt themselves to specific situations. This is the program management expertise of a Lockheed Martin, a Bechtel, or an Accenture.

Contrast that with the deterministic processes of a volume-operations effort, the sort of thing that leads to every pill in a prescription being identical to every other pill. To be sure, there is always some variability, but here the goal is not to embrace it but to design it out. The Toyota manufacturing system, the 99.999 percent uptime of telephony, the good laboratory practices for pharmaceuticals manufacturing—all are rooted in mechanistic statistical quality control, a far cry from the kind of organic personal judgment needed to run the complex-systems model.

Move on to Market, and the contrasts are equally as stark. With complex systems, no one member of the value chain can provide all the products and services end to end. A key concern of marketing, therefore, is aligning properly with partners and allies. To install SAP's enterprise resource planning (ERP) system, for example, requires direct involvement from companies like HP, Accenture, and Oracle and the indirect involvement of companies like Cisco, EMC, and Microsoft. The most valuable marketing asset a company has in this context is a *reputation* that gives it permission to lead and makes others want to recruit it for their teams.

Contrast this with a volume-operations model where the entire offer is inside a package, the entire value chain is preassembled, and the only variable to manage is consumer choice. That is what Apple has accomplished, first with the Macintosh, and more recently with iPod. The challenge here is to win a battle for preference within the mind of each consumer, and the most valuable marketing asset is brand image.

Comparing the two models with respect to Sell processes reveals more of the same. Complex-systems sales cycles take months and require enormous care to bring together all the customer interest groups that impinge on the buying decision. Think of the effort your company puts into selecting an employee benefits vendor or the human resources (HR) system to run behind it.

By contrast, volume-operations purchases are simple transactions that do not require and often do not appreciate the intervention of a sales assistant. Here the focus is on *buying*, and whatever selling is to be done is accomplished through the package itself and any point-of-sale displays accompanying it. Children's toys and breakfast cereals are particularly adept in making the package reach out and speak.

And, finally, look at Service. In the complex-systems model, service makes up a major portion of the total solution budget, typically anywhere from 50 to 80 percent. This is the case whether the end product is a hotel building or a catered wedding inside it. It involves both presales and postsales engagements, the former to help customers understand and tailor their investment to the specific situations they face, the latter to get them up and running faster and more reliably.

In the volume-operations model, by contrast, services are either embedded in the offers themselves, as with photo processing or Internet searches, or low-touch transactions after the sale to deal with repairs and returns. These are on the vendor's terms and the service center's schedule if for no other reason than that the alternative paths are not scalable.

To sum up the preceding, what we have here are two distinct and opposing modalities of business. Each one is coherent in its own right:

- In the complex-systems world, qualitative market research scenarios identify requirements that can only be fulfilled through integrated architectures that are in turn sourced with a view toward securing the exceptional elements, built using adaptive methodologies, marketed via orchestrated value chains, sold through high-touch persuasion, and serviced by open-ended consultations. That is the complex-systems way of doing business.

- It stands in direct contrast to the volume-operations way. Here quantitative market research analytics establish requirements that can be met by modular architectures, sourced with a view toward the most common elements, manufactured by deterministic processes, marketed through branding and promotion, sold through low-touch distribution channels, and serviced by close-ended transactions.

The relationship between these two models and innovation strategy has two dimensions. Inside either model, innovation to accentuate differentiation takes very different paths. That is why sharing best practices between the two models is ill advised. If that was all there was to it, we could end this chapter right here. But there is also an interaction between the two models, one that aligns with the category-maturity life cycle, which further shapes innovation strategy. So before we close, we need to take this intermodel interplay into account.

BUSINESS ARCHITECTURES AND THE CATEGORY-MATURITY LIFE CYCLE

The interaction between complex systems and volume operations develops and changes as the category-maturity life cycle unfolds. The key stages of this evolution can be visualized in the following diagram, which illustrates the gradual evolution of computing systems over the last three decades:

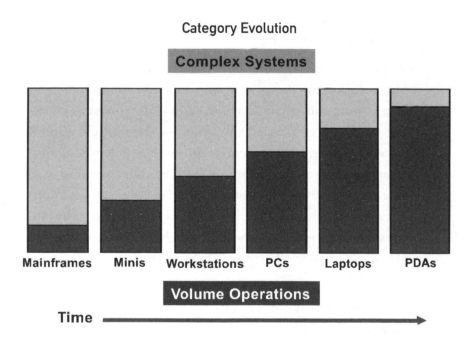

Category Evolution

- Complex-systems architecture pioneers new technologies and new marketplaces with services-led offerings built up from integrated architectures. This is what IBM and its fellow mainframe makers did during the 1960s and 1970s.

- As pioneering offers catch on and proliferate, however, portions of what was initially a purely custom system can now be carved out as component subsystems that can be made more efficiently by leveraging the volume operations model. This is what Digital Equipment Corporation and its fellow minicomputer makers did during the 1980s.

- A symbiotic relationship emerges. Complex systems need ongoing cost reductions in order to maintain margins, and these are supplied in large part by substituting lower-cost volume components for proprietary legacy subsystems. Volume operations need predeveloped market opportunities in order to expand, and these are supplied by those same legacy subsystems. This is what Sun and its fellow workstation makers did, also in the 1980s.

- Over time, however, competitive advantage within categories shifts inexorably toward volume-operations architecture. The various subsystems become sufficiently robust to generate their own end-to-end substitute for the entire complex-systems offer. Initially such offers do not compete well against complex systems on quality or features, but they do so on price, and they typically attract customers who cannot afford the complex-systems offer. This is what IBM and its fellow PC makers began in the 1980s and brought to real fruition with the adoption of local area networks and client-server systems in the 1990s.

- These volume-operations offerings continue to find ways to improve, and by so doing, they displace offers from the complex-systems vendors that were initially their customers. The complex-systems solutions in turn are driven further and further upmarket in search of customers who still need their higher-cost-added value. There are fewer and fewer customers in these rarified regions, and this leads to vendor consolidation at the high end even as volume operations are growing dramatically at the low end. To all outward appearances, it looks as if the complex systems model is toast. Think of the fall of the Digital Equipment Corporation as its minicomputer approach lost out to the PC/local-area-network paradigm.

But the story does not end here! As the following diagram indicates, the complex systems model can and must regenerate itself:

**Business-Model Innovation
at Category Transitions**

When past categories commoditize and no longer need the services of a complex-systems architecture, vendors must set out for new pastures to start the cycle all over again. In doing so, they will leverage their past expertise by designing next-generation systems that incorporate and transcend the commoditizing products they are leaving behind. Thus IBM is reinventing computing architectures around harnessing literally thousands of PC servers into supercomputing clusters, while companies like Siebel, Oracle, and

SAP are building mobile workforce applications to leverage the computing capability of smart phones.

Understanding, then, that complex-systems architectures re-new themselves by inventing new categories of higher complexity, we can now trace out the interoperation of the two business archi-tectures over the course of the category-maturity life cycle:

- In phase A of market development, the complex-systems players play the lead role. During this time there is too little volume for the volume-operations approach to be viable. Moreover, there are virtually no standards in place, and so the added value services of the complex model are critical to success. Therefore, volume-operations players are wise to hold back, take opportunistic component business as it comes, and await further developments.

- These come in phase B. With the maturation of the category, volume operations can now make inroads into the complex-systems position. These inroads create some consternation among the complex-systems ranks, but wise heads welcome them as they help cost-reduce the total offer and there is still plenty of value for complex-systems vendors to create by com-pleting the solution. As a result, the two models are able to coexist and coevolve relatively harmoniously.

- Eventually, however, the market transitions to phase C, where so much of the system value has become incorporated into com-ponent parts that it is folly to persist in maintaining a legacy of integrated architecture. Volume operations take the upper hand for the current category. Complex-systems models must relinquish their claims on that category and redeploy their assets one level up in the systems hierarchy. This is made pos-sible by the very commoditization that instigates it because the complex-systems model now uses the newly created com-modity as an enabling component for a higher-order system.

Over multiple generations of technology, a pattern of cyclical progression emerges as illustrated by the following diagram:

Cyclicality and Strategy

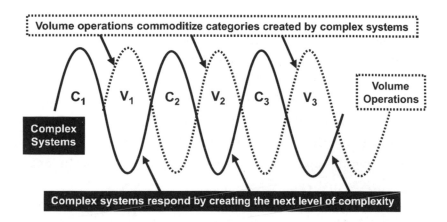

The solid-line sine curve traces the market fortunes of the complex-systems model; the dotted-line curve, those of the volume-operations model. They are 180 degrees out of phase at any point along the curve. Within each pair of cycles, complex-systems enterprises break open the new ground and capture the early returns while volume-operations companies follow behind to extract the residual value.

The correct path for innovating for competitive advantage is to stick to your own business architecture's curve and not covet the other one when it is in its ascendancy. When categories are emerging, volume-operations companies should refrain from envying complex-systems enterprises their fat profit margins and wide-open marketplaces. And as categories mature, complex-systems companies should refrain from envying volume-operations enterprises their lean operating margins and huge installed bases. The truth is, neither model can successfully capitalize on the other's opportunities. Volume operations can never truly embrace complexity, and complex systems can never truly embrace commoditization.

To be sure, as the volume-operations model seeks additional market growth, it does so through systematic occupation of ground formerly staked out by complex-systems enterprises. And as it does, the strategy for complex-systems companies is to resist these incursions and defend their turf for as long as they viably can. That is, although it may never be a question of *if* the complex-systems model will eventually have to capitulate to volume operations, there is always the question of *when*, and there are literally billions of dollars of revenues and profits that hang on the timing of that transition. The most successful complex-systems companies excel at fighting effective rearguard actions, just as the most successful volume-operations companies excel at relentless encroachment.

WRAPPING UP

We have been exploring the nature and interaction of two business architectures in order to provide a proper backdrop for understanding how innovation creates competitive advantage in business. Instead of there being one path to follow, we discover there are two. Each is so different from the other that best practices for innovation should not be shared between them.

And that, in turn, establishes the first question a competitive advantage strategy must answer: Are we going to play the complex-systems or the volume-operations game? This represents our first step toward competitive differentiation. It is so fundamental that, once taken, one need take no other measures to differentiate from competitors of the opposing architecture. Innovation instead focuses on either delaying or increasing the pace of category commoditization, depending on which hand is on the tiller.

But when competition comes from companies with the same architecture, differentiation becomes critical. This is where the innovation types model comes to the fore. We will employ it both to determine what kinds of innovation our competitors are using to differentiate from us and what type we will use to differentiate ourselves from them.

CISCO'S BUSINESS ARCHITECTURE

With the exception of a single division, Cisco is a pure-play complex-systems company. It is organized along functional lines, with the bulk of its resources in engineering and sales, supported by customer services, marketing, manufacturing and logistics, information technology (IT), finance, legal, and human resources. The one exception to this functional structure is its consumer products division based upon its acquisition of Linksys in 2003. That division markets products for the home and to a lesser degree for small to medium businesses under its own brand. It is a volume-operations enterprise run autonomously to ensure that its business model is not overburdened by complex-systems overhead.

As a complex-systems enterprise organized around line functions, Cisco must wrestle with a number of innovation challenges at all times. The first lies in managing cross-functional business processes. Functionally organized enterprises tend to optimize their operations around each line function, creating stovepipes that do not adapt readily to cross-functional process demands. The global corporations that such companies serve, however, have complex requirements calling for highly orchestrated responses across the various functions. How can one retain the internal efficiencies of centralized functions and still adapt to the external demands of the marketplace? What are the best practices in this situation?

For many companies, the answers have required reorganizing by business unit, focusing each unit on a particular vertical market, and optimizing operations in service to market-specific solution sets. This creates not only smoother relationships with customers, but it also provides a breeding ground for grooming CEO succession candidates. It does so, however, at an often considerable sacrifice of gross margins, for inherent in the business unit model is the decentralization and concomitant duplication of a number of functions. Cisco is able to retain extraordinary gross margins—in excess of 65 percent—in part because it refuses to abandon its functionally organized model.

Instead, Cisco's approach has been to form cross-functional business councils made up of senior line executives. There are three such councils organized around market sectors: the enterprise council for global corporations, the service provider council for telecommunications customers, and the commercial council for small-to-medium business customers. The purpose of each is simple: process customer-driven demands and develop end-to-end responses to them. Getting them to work properly, however, has been a real challenge.

From the outset, these councils ran against the grain of Cisco's management culture, the style of which is to assign even very complex problems to a single problem owner and have that person drive to a resolution verified by one or more specific metrics. The councils, by contrast, discuss and socialize issues driving toward a consensus that is then executed within the functional organizations. For a company used to *making* things happen, it is very hard to convert to *letting* them happen.

In particular, there were several executives for whom such teamwork simply was not in the cards, and despite their strong skills in other areas, they had to move on. With their departure, there has been a notable uptick in teamwork, further encouraged by a compensation system that uses peer reviews of team behavior. As a result, over time the councils have gotten more traction, particularly where a competitive situation has demanded a cross-functional response. All in all, it has been a slow progression, but one that CEO John Chambers is willing to be patient with. And it is that very patience, I would argue, that is the best practice at stake here.

Look at the track record. In the first year none of the councils were effective. In the second, the enterprise council got its act together, but since most of Cisco defaults to enterprise market orientation anyway, this was no great feat. In the third year, however, the commercial council had a breakthrough. It was able to orchestrate an end-to-end solution-oriented set of programs with partners to adapt the enterprise-oriented complex systems model to a more cost-sensitive market sector. This included product reengineering to simplify the installation, management, and ease of use of its products, special incentive programs for sales partners to encourage them to develop new accounts and new applications, unique financing to support distributors, resellers, and end-user customers, and training resources that repackaged expensive Cisco know-how into lower-cost partner-deliverable services. All these innovations have worked to extend the tail of the market that Cisco's complex-systems model can exploit, without sacrificing the company's higher-gross margin targets.

Now it is the service provider council's turn. It faces the single biggest challenge of all: namely, how to compete in a telecommunications sector that takes for granted that its vendors will dedicate market-specific resources to both product and service offerings. Here more than anywhere else the temptation is simply to create a separate business unit with significantly lower-gross margins and be done with it. But that would be shortsighted in light of Cisco's long-term view, which is that telecommunications networks and enterprise networks will ultimately merge into a single network of networks. In the long term, the company's best strategy is to partner with telecommunications-focused enterprises to serve market-specific needs of this sector.

Unfortunately, most of the desirable partners have major product lines that compete with Cisco directly, so for the short term the company must innovate on its own. Here it is focusing on early adopting visionaries who seek competitive advantage by being the first in their sector to offer next-generation network services atop an all-IP backbone. These trailblazing customers have become the focus for the service provider council. By rallying around their demands, the council is galvanizing its own capabilities to effect cross-functional change.

The council system at Cisco is still a work in progress, but it is demonstrating that a complex-systems enterprise can retain a functional organization far longer than normally imagined and by so doing, achieve enviable gross margins. Another part of this same strategy is the company's emphasis on product revenues as opposed to services revenues. Once again there is a best practice at stake.

The complex-systems model does not specify how much of the total solution should come from product and how much from professional services. It does, however, reward product-based delivery with higher-gross margins, presuming the company can secure sufficient market share to pay back the up-front investment. To the degree that they cannot meet their revenue objectives by product licensing, complex-systems companies take on more and more of a service-based business model. This leads to a degradation in gross margins and increasing exposure to the commoditizing competition of offshore service providers. A far better tack is to focus professional services on accelerating the adoption of the next generation of product offerings. But how do you do that without jeopardizing gross margins over all?

Cisco's response to this challenge might be called cavalry and weaponry—with no infantry. That is, Cisco deploys consultative teams (cavalry) to support next-generation architectures and products. These teams engage with flagship customers in transformational projects to push the state of the art. Each one of these projects has two critical deliverables: first, a satisfied customer, and second, a body of knowledge that can be repackaged for subsequent use (weaponry). The projects, in effect, are paid-for R&D that creates service offerings which, over time, will be fulfilled either by automated systems or Cisco partners (infantry). In this way, the company makes a market for its partners, thereby further securing its market-leading position, while at the same time avoiding building a dependency on lower-margin service revenues.

This best practice works as long as your company's next-generation offers enjoy marketplace acceptance. That begs the question of what to do when they don't. Cisco has yet to face this problem, but other clients of ours have, and we have a best practice of our own to share here.

To put it in perspective, we should note that standard practice is to do whatever it takes to maintain revenue growth, inevitably leading to building increasing dependency on services. This violates an important principle, however, which is that the hardest thing to change successfully in any company is its gross-margin model. Every such change leads to radical downsizing and reorganization, but this is rarely accompanied by wholesale replacement of the executive team. There is no infusion, in other words, of the new skills required to make the new margin model work. Instead there is an increasingly strained old guard struggling to adapt to patterns and problems it has no experience in handling.

In our view, therefore, the best practice for dealing with a failure to gain marketplace acceptance with a current generation of offers should be to undertake an immediate restructuring designed to maintain the margin model over a smaller base of revenue and to focus on getting the following generation of offers back into the mainstream. This keeps the enterprise within the experience base of the current management team and maintains a financial model that can support its current organizational model, albeit at a smaller scale. It does require the executive team to own up to its shortfall in performance instead of burying it beneath an alternative revenue stream that defers the reckoning to a future quarter. And it likely means also embracing a potentially deferrable decrease in personal compensation. In return, however, it provides a more authentic platform for making future management decisions and leads to a healthier enterprise overall.

Returning to lessons to be learned from Cisco, let us now turn to its one volume-operations division, Linksys, and how its acquisition has been incorporated into the overall enterprise. From the outset, the company has been careful to maintain the autonomy of this operation, thereby allowing it to retain its volume-operations virtues. These include both a low-cost, fast time-to-market business model that outsources much of its R&D along with all of its manufacturing and logistics as well as a go-to-market model focused on retail marketing and distribution. To ensure that this autonomy is maintained, the division reports to a very senior Cisco executive whose primary role is to protect it from being overtaxed by demands from one or another of the powerful complex-systems–oriented line organizations.

To date this has been successful, and the division has doubled in size during the two years Cisco has owned it, reaching just under a billion dollars in revenue. As long as it focuses on reaching the consumer market through retail, the current arm's-length strategy should continue to serve. Longer term, however, Cisco envisions a more closely coordinated interaction between Linksys and the other product groups as home products become integrated volume-operations components of complex service-provider networks. Under this view of the future, service-provider business will be served by complex-systems solutions that incorporate volume-operations elements that have been specifically engineered to play an integrated role in the overall system. How will Linksys be able to pay for such engineering and still maintain its lean operating margins?

Cisco has yet to face this problem, but the principles of business-model architecture already make clear what it must do. It must preserve Linksys's operating model. Therefore, it must find ways to absorb the costs of greater complexity within the margin model of the complex-systems divisions. To pay for these costs, it should also assign an appropriate share of the higher margins to the same cost-bearing source. In this way, Linksys can operate as a virtual original equipment manufacturer (OEM), providing volume-operations components to a complex-systems prime contractor who takes upstream responsibility for the nonrecurring engineering and downstream responsibility for sales and service.

For the time being, however, Cisco as a whole continues to operate as a complex-systems–oriented enterprise and enjoys the synergy gained from optimizing all its functions in support of this architecture. Its research, design, sourcing, manufacturing, marketing, sales, and service all reflect a complex-systems approach. When it needs to adapt quickly to a changing market or a challenging competitor, its various line functions interoperate smoothly because they share a common financial model and a common approach to creating competitive differentiation. This is the best practice of a single-architecture enterprise.

PART TWO

MANAGING INNOVATION

T he purpose of this section is to help you and your colleagues come to a unanimous consensus around the single most compelling question that drives innovation strategy: What type of innovation will we so excel at that we will leave all our competition behind?

We ask you to think of each innovation type as an independent vector, an arrow pointed in its own unique direction. Any vector sufficiently amplified will achieve breakaway separation from your competitive set. What then would cause you to choose one over the other? There are three such factors in our view:

1. *Core competence.* Different companies have different assets to exploit—some latent, some realized, in part a function of their business architecture, in part a function of their particular histories.

2. *Competitive analysis.* Different sets of competitors leave different openings to exploit, either by neglecting them altogether or by targeting them but underperforming.

3. *Category maturity.* Different stages of the category-maturity life cycle reward different forms of innovation. As categories mature, certain forms of innovation become outmoded and new ones are called for.

The first two of these factors are specific to every company, and we will leave it to you to bring them to bear on your innovation strategy. The third, however, transcends company-specific issues, and it provides the backdrop for the material to follow. Our premise is that you should commit to an innovation type appropriate to the maturity of your category and forgo types that are not. By mapping innovation types across the category-maturity life cycle, we will give you a framework for debating their relative attractions on your way toward choosing one for a strategic focus.

It may seem that committing to a single vector of innovation entails great risk and requires exceptional courage. Actually, however, it is the lowest-risk choice in any Darwinian competition. Consider the alternatives: You could delay or abstain, but that will leave you increasingly exposed to more competitive offers with no defense. You could bet the field of innovation types, but that will ensure that you get no separation on any vector and again leave you exposed. You are much better off making the following wager instead:

Focusing on our chosen innovation type
for this particular market category
within this defined scope of time,
we will so outperform our competitors
that prospective customers and partners
will cease to entertain them as legitimate alternatives.

Making such a bet is, of course, a fateful decision, and as such, it needs to be managed. Managing implies a process that it is led from the top. This makes an odd pairing with innovation, which normally is perceived as bubbling up from the bottom. But the two can be aligned. Managing innovation requires executives to foster a bottoms-up stream of innovation opportunities, thereby keeping their portfolio of options open, but at the same time to commit top down to a single innovation vector along which separation will be gained. Once that commitment is made, other forms of innovation are expected to align with or subordinate themselves to the chosen vector.

One more thing: It is not just one bet. Managing innovation also implies maintaining a portfolio of strategies because different categories will respond to different types of innovation. This creates a level of complexity that can create confusion in the broader organization, with teams being asked to pursue one form of innovation here and another there. To ensure consistent and effective execution across the portfolio, management must orient the organization to the logic behind the different choices and the importance of keeping them distinct from one another.

The innovation-types model that follows helps with all these responsibilities. It offers a broad universe of innovation strategies to choose from. It makes clear where in the category-maturity life cycle they are most effective. And it explains how each one is distinct from all the others. It is, in effect, a taxonomy that will help you and your team to frame your alternatives properly and then make the best choice.

CHAPTER FOUR

TYPES OF INNOVATION

henever we hear the word *innovation,* we tend to call to mind its most dramatic form—*disruptive innovation*—the sort of thing brought to life by brilliant inventors, rebellious artists, and daredevil entrepreneurs. That is indeed an important type, and it has pride of position at the far left of the diagram below. But as the diagram indicates, it has a great many brothers and sisters with whom to share the category life cycle.

A Broad Universe of Innovations Types

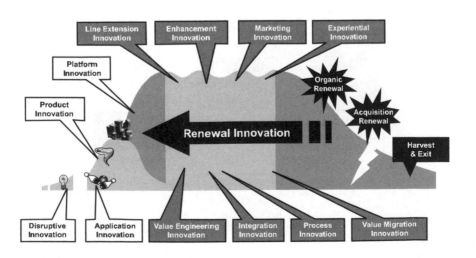

We are going to sort through this cornucopia of innovation types in the chapters that follow; for now, just register the range of opportunities represented above. When you hear someone say, we can't innovate around here anymore, realize that that is almost certainly not the case. All established enterprises have the opportunity to innovate all the time, and most do, often at considerable expense. The problem, as we outlined in a prior chapter, is that many do not achieve competitive separation through their innovations, and thus are not economically rewarded for them. Over time these companies shrink their footprints, layoff by layoff, thereby discouraging their rank and file, leading to the loss of confidence just expressed. But it is not for lack of the opportunity to innovate, not even late into such cycles of decay.

Our goal is to use the innovation-types model to help turn such performances around. The first step down that path is to organize the various innovation types into clusters, both to understand them better and to facilitate calling them to mind. Our clustering principle is supplied by the concept of value disciplines, first introduced by Michael Treacy and Fred Wiersema in *The Disciplines of Market Leaders*. Using this construct, the innovation types highlighted below fall into four clusters or innovation zones, as follows:

Four Innovation Zones

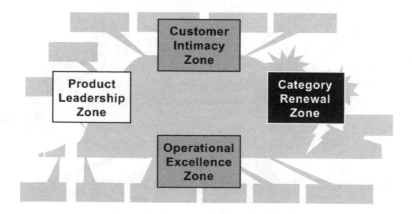

Three of these zones are named for the value discipline that provides the driving force behind the cluster of innovation types it hosts. As you can see, innovation types in the Product Leadership Zone are privileged during the growth phase of a category, whereas those in the Customer Intimacy and Operational Excellence zones are privileged during the mature phase. Value disciplines in general represent different paths for creating value within the same category. The zone on the right, Category Renewal, is for categories that have lost the ability to sustain future value creation. Enterprises operating in these categories need to renew their franchises by transplanting their focus elsewhere.

The table below shows the grouping of the various types into these four categories.

Clustered together like this, there seem to be an awful lot of ideas vying for a limited amount of mental space. But realize what an exciting and encouraging observation that is. Each one of these types is different from every other, so look how many possible

PRODUCT LEADERSHIP ZONE	CUSTOMER INTIMACY ZONE	OPERATIONAL EXCELLENCE ZONE	CATEGORY RENEWAL ZONE
Disruptive Innovation	Line-Extension Innovation	Value-Engineering Innovation	Organic Innovation
Application Innovation	Enhancement Innovation	Integration Innovation	Acquisition Innovation
Product Innovation	Marketing Innovation	Process Innovation	Harvest and Exit
Platform Innovation	Experiential Innovation	Value-Migration Innovation	

vectors for breakaway differentiation there are for you to choose from! Like all ecosystems, markets encourage and reward a variety of strategies. That is why we can be so optimistic whenever we engage with clients who have fallen on hard times and are seeking to recapture their old form.

INNOVATION TYPES IN THE PRODUCT LEADERSHIP ZONE

A word about the phrase *product leadership*. Despite its literal sense, it can be applied to any type of commercial offering, be it a product or a service. Indeed, throughout this book the word *product* should normally be considered to be synonymous with *offer*. A focus on product leadership is intended to contrast with strategies that do not differentiate the offer but rather the customer's experience of it, *customer intimacy*, or the value chain's effectiveness at delivering it, *operational excellence*.

There are four primary types of innovation that leverage product leadership as their underlying value creation engine:

DISRUPTIVE INNOVATION. This type of innovation creates new market categories based on a discontinuous technology change or a disruptive business model. Examples include the technological discontinuity of digital photo processing introduced by Shutterfly and Ofoto and the business-model disruption of digital media distribution heralded by Napster and made far more palatable by Apple iTunes. Disruptive innovations are incompatible with existing standards and the existing value chain, and they develop their markets de novo.

APPLICATION INNOVATION. Also known as solution innovation, this type develops new markets for existing products by finding unexploited uses for them, often by combining them in novel ways. Examples include the use of fault-tolerant computers to run ATMs in banking, the use of engineering computers to run financial trader workstations on Wall Street, the use of document management systems to dramatically accelerate the new-drug application process in pharmaceuticals, and the adaptation of the Macintosh to desktop publishing in advertising and media. Application innovations introduce new standards but leverage existing value chains, albeit by giving them a new focus.

PRODUCT INNOVATION. This innovation type focuses on existing markets for existing products, differentiating through features and functions that current offers do not have. This form of innovation is normally highly dependent on fast time to market, although patents can sometimes keep competitors at bay for prolonged periods. Examples include the hybrid engines in automobiles, cameras in cell phones, wireless connectivity in laptop computers, and flat-screen plasma displays for entertainment centers.

Product innovation has an additional dimension stemming from the fact that all products participate in a hierarchy of components, products, and systems. That is, every product is both made up of components and is itself a component in some larger system. So in addition to better performing an existing role in the hierarchy, product innovation can also enable a shift in roles within the stack, either moving down to the component level for more volume or moving up to the system level for more value. Examples of moving down for more volume include Canon supplying its print engines to HP laser printers and Gillette refocusing its shaving business from razors to razor blades. Examples of moving up for more value include Microsoft Windows moving up from operating a stand-alone PC to a home media center and IBM moving up from mainframes to grid computing.

PLATFORM INNOVATION. This type of innovation interposes a simplifying layer to mask an underlying legacy of complexity and complication, thereby freeing a next generation of offers to focus on new value propositions. Part of the innovation activity here, therefore, includes recruiting and supporting the partners who complete the value chain. The most successful platform innovations reposition an already ubiquitous product to take on this new role. Examples include Microsoft and Intel repositioning DOS and the 8086 microprocessor family from being component ingredients of IBM's PC to being PC clone enablers, Oracle repositioning its relational database from a component ingredient of the minicomputer to a universal enterprise application software enabler, and Qualcomm repositioning its CDMA technology from a product-differentiating ingredient in its own products to an enabling element for 3G wireless telephony.

All four of these innovation types entail heavy R&D expense and significant market risk. This sets the product leadership zone apart from the other zones and is the reason it is most appropriately used in growth markets. To warrant the risk and expense, the reward must not just be winning a sale but winning a new customer with potential for follow-on sales. The focus, therefore, is first on winning market share and then on maximizing profit. This will not be the case with either of the next two zones.

INNOVATION TYPES IN THE CUSTOMER INTIMACY ZONE

Innovation types in mature markets all have an optimizing flavor. They are either leveraging customer intimacy to make the offer a little bit more attractive to the customer or leveraging operational excellence to make it a little bit more profitable to the vendor.

In the customer intimacy zone, there are four innovation types to choose from, arranged in a sequence migrating from closest to the product to closest to the customer:

LINE-EXTENSION INNOVATION. This type of innovation makes structural modifications to an established offer to create a distinctive subcategory. The goal is to expand a maturing market by engaging with a new customer base or reengaging more compellingly with an old one. Examples include the introduction of the minivan and SUV in the automotive sector, the running shoe in sportswear, and both the laptop and work-group server in personal computers. In each case, the preponderance of the underlying infrastructure remains unchanged, thereby allowing the vendor to leverage amortized investments and keep development risks low. The differences at the surface, however, are enough to elicit preferential treatment from customers who might otherwise treat the category as a commodity.

ENHANCEMENT INNOVATION. This type of innovation continues the trajectory begun by line extensions, driving innovation into finer and finer elements of detail, getting closer and closer to the surface of the offer with less and less impact on the underlying infrastructure. The goal is to improve existing offers in existing markets by modifying a single dimension, thereby reawakening customer interest in what was becoming an increasingly commoditized category. Examples include ice makers in refrigerators, navigation systems in cars, Teflon in frying pans, and cherry flavoring in Coke.

MARKETING INNOVATION. This type of innovation focuses on differentiating the interaction with a prospective customer during the purchase process. The goal here is to outsell your competitors rather than outproduct them. Examples include using viral marketing on the Web to create buzz about a new movie, product placements in TV shows, peer-to-peer marketing of social networks, and single-vendor showcase stores.

EXPERIENTIAL INNOVATION. The ultimate refinement in this trajectory of customer intimacy is experiential innovation, where the value is based not on differentiating the functionality but rather the experience of the offering. It is particularly suited to consumer markets where the product has become a commodity, and the purchase decision has become risk free. Examples include business hotels that remember your newspaper preference, restaurants that supply patrons with pagers so they can roam while waiting for a restaurant table, and coffeehouses with a European ambience.

These types of innovation are distinctive in part because the core offer is not. That is, in mature markets products per se become increasingly commoditized as more and more vendors meet the same relatively complete design specification. In such markets, additional investment in product leadership creates no returns. Conversely, earlier in the life cycle, when a product category still has headroom for significant functional improvements, customer intimacy is much less effective because customers are still looking at price/performance as their primary evaluation criterion. This simply underscores our theme that innovation strategy must be situational in selecting its preferred innovation types. Customers always need a reason to prefer one offer over another, and winning that preference battle is the key to economic success. The only question is how.

INNOVATION TYPES IN THE OPERATIONAL EXCELLENCE ZONE

Complementing the customer intimacy zone's focus on differentiating the offering on the demand side of the market, the operational excellence zone focuses on differentiating on the supply side. Here the primary reward is a lowered cost structure that enables either price reductions, capital reinvestment, or higher profits. In addition, there is a secondary focus on time to market and speed of adaptation to market changes, both of which are keys to success in markets that have low barriers to competition.

Innovation types in the operational excellence zone include the following, organized in a sequence migrating from closest to the product to closest to the processes that enable it:

VALUE-ENGINEERING INNOVATION. This type of innovation extracts cost from the materials and manufacturing of an established offer without changing its external properties. Typically it calls for substituting low-cost standard parts and preintegrated subsystems for an earlier design's high-cost manually integrated custom components. Examples include the TV, PC, cell phone, as well as the aircraft engine and the mainframe computer, all of which have been substantially cost reduced through value engineering.

INTEGRATION INNOVATION. This type of innovation reduces the customer's cost of maintaining a complex operation by integrating its many disparate elements into a single centrally managed system. Typically it permits backward compatibility with existing systems, buffering them with a management and integration layer that allows changes outboard while keeping things constant within. Examples include mutual funds, data center management software, and all-in-one printer/fax/copiers.

PROCESS INNOVATION. This type of innovation focuses on improving profit margins by extracting waste not from the offer itself but from the enabling processes that produce it. The goal is to remove nonvalue-adding steps from the work flow. Examples include Wal-Mart's vendor-managed inventory process, Toyota's kanban manufacturing process, and Dell's direct-retail model.

VALUE MIGRATION INNOVATION. This type of innovation consists of redirecting the business model away from a commoditizing element in the market's value chain toward one richer in margins. It is essentially a response to a phenomenon described by Adrian Slywotzky in his seminal book, *Value Migration: How to Think Several Moves Ahead of the Competition.* Examples include the switch in focus from products to consumables, as with razors to razor blades or printers to ink-jet cartridges, as well as one from products to services, seen when answering machines were supplanted by voicemail or when aging systems companies refashion themselves as consultants and outsourcers.

Taking both the customer intimacy and operational excellence zones together, mature-market innovation types as a whole are optimized for deepening relationships with existing customers rather than for acquiring new ones. Because the relationship is already established, these innovation types need not be as powerful in their impact as those in the product leadership zone, where the focus is on new customer acquisition. But they must be increasingly less expensive and more capital efficient in order to maintain attractive vendor margins while meeting customer cost-reduction objectives.

INNOVATION TYPES IN THE CATEGORY RENEWAL ZONE

Sooner or later all market categories enter into a decline. It is important to remember that when you are faced with a declining market, any market that is still a going concern is in itself a valuable asset. That is, markets provide a necessary context for commerce, and they are both expensive and risky to create. Thus even in a declining market, both customers and incumbent vendors have an incentive to stay engaged.

From the vendor's point of view, there are two basic options to explore, normally in tandem: Renew your franchise by refocusing the majority of your resources on a new category while simultaneously optimizing returns for the remainder of the present category's useful life following a harvest-and-exit strategy. Here are the types of innovation that pertain:

ORGANIC INNOVATION. On this path the company uses its internal resources to reposition itself into a growth category. In industrial markets, this repositioning typically involves reconnecting with its most valued customers and finding new problems to solve for them, following the approach laid out in application innovation. That is what IBM did when it repositioned itself as an e-commerce-enabling company. In consumer markets it typically involves reconnecting with a new tornado market, as Microsoft did during the browser wars with Netscape and as Kodak is seeking to do today with digital cameras. This represents a return to product innovation. In all cases, the vendor stays within the same sector but repositions its product line.

ACQUISITION INNOVATION. Acquisition innovation solves the problem of category renewal externally through merger and acquisition. One can play this game either as an acquirer or an acquiree. Thus by acquiring the Web application server software company WebLogic, BEA repositioned itself from the Unix market to the Internet and dramatically improved its performance. On the other hand, when the PC software company Lotus could not renew itself organically via its Notes platform, it took the structural path of selling itself to IBM, thereby acquiring the sophisticated distribution and services capabilities that Notes required to be successful.

WRAP-UP

The category-life-cycle model provides a framework for analyzing the market forces affecting your competitive advantage strategy. The innovation-types model allows you to target a specific vector of differentiation to gain definitive separation from your competitive set. Taken together they lay out the landscape upon which you will define your core.

The single most important act of strategy leadership is to select the innovation vector upon which your company will develop its sustainable competitive advantage—its core. To do this properly requires a deeper understanding of the properties of each of these innovation types. That is the function of the remaining chapters in this section. In them we will delve into each innovation type and provide case examples of companies that have used it to achieve persistent differentiation from their closest competitors. We will then bring the section to a close by outlining a process by which management teams have successfully applied these models to selecting their strategic focus.

CHAPTER FIVE

MANAGING INNOVATION IN GROWTH MARKETS

I nnovating in growth markets is all about leveraging category growth. You are sailing with the wind, and the goal is to set your course and your sails to take maximum advantage of this condition.

As we noted in our initial discussion of innovation types, the principal value discipline to be leveraged in growth markets is product leadership. This discipline underlies four innovation types, as indicated in the table we presented on page 61. As we also noted at the time, each type correlates directly with a specific inflection point in the technology-adoption life cycle, as follows:

Innovation Types for Growth Markets
The Product Leadership Zone

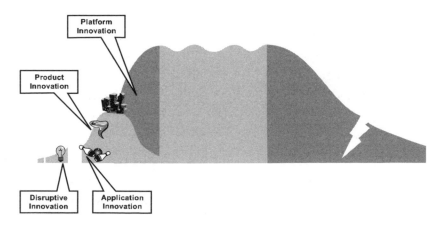

- *Disruptive innovation,* in which the category is making its first appearance in any form, correlates with the early market phase of the technology-adoption life cycle.

- *Application innovation,* in which the category is gaining adoption by virtue of addressing a single, specific application need, correlates to the bowling-alley phase.

- *Product innovation,* in which the category is gaining widespread adoption for many applications by virtue of its price/performance becoming increasingly and significantly enhanced, correlates to the tornado.

- *Platform innovation,* in which the offer becomes an enabling component of one or more whole new classes of offerings, is a posttornado phenomenon that actually participates in follow-on future tornados, a notion that will require some elaboration when we dig into this innovation type.

Because the technology-adoption life cycle is the governing model for setting strategy in growth markets, the first step is to concur with your colleagues about where you collectively believe the category to be in its progression through these stages. This in itself can be challenging, since markets can demonstrate one behavior in one segment and another elsewhere. (So, for that matter, can colleagues.) At the end of the day, however, you must come to a consensus to establish a baseline for further discussion.

When that baseline is set, one of the four innovation types automatically becomes the lead candidate for your innovation strategy, essentially by default. But that does not mean you cannot consider alternatives. It just means that to the degree these other types are out of synch with the category's adoption dynamics, they will struggle to create their effects, and you will have to make additional accommodations to make them viable. One reason you might decide to do this is that a powerful competitor has already preempted the default strategy, and you believe they have too much of a head start for you to wrest it from them.

The other major consideration in focusing innovation in a growth market is making sure you are adapting the innovation type to your dominant business architecture. Complex systems and volume-operations enterprises engage with each of these innovation types in very different ways, so it is important to make sure your entire team is looking at things through the same lens. As we work through the various examples below, be sure to discuss whether it applies to your situation or whether it might be more useful as an illustration of what a competitor with the opposing architecture might be up to.

With these thoughts in mind, let us now turn to a consideration of each of the innovation types in the product leadership zone. Your goal in this chapter, as with the next two, is to read through the material on each type and ask yourself at the end, does this sound like something we could do? If the answer is yes, put it on the list of types to prioritize. If the answer is no, get specific about why you think so and socialize your ideas with your colleagues. Focus is achieved by a process of first winnowing out the inappropriate types and then selecting from the remaining set the one that best fits your competitive situation and current capabilities.

SHOULD WE FOCUS ON DISRUPTIVE INNOVATION?

There are two kinds of disruptive innovation to look into here: one that favors the complex-systems model and the other, volume operations. The former is grounded in a disruptive technology, the latter in a disruptive business model. In both cases, vendors are tackling two new things: a new type of offer and a new type of market. This makes disruptive innovation the riskiest type there is, which in turn means it should be used only to target high-reward opportunities.

In particular, it needs to target very large potential markets and seek to create a prolonged competitive advantage period in order to create a proper risk-adjusted return.

Turning specifically to disruptive technologies, they have two defining attributes. The first is astounding price/performance advantage compared to the current in-market technologies, typically of an order of magnitude. Consider, for example, the properties of carbon nanotubes, which are stronger than steel yet as supple as rope. If science and industry can harness these properties, all kinds of currently unimaginable structures could be created, including a space elevator for getting up and down from space stations.

The second attribute of disruptive technologies is that they are fundamentally incompatible with current market standards. Think of hydrogen fuel cells or Internet telephony. Both call for a rip-and-replace approach, something which is appealing to visionaries (they are just looking for an excuse to junk the old stuff and are elated by the new possibilities) and appalling to everyone else. As a result, for the purposes of initial market development, the only viable customer sponsors are visionaries.

To win their business, you must wrap your discontinuous technology in a blanket of services that will fulfill the promise of delivering dramatic competitive advantage. Products at this stage are really more like projects, with consultative sales teams working hand in hand with professional services organizations to scope the work and deliver it. This plays directly to the strengths of a complex systems vendor.

Examples of complex-systems companies that have succeeded bringing disruptive technologies to market, thereby gaining sustainable competitive advantage, include:

- **ORACLE**. At a time when databases primarily came from computer systems vendors, Oracle championed a portable database that ran on many different computers. Moreover, it was a relational database that used the familiar metaphor of a table to organize information into columns and rows. These two innovations attracted first laboratory scientists and then independent software vendors, both of whom were attracted by the ease of reporting and the ability to run on multiple platforms. By the end of the 1980s, the company was the clear market leader in relational databases with every major computer vendor supporting its software and every major application vendor using it as a platform.

- **BOSTON SCIENTIFIC.** Stents are plastic tubes that are inserted into blocked arteries to open them and keep them open. The problem is that blockages often reform around the stent, requiring additional intervention. Boston Scientific pioneered the introduction of drug-eluting stents that release plaque-reducing chemicals at the point of use. These stents have revolutionized the treatment of arterial sclerosis, and the company, along with fast-following competitor Johnson & Johnson, dominates the market.

- **APPLIED BIOSYSTEMS.** The company acquired the patent rights to a process central and critical to genetic research called polymerase chain reaction, or PCR. This allowed it to disrupt the field by creating PCR machines that vastly outperformed prior manual methods. The result was a company with $1.3 billion in revenues a decade or so later. The company was subsequently instrumental in a second disruptive event, led by its now sister division, Celera, which accelerated the Human Genome Project. The two have combined into one company, Applera, which is the leader in the category of genetic research tools.

- **XILINX.** Prior to this company's disruptive innovation, field-programmable gate arrays, or FPGAs, companies basing their devices on new chips had to spend heavily both in time and money to build up an application-specific integrated circuit, or ASIC, layer by layer. FPGAs have prewired circuitry that is edited to carve out the desired logic paths. Although considerably more expensive per chip, they are much less capital intensive to use, and prototypes can be in market in a matter of weeks rather than months. Pioneer Xilinx and fast-follower Altera have dominated this market from the outset.

In contrast to the companies cited above, when volume-operations enterprises introduce disruptive technologies, they cannot directly provide the consulting services and systems integration needed to serve the early market. Instead, they must recruit partners to do so. This is possible but rarely easy, as the following examples will illustrate:

- **APPLE**. The company revolutionized the personal computer market with its graphical user interface (GUI), but it had no IBM to help it recruit partners and serve early customers. As a result, it had to wait for desktop publishing to evolve organically, through the independent efforts of companies like Adobe and Aldus, before its technology could cross the chasm. This gave rival Microsoft time to catch up, replicating the entire system to run on top of its already prevalent DOS software. The end result was that Microsoft, not Apple, took GUI technology into the tornado.

- **LOTUS**. Hugely successful with its 1-2-3 spreadsheet, an adaptation of VisiCalc optimized for the IBM PC, Lotus subsequently struggled to bring its more revolutionary product, Notes, to market. Again the company's pricing and distribution channels were oriented for volume-operations transactions, but customers required significant services to make use of Notes's information-sharing features. Lotus recruited value-added resellers, or VARs, to provide this service, but progress was laborious, and eventually the company had to sell itself to IBM. There, given access to a complex systems support infrastructure, Notes thrived. But by then it had already lost key market momentum to the Internet, and it never did fulfill its initial potential.

- **QUALCOMM.** This company reinvented cellular telephony by patenting a novel technology, CDMA, which multiplexed concurrent phone calls one atop the other in a highly efficient way. The cellular industry fiercely resisted adopting the company's offers until it spun off its network equipment and handset businesses to an established complex systems partner, Ericsson. That relationship got its technology across the chasm, but still the industry as a whole resisted paying high tariffs to a single proprietary source. Only after rival vendors were able to work around a portion of the patent portfolio and maintain greater compatibility with the prior technology did the technology reach the tornado. Fortunately for Qualcomm, its patent position was strong enough to withstand the wait.

A more straightforward path to engineering a volume-operations coup in the early market is to forgo the path of discontinuous technology altogether and to focus instead on introducing a disruptive business model. The goal is still to generate a 10X (ten times) price/performance improvement, calling for a rip-and-replace approach to adoption, but this time it is the intermediaries in the value chain that get ripped and replaced. Consumers are largely untouched by all the reengineering, getting to enjoy the prices and convenience of a volume-operations service where before they had to pay up or make custom arrangements for the privilege.

Volume-operations companies that have successfully created competitive separation following this path include:

- **CHARLES SCHWAB.** The company revolutionized wealth management for middle America by designing a no-frills stock trading platform and recruiting independent financial advisers to service its customers. In so doing, it eviscerated the business models of stock brokers like Dean Witter and Smith Barney but was relatively nondisruptive to the end user. In the turbulence of the dot-com era the company lost some of its momentum, but it is still a highly valuable franchise.

- **FEDERAL EXPRESS.** Who would have thought the most efficient way to send a package from San Francisco to Los Angeles was through Memphis? Fred Smith. Since its founding, Federal Express has revolutionized package delivery, eviscerating the business model of the United States Postal Service and local couriers by giving end users the assurance of absolutely, positively overnight delivery. The company continues to be one of the most respected best-performing enterprises in American business.

- **SOUTHWEST AIRLINES.** What do you get when you redesign an airline from scratch in order to economize on every single process and function? You get an airline whose market capitalization equals the sum of all of its competitors combined. From work rules to employee compensation, from reservations to pricing, from equipment to airport selection, Southwest eviscerated the established hub-and-spoke business model, driving market leaders like United Airlines, Continental, and US Airways into bankruptcy, all the while providing a popular no-frills service to its clients.

- **EBAY.** In the case of eBay, there were no predecessors to eviscerate. Instead, it pioneered an entirely new market category, the online auction, leveraging the tornado adoption of the Internet with a novel business model. What looked at first to be a forum for hobbyists at the fringe of the economy has subsequently developed into a mainstream distribution channel where dynamic pricing, the technical term for auction-set prices, enables a wide variety of transactions that otherwise would not or could not occur. Today eBay is poised to become the dominant economic channel for microbusinesses worldwide, not to mention a key route to market for major corporations seeking to dispose of obsolete inventory.

The reason why volume operations find it relatively easy to succeed with disruptive business models while they struggle with discontinuous technologies is a simple one: The market for the new product or service already exists. What the disruptive model is doing is providing a highly unconventional but still readily recognizable version of that offer at a radically lower price. There are no new behaviors for the end consumers to adopt, no incompatibilities to be engineered around, and hence no great need for consultative assistance. The market must simply be persuaded that it is safe to transfer its purchasing commitments from one class of offer to another. As that is proven to be the case, it is not the customer but the competitor who bears the brunt of this disruption.

To conclude, both complex-systems and volume-operations architectures can succeed with disruptive innovation. If you are in the complex-systems camp, you should focus on discontinuous technologies that impose high service needs on customers, supplementing your product leadership with customer-intimate domain expertise. On the other hand, if you are in the volume-operations camp, you will more likely succeed with disruptive business models that destabilize established markets. Here you will want to supplement your product leadership with operationally excellent systems to ensure you can ramp volume rapidly and maintain it reliably.

In both cases, the number one success factor is having an offer that is truly revolutionary, meaning it creates an order-of-magnitude 10X differential between itself and the current market standard. The next key element for success is total commitment to the new path. Early markets cannot be finessed. They have to be attacked head on. That is why established enterprises are rarely successful with disruptive innovation. Their go-to-market efforts are typically compromised by lingering commitments to the prior paradigm. These undercut the offer even before it gets to market. As a result, most established enterprises are better off adopting a fast-follower strategy, allowing the disruptive innovation to make its own way across the chasm, and then either acquiring it or replicating it after it reaches the other side.

So to bring this discussion to a close, ask yourself, does this sound like us? Do we have a disruptive technology or a disruptive business model to exploit? Could we imagine ourselves making the no-compromise commitment needed to bring it to market? If so, then put disruptive innovation on the short list, and move on to consider the remaining forms of product leadership innovation.

SHOULD WE FOCUS ON APPLICATION INNOVATION?

Unlike disruptive innovation, which involves both a new product and a new market, application innovation focuses primarily on the latter. That is, it leverages existing product capabilities already in the market, innovating by redirection rather than by inventing from scratch. It targets customers who have a pressing unmet need and are thus predisposed to give the new offer generous consideration. Moreover, if the offer proves successful, these same customers are likely to evangelize on its behalf to their friends and colleagues, further accelerating its adoption. And finally, because the need is at present unmet, there is typically little competition and hence a relatively straightforward path to creating genuine and sustainable separation. What's not to like?

Well, there is market size for one thing. Application-focused markets are essentially niche markets. They are not blockbuster in size. This is not a problem for a small business or a venture-backed start-up crossing the chasm for the first time because from their point of view a single new niche market is big enough to fill the need. But for established enterprises expected to achieve percentage growth targets relative to an increasingly large revenue base, it becomes harder and harder to justify the time, talent, and attention required to pursue niche opportunities. Moreover, sales and marketing channels for niche markets must develop specialized domain expertise if they are to fulfill their role in the value chain. If these same channels are also being asked to serve as operationally efficient generalists in other markets, the result is frustration and underperformance. So as you look into application innovation as an opportunity, be thinking about how your organization might deal with these issues.

For complex-systems companies serving enterprise customers, there are three keys to application innovation. The first is focus, and it is typically achieved through vertical marketing, wherein an executive-sponsored cross-functional team champions a target market initiative to fully address a specific unmet need in a particular and distinct business community. Such focus allows the second key to materialize: an end-to-end preassembled solution to meet that unmet need, the end result of what we call whole product management. Committing to be accountable for a whole-product outcome, in turn, means not only marshaling all the product and service resources your own company can bring to bear but also orchestrating a value chain of partners to complete the ensemble. We usually call this last function alliance marketing.

Complex-systems companies that have successfully leveraged the three disciplines of vertical marketing, whole-product management, and alliance marketing to create competitive separation via application innovation include:

- **SUN MICROSYSTEMS.** In the heyday of workstations, there were six competitors vying for the market lead: Sun, HP, Apollo, DEC, Silicon Graphics, and IBM. Part of what allowed Sun to break out from the pack and dominate the category was its extraordinary success in the financial services market. Partnering with relational database supplier Sybase, the company focused on the insatiable appetite financial market traders have for information at the point of transaction. The result was virtual standardization across the segment on Sun-based trader workstations. This high-margin segment gave the company a protected home base from which to fight bloody price battles in other segments.

- **JUNIPER NETWORKS**. Faced with an increasingly dominant category leader in Cisco Systems, the company wisely retrenched to focus on the specific needs of telecommunications service providers, the very customers that Cisco had alienated with its "voice will be free" messaging. By staying out of optical equipment and other competing product lines, the company has positioned itself as the IP-router supplier of choice for traditional telecom system suppliers. This ensures its highly technical offers get the domain-specific service expertise they require without having to bear that cost on the Juniper payroll. It also has allowed the company to focus specifically on telecommunications traffic, outperforming its rival in raw throughput while meeting the exacting standards of carrier-class reliability at the same time. In a marketplace that demands at least two suppliers, the company has a highly sustainable competitive advantage position.

- **SYMBOL TECHNOLOGIES**. This company has carved out a dominant position in the retail systems segment, first in the category of bar-code readers, then more recently, in mobile information systems. Profit margins in retail are razor thin, so increasing turns on inventory and reducing labor costs are key. The company has assembled an ecosystem of partners that integrate its handheld computers and wireless network access devices with software and services to meet highly specific customer demands. This allows the company to focus on customizable systems that can be readily configured for use in warehouses, trucks, or on the sales floor. At $1.3 billion in revenues it is far and away the leader in the segment.

- **SILICON VALLEY BANK.** During the rise of venture-backed start-ups in the 1980s, traditional banks were loath to lend even the most successful of these companies money to grow their operations, for the only assets they had walked out the door at the end of the workday. Silicon Valley Bank focused on this unmet sector need and developed innovative ways to absorb this new class of risk, including developing the specialized expertise needed to distinguish the winners from the losers and taking stock warrants in the firms as an additional form of compensation. The result is that it established a niche position that lets it hold its own against much larger competitors and gives it access to a perennially active financial services market.

Vertical market focus, whole-product management, and alliance marketing—as these examples illustrate—are the keys to application innovation in the complex-systems model. But they are not tactics that a volume-operations architecture can embrace, for they require high-margin pricing to pay back the investment in time and talent they entail. How, then, should a volume-operations enterprise approach application innovation? Actually, rather by accident. Normally when volume-operations models seek to explore new markets, they do so through line-extension and enhancement innovations. These are much less ambitious undertakings that modify an existing application rather than create a new one. Occasionally, however, they actually create wholly new markets, usually as a result of serendipity, as the following examples will illustrate:

- **VIAGRA.** Pfizer developed the drug to address high blood pressure, but it failed to perform as intended in clinical trials. It was only when trial patients refused to return the remainder of their drug samples that the company discovered the side effect that led to a whole new market category.

- **SILLY PUTTY.** During World War II, the government sought to develop a synthetic rubber to remove a critical dependency on foreign resources. It was only when playful scientists discovered its bounciness and an entrepreneur took it to market that the toy was born.

- **POST-IT NOTES.** What do you do with glue that doesn't stick very well? One enterprising individual at 3M came up with sticky notes. It took a lot of evangelizing to get it to market, but now it is a staple in any office supplies store.

- **SKIN SO SOFT.** Avon thought it was creating a cosmetic. Who knew it was actually a bug repellent? Now it is one of the company's perennial top-ten best sellers.

The reason volume-operations companies do not target such application-specific offers from the outset is that they appear to address markets too small in scope to warrant a volume approach. The exception to this rule is when software applications are designed to run on top of consumer devices such as PDAs and cell phones or adaptations thereof. This has led to a host of successfully differentiated application innovations, including the following:

- *RIM Blackberry,* a portable e-mail device

- *Nintendo Game Boy,* a portable gaming device

- *TomTom Go,* a portable navigation device

- *SkyCaddie,* a golf-shot distance finder

The key to volume-operations success with application innovation is to target demographic segments instead of vertical markets. Both targets create applications focus, but the former lends itself to a consumer-oriented infrastructure for sales and support. That is, demographic segments integrate seamlessly into the general consumer flow through the direct marketing and retail transaction system. They are thus easy and economical for a volume-operations model to reach.

To do so, vendors must segregate and aggregate demand through audience-specific messaging that attracts qualified consumers to actively seek out the offer. The offer itself is typically modified in only one or two dimensions so that it can leverage volume operations' economies of scale. Effectively, companies are doing product marketing, not solutions marketing. But most important, the distribution channel does not have to be modified at all—it is not asked to assume any customer-domain expertise—meaning there is *no service component* to the offer, or at least none provided by a human being (downloading from a Web site, on the other hand, is fair game). The only limit to scalability, therefore, is the size of the demographic segment.

That said, there are boundary conditions that limit the use of application innovation in a volume-operations model, and they are set by the elasticity of the company's brand image. The more a company expands its application reach, the greater the risk of diluting or blurring its brand image. Thus when Phillips sought to market a cell phone and failed, it learned from its focus groups that it was perceived as a maker of kitchen appliances—too much of a stretch. Similar brand limits have prevented HP from being successful in the copier market, even though the technology is virtually identical to that of its printers and scanners. Although brands can be repositioned, the process is both expensive and risky, so compatibility with current brand image is a good criterion to apply to application-innovation opportunities in a volume-operations enterprise.

To sum up, application innovation is a customercentric discipline that works backward from the peculiar interests of a defined segment to construct a fit-for-purpose offer. It builds strong competitive advantage positions by securing customer preference and then loyalty, and many wonder why it is not more universally exercised. The primary reason is that it is hard to scale operationally. It is far easier to build a more universal offer and let other institutions downstream make the customer-facing modifications. That is the tack taken by product innovation, to which we will turn next. Before we do, however, ask yourself whether the virtues of application innovation outweigh its vices in your case, and then either put it on or strike it off your short list.

SHOULD WE FOCUS ON PRODUCT INNOVATION?

Product innovation is in some sense the obverse of application innovation. Whereas the latter focuses on adapting an existing product to serve a new market, product innovation addresses an existing market with new products. In this it is distinct from disruptive innovation, where neither the product nor the market exists at the outset. It is much more closely related to line-extension and enhancement innovation, which also serve existing markets, but they do so by modestly modifying existing products. The essence of product innovation, by contrast, is to make deep and fundamental changes to the product, entailing high costs and significant risk.

The desired return from such big bets is to gain market-share dominance in a growing market. By riding a wave of category growth, you can enjoy market dynamics that bring customers to you rather than your having to go to them. And when you win those customers, depending on how high the switching costs are, you have a good chance of retaining them. This means their net present value to an investor goes beyond the revenue of the first sale to incorporate the probability of future revenues. Moreover, if you are fortunate enough to achieve market-leader status in the category, future new entrants will more likely choose you over the competition, even when the latter's offers have better price/performance. Only the market leader can offer the "safe buy" value proposition that pragmatists value so highly. And finally, since this phenomenon is not lost on partners, you will have other companies vying for your favors, bringing you customers you would otherwise not see under terms more favorable than other vendors will get. In sum, a winning product in a tornado market is a very big win indeed.

Tornado markets served by product innovation are where the volume-operations model shines, as the following litany of household names will indicate:

- *Google* with a better search engine
- *Pampers* with disposable diapers
- *Nike* with running shoes
- *Duracell* with alkaline batteries
- *Swingline* with easy-to-refill staplers
- *Cuisinart* with food processors
- *Titleist* with golf balls
- *Gatorade* with sports drinks

Each of these companies was able to capture dominant market share extremely rapidly by offering the market a significantly improved version of something it already had. There was no need to educate either the consumer or the distribution channel. All they had to do was make their claim and back it up and then get themselves out of the way.

Hence the three success factors for gaining competitive separation through product innovation in the volume-operations model are as follows:

1. R&D that creates a genuine product breakthrough
2. Marketing that drives home a single game-changing claim
3. Manufacturing and logistics that create an uninterrupted ramp of supply

Please note that all three are key.

Consider the following "partial" successes:

- *Apple's Newton,* whose marketing drove home a single game-changing claim that its product R&D could not fulfill

- *IBM OS/2,* whose R&D could never be captured in a single game-changing claim

- *Microsoft's BOB human interface,* which whiffed on both R&D *and* marketing

- *Chiron's flu vaccine,* which in 2004 had compelling R&D and a can't-miss marketing message, but no supply

And to make matters worse, volume-operations markets give no second chances. Smoking craters are all that remain where these products once were.

In sum, there is not a lot of subtlety to product innovation strategy in the volume-operations model. You are trying to capture millions of customers in a matter of months, so there is no percentage in getting fancy. It is simply a matter of taking a single breakthrough idea and executing like crazy.

By contrast, when tornado markets are served by complex-systems offers, there is a great deal of subtlety involved. Here you are trying to capture hundreds to thousands of customers over several years, with no two customers ever getting precisely the same offer. Moreover, to completely fulfill your value proposition, you have to incorporate partner-supplied products and services into the whole product, thereby further complicating the mix. Marketing is never as simple as making a single game-changing claim; there are far too many constituencies involved in the buying decision with far too many separate interests for that. And as for manufacturing and logistics, there is so much complexity involved in every installation that sooner or later something always goes off the track. In sum, to serve a tornado market with a complex systems offer requires nerves of steel.

Nonetheless, a single tornado success can put a company permanently on the map. Consider the following success examples:

- **XEROX.** The company introduced the photocopier in 1960, building the franchise in both a complex-systems direction, with copy-center systems like DocuTech, as well as in the volume-operations direction with desktop copiers. Despite failing to commercialize on many of its other product innovations, including Ethernet, Smalltalk, and graphical user interface computing, this one major success has led to a $15 billion global corporation.

- **MEDTRONIC.** The company introduced the pacemaker in 1960 and remains the worldwide market leader today, earning about half its $9 billion in revenue from cardiac rhythm management products.

- **APPLIED MATERIALS.** The company introduced the first multichamber semiconductor manufacturing device that integrated multiple steps of wafer fabrication within a single environment. The product revolutionized the industry, earning a place in the Smithsonian, and established the company as the market leader in the sector at $8 billion in revenue.

- **EMC.** Already a billion-dollar corporation in 1995, the company introduced the first platform-independent storage system, a breakthrough that freed corporations from having to pay captive prices for storage to their computer-systems vendors. Today the company is the $8 billion leader in the storage-systems market.

All of these success stories are based on making major bets on massive R&D efforts. How can executive teams decide if such risks are prudent? How do you know in a complex systems company when product innovation is the bet to make? When making this call, there are at least three operating principles to keep in mind:

First, be confident there is a killer app. *Killer app* is a technology-industry expression for a market characterized by enormous immediate demand. In the case of Medtronic's pacemaker, that market is cardiac arrhythmia patients. In the case of Applied Materials, it is the semiconductor industry's ongoing requirement to increase the content it can put onto a single chip. In the cases of Xerox and EMC, it is the explosion in document creation, distribution, and storage brought on by computerization, the Internet, and the World Wide Web. Whenever there is such a forcing function for continued investment, product innovation can target the kind of returns it needs.

The second principle is focus. Massive R&D budgets attract an entourage of ancillary projects that seek to feed at the main trough. Marketing can fall into a similar trap of hedging its primary messaging with a lot of secondary-value propositions. The end result is an overfeatured offering that lacks a clear identity. Such products lose ground in tornado markets because they are hard to explain and harder still to cost-justify. Winning offers, by contrast, overdeliver in one or two critical dimensions—the ones that are driving the market adoption demand in the first place—and are dead simple everywhere else.

And that leads us to the third and final element needed to capitalize on product innovation in a complex-systems market—whole-product management. Whether it is recruiting the network of sales agents and repair services for copying machines; ensuring that insurance companies, hospital administrators, doctors, and nurses all support your pacemaker; working with the other capital equipment and chemical suppliers in the semiconductor value chain; or interfacing with each of the computer systems and application-software companies who use your storage; you have to make sure a tornado offer works end to end with no snafus. As in an automobile race, even a minor glitch can force you to make a pit stop and cost you valuable ground during the heart of the race.

A killer app calling for restricted focus leading to a whole product—this is not the sort of language people call to mind when they hear the phrase product innovation. Where are the bells, the whistles, the wow factors, the cool? Well, except for fashion items— where cool *is* the killer app—all these elements belong to a later stage in the market's development. They inhabit the world of enhancement innovation's delighters and have their biggest influence in mature markets after the first wave of category adoption has passed. They have no place among the first generation of enablers that leverage the radically simplifying, industrial-strength forces of the tornado in a quest to acquire new customers.

To summarize, as you think about product innovation as an investment candidate, test your situation first to see if there is sufficient categorical demand to warrant the risk, and if so, see if you measure up well against the respective success factors that drive volume operations and complex systems success. If the scores come up positive, you can probably curtail your search, because the returns here will not be exceeded elsewhere. There is a form of innovation that can produce higher returns than product innovation, but it typically builds upon a prior product innovation success. That innovation type is platform innovation, to which we shall now turn.

SHOULD WE FOCUS ON PLATFORM INNOVATION?

Platform innovation rejuvenates stagnating markets by supplying a layer of abstraction that masks an underlying complexity of legacy systems. Future offers are thereby freed from having to engage with this complexity. Instead, they simply interface to the platform, and the platform takes care of all the rest. Of course, there is a price to be paid for this service, but typically it is nominal from a new vendor's point of view. If there are enough of these new vendors, however, the total revenues to the platform provider are anything but nominal, as the following companies can bear witness:

- Oracle, in relational databases

- Microsoft, in personal computers

- Intel, in servers

- Sony, in video game machines

It doesn't take much of a look at the market valuations of these companies to stimulate the ambition to become a platform provider yourself, but it is fair to say that the world of true platform providers is a very exclusive club. Other vendors have a hard enough time making money without having to pay tribute to platform providers, so they are always trying to get their platform services for free. And customers do not like to be locked into platform providers with no competitive alternatives to keep them honest. As a result, markets spontaneously self-organize to defend themselves against proprietary platform plays by promoting wherever possible open platforms, as they have with Linux, for example, and by crying foul whenever they see a proprietary platform gaining traction, as they now do routinely with Microsoft, whether it be in set-top boxes or cell phones.

Of course, proponents of platform plays are well aware of these concerns and the defense mechanisms they engender, and so it is a rare platform plan than does not highlight its Trojan horse strategy. That's how the first and arguably greatest winners of this game— Microsoft and Intel—came to power, buried inside the IBM PC. These days, however, if you leave a large wooden horse in front of a walled city, the inhabitants are going to look inside before they bring it in. Then they are going to require that you evacuate the horse, and *then* they are going to accept the gift—all of which is great for them but not for you and your investors. That, arguably, is what happened to Sun with Java. The moral here is that it is easy to be in the platform business as long as you give up all claims to an economic return, which is not a goal your investors will approve.

So how *do* you play this game?

There are two paths to take with platform innovation, what we might call the direct and the indirect routes. The first is more suited to a volume-operations model, and the second, to a complex-systems one.

In the direct path you declare for the platform goal from birth before you have shipped your first product. The simplest tactic on this front is the free-platform approach so powerfully employed by Netscape during the 1990s. Adobe has taken this road with its Acrobat Reader, positioning it as an alternative document platform to Microsoft Office. The trick here is to "monetize" the position of ubiquity only after it has been achieved, something that was presumed to be inevitable during the dot-com boom and that subsequently proved discouragingly elusive during the dot-bomb bust. The key criterion, it turns out, is switching costs. They were not high enough for most dot-com plays, as was most visibly illustrated by Netscape's demise. But they are high when it comes to Adobe Acrobat. Given these high switching costs, the company's current path is a promising one: providing value-added services over and above the basic reader—ones that customers are willing to pay for—including automatically routed workflow, secured delivery, and enforced privacy. From there Adobe can then license the resulting network to software and service providers who must incorporate document transmission as part of their workflow.

A more challenging version of the direct route to platform dominance is one that promotes a proprietary solution for which you charge a high price right from the outset. This has been the path that both Rambus and Qualcomm have taken, the former in high-speed memories, the latter in high-speed chips for cell phones. Both have bet heavily that their strong patent positions would block any workarounds, and for the most part those bets have stood up—but at a severe cost. For so abhorrent was their proposition to their would-be licensees that both companies have been dragged through hideously expensive litigation and vilifying PR attacks that not only jeopardized their financial viability but delayed their respective tornadoes. As a result, subsequent adjacent technological developments, such as DDR in memories and Wi-Fi in wireless, have had time to steal some of their thunder. Nonetheless, both can claim a reasonable amount of success with platform innovation.

Turning to companies that employ a complex systems model, the path forward takes a more indirect route, one based on breaking platform innovation into two separate acts. In act 1, the goal is to achieve ubiquity not as a platform but simply as a product of value in its own right. The key here is for the product to be anchored in proprietary technology and to entail high switching costs. As a result of these two factors, once it has achieved ubiquity, it will enjoy long staying power.

By that criterion, the following vendors have achieved the goals of act 1 of the indirect approach to platform innovation:

- Cisco, based on its network ubiquity

- SAP, based on its business-process application software ubiquity

- EMC, based on its enterprise storage ubiquity

Now comes act 2, in which the goal is to convert these well-ensconced products into platforms. This change in state implies that third parties could build offers atop these products-become-platforms, thereby leveraging the capabilities already developed and available within them while also gaining access to the customers that already own them. For this to occur, the sponsoring vendors must open up their existing products to expose "the platform layer within" for use by their platform partners.

Such an effort goes by many names—modularization, componentization, conversion to services-oriented architecture—but in every guise the result is the same. What was heretofore a monolithic structure with a single layer of interfaces is now revealed to be a multilayered structure with a "public" interface for normal customers and a "private" entrance for platform partners. Taking the private entrance lets the platform partner use the underlying product's capabilities for its own purposes.

Now as it turns out, all the vendors noted above are already conducting this kind of remodeling project, independent of their platform ambitions, because it is necessary to simplify and organize their own ongoing maintenance and development efforts. In effect, their next-generation R&D itself needs to treat their current product as a platform. So technically the challenge of act 2 is not particularly daunting to them, and in some cases it has already been implemented.

The as yet unmet challenge is figuring out how to present their platform to third parties as the center for a new and potentially vibrant ecosystem. Every market leader in the technology sector is contemplating this challenge. They all know that maybe one or two companies are likely to achieve this outcome in the coming decade. If they can make it their company, they will graduate into the highest rank of the technology elite. If that goal is too ambitious, they have the still-daunting task of deciding which partner bid to endorse, which ecosystem to join.

To bring consideration of the platform innovation type to a close, let me be the first to admit that unlike all the other innovation types, this one is anything but an exact science. Therefore, I have no simple rules for you to follow. The key principles are to bring two highly valuable assets to the would-be partner community: access to a market they otherwise would struggle to reach and access to functional capability they otherwise would struggle to create. If you can time this offer with a market-growth curve that forces vendors to act quickly or be left behind, you have as good a shot as anyone at winning the platform innovation game.

WRAPPING UP

In this chapter we have been reviewing types of innovation that feature product leadership and are adapted to growth markets. A simple way to sort out the four types is to align them with a product/market analysis matrix, as follows:

Innovation Types for Growth Markets

	Product	
	New	**Existing**
New	Disruptive Innovation	Application Innovation
Market		
Existing	Product Innovation	Platform Innovation

The diagram represents the relationships among disruptive, application, and product innovation reasonably straightforwardly. It is taking liberties, on the other hand, with platform innovation. Still, it makes the key point that the platform innovator gives its partner clients access to existing product capability in an existing market. Moreover, the matrix as a whole helps make another key point about innovation types in growth markets: *They do not play well together.*

Each innovation type calls on different strategies and skills. Management teams noted for their success in any one of these forms of innovation are often equally noted for their failures in alternative modes. In start-ups, for example, the entrepreneurs who champion disruptive innovation, and are the darlings of visionary customers, are typically moved aside into support roles once the market crosses the chasm and pragmatist customers become the target. These pragmatist customers resonate with the whole-product orientation and domain expertise of application innovation. They do not want to hear any more future promises from the founder; they are looking for much more prosaic commitments in the present.

But if the market goes into the tornado, product orientation trumps customer orientation in the battle for ubiquity. Now the pragmatists, more than anything else, want to go with the market leader. Application innovators end up being positioned as nice guys finishing last. The new winning formula calls for highly competitive sales-and-engineering-oriented executives to come to the fore. They drive the industry to common standards by imposing their own proprietary technology as the de facto standard.

Finally, if there is to be a platform opportunity, it will call forth a fourth form of leadership, one that is able to look beyond the parochial competitions at the current level of the systems hierarchy and orchestrate an entire industry of players in populating the next layer up to emerge. Here collaboration, diplomacy, and vision must displace hard-charging competitiveness to achieve the desired result.

And so the final lesson to take from this chapter is this: *If you are innovating in a growth market, you must focus on one, and only one, innovation type.* As we have discussed, the factors that influence your choice include where your category is in the technology-adoption life cycle, what positions your competitors have already staked out, and what type of innovation you are most likely to excel at. The model does not dictate an answer. It sets up the questions. The goal is not to arrive at Truth with a capital T. The goal is to get the entire team on the same page, focused on the same type, so that all functions within the enterprise commodify their process to reinforce the desired outcome of differentiation that creates separation.

CISCO INNOVATING IN GROWTH MARKETS

As you may recall from an earlier installment, although Cisco's major markets have transitioned from growth to maturity, a number of advanced technologies are going through the technology-adoption life cycle at present. Here we are going to examine how the company has applied the principles of growth market innovation to setting strategy in each of these categories.

Let us note at the outset that Cisco has an intentional bias toward product innovation. There are several good reasons for this. First, as the gorilla in the network equipment category, its products set the standards for the sector. As such, customers are more willing to adapt their applications to Cisco's products than they are to other vendors'. Both the company and the customers are served by having a common product layer. By contrast, a competing vendor with a different architecture has to carve out a niche space for itself, and thus will be more attracted to application innovation.

Second, Cisco's functional organization is optimized for product innovation. In an enterprise organized by market-specific business units, by contrast, research, design, and product marketing become segmented by unit, and product innovation does not cross easily from one to the other. In return, application innovation is much easier, since each unit has a single segment to serve and need not compromise its product requirements to meet the needs of other segments.

Finally, tornado markets, as we have repeatedly noted, privilege product innovation over all other types. Cisco is specifically interested in advanced technologies precisely for their potential for hypergrowth adoption. CEO Chambers talks about lining up an array of billion-dollar market opportunities and knocking them down one after the other. Product innovation in tornado markets is the most efficient path to that goal.

Keeping this strategic intent in mind, let us turn to some specific examples of how it plays out:

- **SECURITY.** With the massive shift of customer service and commercial transactions to the Internet well under way, criminal elements have targeted this new medium for identity theft and fraud. Moreover, hackers continue to test their wits against the system. These twin sources of attack are forcing both private and public enterprises to invest heavily in security, and the market for security products is inside the tornado and likely to stay there for some time.

Cisco's primary competitive advantage in this market is location. The best place for security products to intervene is at the earliest point of contact, and that will always be in the network. Because Cisco runs so many of the world's networks, and because security wants to be hosted in the network, the market looks to it to populate the network as rapidly as possible with as many security devices as are required. Although other companies may be expected to out-innovate it on a product-by-product, feature-by-feature basis, Cisco is positioning its offerings as an integrated *system,* architected end to end to address security issues in a comprehensive rather than piecemeal way. For something like security this position is extremely compelling.

The best practice to take away from this is something Cisco calls the evolution from product to system. There are actually two states of product innovation in a complex-systems model: the state before commoditization forces you to move up a level in the systems hierarchy and the one after. Systems over time become products that then must be integrated with other systems that have become products to create a new higher-level system. That is what product innovation means in the complex-systems business model. Engineers who thrive on fighting product-versus-product battles, feature by feature, often miss this point, and they fret that the competition is getting ahead and that their company is not innovating. For challenger companies that do not have significant installed bases, this is a healthy attitude. But for established enterprises, the move from product to system orientation is key to sustaining competitive advantage.

- • **WIRELESS**. With the rise of a wireless networking technology called Wi-Fi, championed in particular by Intel's Centrino technology that goes into every laptop today, the world is converting its local access to networks from wired to wireless. Whether you are at Starbucks, at an airport, in your hotel room, or in your home, you no longer need to plug into a specialized cable to get on the Internet.

This market opportunity is best suited to a volume-operations business model, since the bulk of its revenues comes from selling individual access points. As a complex-systems vendor, Cisco approached the market more comprehensively than was necessary, and its architecture was seen as overkill. Meanwhile, nimble disrupters like Symbol Technologies, Airespace, Aruba, and Trapeze were taking market share. Cisco still had the leading market share by virtue of its size and access to the customer, but it was not content just to sit there. Instead, it has acquired competitor Airespace to shore up a simpler set of offers and drive its wireless business to $1 billion in short order.

The best-practice idea to take away here is what Cisco calls no technology religion. It learned this lesson during the heyday of the Internet boom when the market's focus began to shift from routers, where Cisco was the established leader, to switches, where it had no products to speak of. Instead of fighting this trend, the company capitulated to it and in short order acquired four switch companies: Grand Junction, Kalpana, Crescendo, and Granite. Meanwhile, its major competitor, Bay Networks, which was actually better positioned at the time because it had the market-leading franchise in network hubs (which are simply a more primitive form of switch), refused to capitulate to the change and eventually was acquired by Nortel.

- **VOICE-OVER IP.** This technology is earlier in the life cycle. It has crossed the chasm in call-center operations where it provided low-cost connections between customers and offshore operators. More recently it is gaining share in the small-to-medium business market where the integration of telephone and PC creates a unified messaging environment that makes it easier for multitasking workers to keep up with voice and e-mail. At the same time, consumers are getting into the act with home adapters to get their international calls for free.

VOIP lends itself to both a complex-systems and a volume-operations approach, depending on whether you are displacing a PBX or a desk phone. Cisco's Linksys division has gone after the latter with a vengeance and is the dominant market leader in the category. Cisco's complex-systems divisions went after the former, but with much less success out of the gate. The problem was that Cisco's best customers had such complex systems that they needed a telecommunications service provider's support, not a network equipment vendor's. Meanwhile, the part of the market that wanted a Cisco-like solution needed something easier to install and maintain. Once again, the company's complex system was too complex.

This is where the company's Commercial Council, focused on the small-to-medium business market, swung into action. It drove an overhaul of the product, the installation process and software, the pricing, and the channel partner support programs—all to refocus the company's market penetration efforts where they could have the most effect. The net result is that the company is overtaking Avaya, the spinout from Lucent that is dedicated to voice systems, as the market leader.

The best-practice idea here is what Cisco calls being customer driven. That's a cliché in most companies, and normally it stands for little more than a salesperson's way of getting the latest deal's special terms and conditions approved. But at Cisco it means something else. It means letting the market pull you where it wants you to go. If you approach the market with the thought of serving it, and you find customers you can trust—customers who will keep both their interests and yours in view—then when those customers give you input, follow it. Cisco conducts customer advisory board sessions in support of each of its business councils, assigns members of the senior executive staff to interface with each board, ends each session with a list of action items, and reports back at the following session on how they have followed up. By making itself accountable in this way, the company gives a much stronger meaning to being customer driven.

- **STORAGE AREA NETWORK SWITCHES**. This market is in rapid growth, being part of the overall effort in data centers to get more bang for their bucks. By putting a lot of storage devices on a single high-speed subnetwork, one gets better overall resource utilization.

Cisco does not participate in this market directly. Instead, it provides its switches to EMC, which then repackages them to sell as part of its whole product. The amount of revenue that goes to Cisco is relatively small, and this is the slowest moving of its billion-dollar-market initiatives. Even so, the company is competing fiercely to win market-share leadership from Brocade and McData, the two vendors who championed the space originally. Why is the company paying so much attention to it? The answer is twofold:

First, SAN technology today still depends on a pre-Internet protocol called Fibre Channel. In the future there is every reason to expect this to be replaced by IP. When it is, Cisco's enormous investments in IP will give it a dramatic edge in future generations of the product.

Second, subnetworks for storage are entry points into a whole variety of other subnetworks that hook other data center devices one to another. Ultimately this leads to a vision of the data center it-self as simply a network of devices hooked to a common backplane, optimizing resource utilization across the entire portfolio of equipment. That vision is called data center virtualization, and it represents a market opportunity as large as the current network market Cisco dominates. So getting one's toe in the water early is a very good strategy, and that is precisely what the company is doing with SAN switches.

The best practice to note here is part of a strategy Cisco calls build, partner, acquire. These are largely mutually exclusive paths, although from time to time partnering can lead to an acquisition down the road. Cisco wants to *build* things that are core to its competitive advantage strategy, *partner* for things that are context for that strategy, and *acquire* things where their build strategy did not hit the market's sweet spot. In the case of SANs, storage products in general are context, not core, for Cisco, so it wants to partner there. The part that is core, the subnetwork provided by the SAN switch, is what the company builds. In actual fact, however, the group that builds the switch was chartered as a spinout called Andiamo, which was acquired the day it announced its first product. Thus the category exemplifies all three elements of the company's three-pronged approach to product innovation.

In addition to the four markets noted above, all of which are well into their technology-adoption life cycles, there are three longer-term opportunities Cisco has on its radar. Each represents the possibility of a major new market sector, so they are very much worth management's attention. But none of them has crossed the chasm, and so it is hard to apply product innovation to them in their current state. Indeed, it is possible that one or more of these markets may never come to fruition, or at least not in the form currently envisioned. So as a management team, what you want is to buy an option on being in the market at some future date. This, too, is part of innovating for growth markets, and so it behooves us to look into what Cisco is doing here as well.

- **NEXT-GENERATION NETWORKS FOR SERVICE PROVIDERS**. This is the market opportunity that is closest to crossing the chasm. Basically, it represents the wholesale conversion of traditional circuit-switched networks, the kind that have carried our phone calls for the past century, to IP networks, the kind that have to date carried our Internet traffic. This represents a massive investment in capital equipment by the telecommunications service-provider sector, a once-in-a-lifetime procurement boom that will establish a lasting market-share pecking order. It is a must-win battle for every network equipment provider, including Cisco.

The challenge for Cisco in this market, as already discussed, is that service-provider customers expect domain-expert professional services teams to be dedicated to their accounts. Cisco does not have a large store of these people, and the business itself is inconsistent with its gross margin model. How can the company innovate its way out of this dilemma?

Here it has been the Service-Provider Council's turn to affect the company's operations. It is clear from working with customers that a major concern about moving to an IP network is loss of control over the service once a customer gets on the Internet. This makes it impossible for service providers to bill properly for added-value services or to prevent low-paying customers from using up huge amounts of network resources. Cisco is responding to this problem by building specifically for service providers a new layer of network architecture, called the Service Exchange, which ensures that all traffic carried can be monitored and controlled by the service provider. This will allow users to be authenticated, policies to be set and enforced, and reliability to be ensured.

The best practice here represents the extension of product-to-system innovation to product-to-system-to-solution. The third element in the chain is a nod toward application innovation. Cisco does not expect to provide the applications needed to leverage the Service

Exchange, but it will partner with those who do, and by so doing seek to co-opt some of the domain expertise it needs to serve this sector.

- **DATA CENTER VIRTUALIZATION.** This opportunity is still more of a theory than a fact, although as already mentioned, tactical steps in this direction, such as storage area networking, are already well under way. In its full realization, however, the entire data center would be like one giant computer, and the bus upon which all data would travel back and forth would be governed by IP network switches.

The biggest challenge to this vision's realization is the resistance of incumbent systems and software providers to the breakdown of category barriers needed to make it happen. These barriers create both product and market inefficiencies that produce substantial profits for the current generation of providers. Moving to a more open system threatens to commoditize these positions. What kind of innovation can overcome this problem?

The answer is a modified form of platform innovation. In this situation, no one can offer the benefit of access to the market, since all the players already have that. What they can offer, on the other hand, is technology to deal with context issues cheaply, thereby saving the partner investments in noncore areas and saving the customer money, some of which can fund greater expenditures with the partner. But it is a delicate dance. If the noncore support bleeds into a core area, or if some legacy profit pool is drained in the process, partnering feelings are displaced by enmity and distrust, and the entire effort falls to pieces.

The best practice that Cisco is following in this area is to proceed cautiously, leveraging the partner prong of its build-partner-acquire strategy. Each of its key relationships—with EMC, IBM, HP, Sun, Microsoft, Oracle, and SAP—can go either way depending on how things are managed. Cisco, however, can afford to be patient because at the end of the day a whole host of services will want to be located in the network. That the network should become a platform, in other words, seems inevitable as an evolutionary rather than a revolutionary outcome.

- **THE NETWORKED HOME.** In the networked home market, it is a different matter entirely. Here we have a vision of the future that is not subject to complex-systems vendor planning. Consumer markets rarely develop under the guidance of vendor-sponsored architectures, as Microsoft, Sony, and Oracle have all learned to their chagrin. Instead, they form through spontaneous acts of self-organization, in effect just appearing as if by magic. There is little percentage in trying to anticipate these outcomes, as any retailer will tell you. Instead, the winning play is to hang out near the parade route and jump on whatever bandwagon comes by. The problem for Cisco is that this is not a behavior you can execute within a complex-systems business model. Hence the need to acquire Linksys.

Linksys was founded about the same time as Cisco and rose to market leadership through taking a volume-operations approach to product innovation. In this model, product development is outsourced on a low-cost, low-capital model, allowing the company to test new market waters extremely quickly with a first-generation offer. Where there is failure, the strategy is to discard the idea and walk away. Where there is success, it is followed up with a hard-charging negotiation with sales channels to get top-performing marketing and in-store programs. Throughout its history, Linksys has followed this highly opportunistic path, never giving itself the luxury of self-directed R&D. This may sound like a far cry from Cisco, but the two companies share at root a pragmatic approach to their markets that is product-innovation focused, does not abide technology religion, and is highly responsive to competitive developments.

What is different here is that Cisco's R&D-rich model requires it to lead the market through product innovation, whereas Linksys's R&D-lean approach requires it to be a fast follower. In effect, Linksys, like Dell, only enters market after they are inside the tornado, for that is all a lean R&D model can afford to do. From this single distinction cascades a series of implications for sales, services, marketing, operations, logistics, and finance—essentially the implications charted out by the complex-systems/volume-operations distinction. Hence the challenge of operating the two models in close proximity.

The best practice of note here is a combining of the two models while operating them at arm's length from each other. This creates a built-in hedge against which of two paths a market's development will take—what one might call the path of intelligent design versus that of natural selection, the one implying that all complex phenomena must be designed before they can exist and the other implying that design can emerge without conscious intent interposing itself. Markets develop along both paths: With a hedged approach, if you miss on the complex-systems design cycle, you have a chance to catch up on the volume-operations downstream.

To sum up this installment of the Cisco case study, where the topic has been innovating for growth markets, the company's focus is on using product innovation to gain competitive advantage. This implies an organization optimized for selling and servicing products, using partners to fulfill the more complex needs of systems and solutions. And that indeed reflects the company that Cisco in large part is today.

That said, one major challenge the company faces is that the heart of its market has moved out of the growth phase and into the mature phase. How it can deal with this development is the subject of the next chapter.

CHAPTER SIX

MANAGING INNOVATION IN MATURE MARKETS

O nce a new category's initial wave of adoption is over—when the bulk of the available new customers have been acquired by selling them their first purchase in the category—growth rates subside dramatically. The market settles into a pattern we have termed the indefinitely elastic middle, and the hierarchy of established vendors becomes increasingly entrenched. Compared to growth markets, returns on capital are lower in absolute terms, but when factored by a discount for risk, they are often more attractive. Welcome to Main Street.

In Main Street markets, there is no prevailing wind of mass adoption to fill your sails, no rising tide of category growth to float all boats. Instead there is an ongoing dynamic of refinement that shapes the unfolding of a mature market, one that lends itself to working at increasingly close quarters with your offering, with your customers, and with your processes.

Understanding this change in climate has been difficult for the technology sector. Accustomed to growth markets spawned from the ongoing price/performance improvements enabled by semiconductor miniaturization, it has had little history to help it deal with market maturation. As a consequence, the industry continues to invest in product R&D at a time when the market is not prepared to pay returns sufficient to warrant it. In the PC industry, we have seen three icons—Compaq, IBM, and HP—all fall victim to excessive R&D expense. Meanwhile, Dell, demonstrating a highly pragmatic understanding of the market's actual dynamics, has capitalized indirectly on all its competitors' investments by capturing their R&D on the rebound from the world's supply chain. Dell's greatest risk, ironically, is that if it puts all three out of business, it will have no ready source of free R&D in the future.

To thrive on Main Street requires management teams to reorient their thinking about market dynamics. The model we have found most useful for aiding this reorientation is called market fractalization, and it can be illustrated by the series of figures below:

Fractalization in Mature Markets

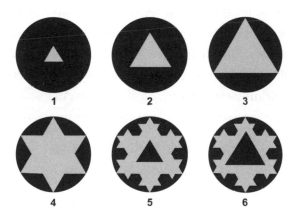

Figures 1 through 3 represent the early, middle, and late stages of a growth market, the sort of thing we looked at in the prior chapter. The circle represents the total available market, and the triangle represents the total market served. As the figures indicate, the driving dynamic at this point is a single-minded attempt to acquire new customers and claim market share.

By the time we hit figure 3, however, the market for the basic offering has become saturated. One can no longer grow simply by adding new customers to the category because the bulk of them have already been added. After virtually every home has a phone, every garage a car, every child a personal sound system, what do you do next?

Figures 4 and 5 show what happens under the pressure for continued growth in revenues and profits. The figure sprouts extensions into the remaining space. The added triangles in figure 4 are intended to represent line extensions, while those in figure 5 represent product enhancements. Thus, from the mass-market Model T car, for example, the automotive industry first generated line extensions: a sedan, a station wagon, a truck, a coupe, a limousine. Then for any one of these it later on created product enhancements by accessorizing any of these vehicles with radios, automatic transmissions, power windows, air bags, cup holders, and, at one point, seats of fine Corinthian leather.

Figure 5 by itself does not represent an end state. Increasingly fine-grained fractalization can and will continue as long as there are discretionary dollars to spend in the system and the category as a whole has not become obsolete. Consider the example of the telecommunications industry:

Fractal Markets: The Nth Device

The Example of Telephones

Larger fractals spawn smaller fractals as innovation continues to seek out finer and finer niches. OK, but surely, one thinks, this has to stop eventually; it can't go on forever. One would think so, but just about the time you are sure nothing more can come out of a category like this one, someone discovers that you can sell ring tones for cell phones, and a multibillion-dollar-per-year market appears out of nowhere!

Finally, figures 5 and 6 also illustrate a companion process that accompanies increasing refinement of the surface of the offer, one represented by a triangle in the center of the figure growing larger over time. This triangle represents increasing cost reduction of the base system as it becomes more and more commoditized. In mature markets customers are willing to pay a small premium for the delighters at the surface, but that premium is relative to a commodity price that is declining. To maintain margins, vendors must therefore cost-reduce the core even as they add value at the surface. In this way, consumer electronics vendors, in particular, have been able to offer an astounding array of new features at the same or lower price points as their previous models. That is because the supply chain behind them is taking out the cost as fast or faster than they can add it back in.

Taking all six triangular figures together, let us note what is changing as we progress through them and what is not. First of all, the area of the figure in the later diagrams is not increasing substantially. Indeed it is bounded permanently by the area of the circle. This is analogous to the total number of customers in the market. Growth from new-customer acquisition reaches an asymptotic limit.

The aspect of the fractal figure that does continue to change dramatically, on the other hand, is its perimeter. Indeed, in the transition from figure 3 to 4, the perimeter is lengthened by 33 percent. Interestingly, in the transition from figure 4 to 5, it is also increased by 33 percent. And had we continued to add smaller triangles to every side of figure 5 when making figure 6, we would have generated yet another 33 percent increase. Pretty attractive growth numbers.

Growth in the perimeter of the figure is analogous to growing the total number of sales in the market. It can be significantly larger than the total number of customers as long as a sizable number of people feel the need for two or more products from the same category. Let's test the idea. How many phones do you have? How many books? How about DVDs? How many TV channels do you subscribe to? How many pairs of shoes do you own? How many watches? Pens? Ties? How many cooking pans? Bottles of wine?

The fractal model makes clear that long after the customer base has made its initial set of in-category purchases, consumption can grow substantially. But for such growth to continue, it must be driven by innovation.

INNOVATION TYPES FOR MATURE MARKETS

As we have already noted, innovation types for mature markets fall into two broad zones, as we illustrated earlier by the table on page 63.

If we now correlate these two zones and their innovation types to the fractal model, we see how they interoperate to create value in mature markets.

The innovation types that leverage customer intimacy create variation at the surface of the offering. The primary offer remains unchanged, but one or more of its secondary attributes is modified. These differentiated secondary attributes sit atop a relatively undifferentiated substrate. Line extensions, product enhancements, marketing programs, improved customer experiences—all these are ways to add value to what from a purely functional point of view is a relatively constant and undifferentiated generic offering. Think of melodic riffs played atop a steady bass line.

As long as vendors can come up with new delighters to deliver, there are untapped pools of returns from which these types of innovation can yield revenue and profit growth. As we noted, how-

Innovation Types for Fractal Markets

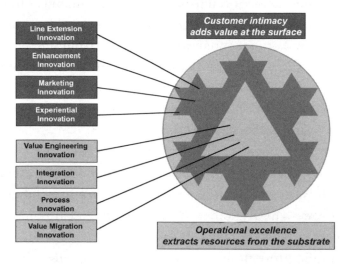

ever, as markets mature, these later returns come with a decreasing premium. That is, as the category becomes more fractalized, there are diminishing returns from each new fractal element. So in order to prosper on Main Street, in addition to generating novel variations at the surface, one must also find ways to economize in the underlying core.

This brings us to the second class of innovation in mature markets, those that leverage operational excellence and which focus on resource extraction from the substrate. In its simplest form it is cost reduction through value engineering—substituting standard commodity components for custom proprietary ones. But there are other ways to create efficiencies in the substrate, from integration innovation to process reengineering to value migration. By combining one or more of these methods with one or more of the first group, one contributes to increases in profits by launching joint attacks not only on the top line but also on the bottom line.

Here we see a substantial departure from innovation in growth markets. There the focus is primarily on the top line, and companies had to choose one innovation type out of four and suppress the rest.

In mature markets there is a combined focus on top and bottom line—more on the top if you focus on customer intimacy, more on the bottom if you focus on operational excellence—with the overarching notion that you should major in one and minor in the other.

This leads us to our mantra for Main Street management:

Add value at the surface;
extract resources from the base.

In order to execute this strategy, organizations need to major in an innovation type from one zone and minor in another from the other zone. This is another way of saying that mature-market innovation must be self-funding. In fact, since overall productivity is expected to improve in the future, the extracting effort has to exceed the adding value budget.

Many companies faced with this challenge throw all their energy into cost reduction, but this is folly, since there is no way to secure adequate returns on capital without investing in ongoing differentiation. Other companies innovate self-indulgently without economizing and then are shocked when the market will not pay enough of a premium to support their high-flying ways. The truth is that there should be no surprises here: The mechanisms of Main Street are well understood, the disciplines known in advance. Just pick up your shovel and walk to the mine.

In so doing, however, keep in mind whether you are playing a complex-systems or a volume-operations game. In mature markets, complex-systems enterprises tend to retain substantial customer intimacy within their installed base if only because switching costs are so high. However, they and their customers both struggle with productivity improvement in the areas of maintenance and total cost of ownership. These organizations, therefore, are normally best served by creating competitive separation through innovation types in the Operational Excellence Zone.

By contrast, volume-operations organizations are typically good at handling the productivity challenges enabled by operational excellence but struggle over time with sustaining customer loyalty in an ever-commoditizing marketplace. Thus they are more likely to gain competitive separation by focusing on the innovation types in the Customer Intimacy Zone, minoring in operational excellence all the while.

With these principles in mind—a major in one innovation type, a minor in the other, and self-funding productivity improvements to pay for all the innovation undertaken—we can now take a closer look at the innovation types optimized for a mature market.

FOCUSING INNOVATION IN THE CUSTOMER INTIMACY ZONE

The four types of innovation that enable customer intimacy—line extension, enhancement, marketing, and experiential—are arranged in a sequence from left to right, moving from those most closely associated with the physical product to those most closely associated with the mind of the customer. This reflects an important element of market maturation: As the features and functions of the un-

Innovation Types for Mature Markets
The Customer Intimacy Zone

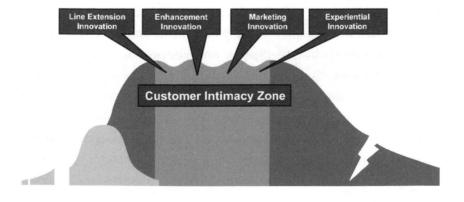

derlying offer become increasingly commoditized, perceived value migrates from the physical world of objects to the symbolic world of personal values and social interactions.

Choosing an innovation type within the Customer Intimacy Zone, therefore, is a life-cycle-sensitive decision. As elsewhere in this model, each type has a sweet spot in the evolution of the category. Outside that sweet spot there still may be a good case for using it, but on a first-pass basis we should look for the type that best matches our market's dynamics.

SHOULD WE FOCUS ON LINE-EXTENSION INNOVATION?

Line extension represents the first filling up of the fractal space by modifying a successful offering in one or more dimensions to better serve one or more relatively large segments. The goal is still to gain market share, albeit in less dramatic fashion than during the hypergrowth phase of category expansion, by adapting a proven solution to a more specific context.

Line-extension innovation lends itself to the volume-operations model in particular because so much of the cost of entering a new segment has already been born by prior efforts. This allows companies to aggressively saturate markets before their competitors can neutralize their competitive advantage. Companies that have succeeded in so doing include the following:

- **TYLENOL**. Having taken the pain reliever market by storm as a safer alternative to aspirin and ibuprofen, Tylenol subsequently branched out into allergy and sinus, cold and flu, and sleeplessness medications, as well as extending their line to children, women with menstrual pain, and arthritis sufferers. Like other examples of consumer packaged goods— Tide and Coca-Cola, for example—this illustrates the power of a strong brand to invade adjacent categories.

- **AMERICAN EXPRESS.** Originally a purveyor of traveler's checks, then moving into credit cards, it has been able to differentiate itself from Visa and MasterCard by extending its credit card franchise into a line of financial services that its rivals are precluded from offering. Thus today you can get a home equity loan, mortgage, or line of credit, open a checking, savings, or CD account, set up an IRA and fill it with mutual funds, or buy insurance for your car or your life. Again, the company's volume-operations brand "covers" this portfolio, making it both comfortable and convenient for you to conduct a series of related transactions with a single vendor.

- **PEOPLE MAGAZINE.** Originally a popular feature within *Time* magazine, it was spun out to capitalize on the inordinate interest it drew. Similar line extensions occur when TV series spin out characters like Joey to form a new series or when movies spawn sequels to *Spiderman* or *Rocky*. In all cases the market is built in and protected from competition—customers are just getting more of something they already have declared their preference for.

- **LEXUS.** This is an example of what a company can do when its brand does not cover the adjacent space it wants to enter. Toyota launched an entirely new brand with a new dealer channel, and then was able to leverage its vaunted Toyota production system to take on Mercedes and BMW directly. This is a higher-risk option, however, as both Honda with its Acura and Nissan with its Infiniti brand have learned.

Line extension is less crisply defined in the world of complex systems. Because offers are typically tailored to each customer, a single class of system can be stretched higher and lower through professional services without having to repackage the base product. Nonetheless, the innovation type still applies, as the following examples illustrate:

- **BOEING 737**. Each class of plane at Boeing is a true product innovation, with all the costs and risks that innovation type entails, but within each class line extensions can maximize returns. This has been particularly true of the 737 line, which has sold more than fifty-two hundred airplanes since its introduction in 1967 (more than all the planes its rival Airbus has sold since its inception). It went through numerous line extensions that provide different size and distance options and convertibility from passenger to cargo—all under the umbrella of a single-service organization and bill of materials. For pragmatist and conservative buyers, incremental improvements to a proven system combined with an ongoing focus on lower costs is the winning formula.

- **EMC**. EMC took the lead in enterprise storage at the high end of the market by allowing storage devices to be shared across computers from different vendors. Subsequently, it acquired Data General's midrange storage line to push its technology down market, significantly increasing its market share and protecting its up-market franchise from a flanking attack. And it has subsequently supplemented this position with software acquisitions that manage data backup and recovery and other data-related processes. All these are natural line extensions that extend the boundary of the franchise at relatively low risk. (This stands in contrast to its expansion into additional software categories beyond storage, a strategy that foreshadows a reorganization of how data is to be managed, one that is more aligned with disruptive innovation than line extension.)

- **SWISS RE**. This 140-year-old company began in response to the insurance industry's inability to handle all the claims of a major fire. Today its has businesses in life and health, property and casualty, and financial services focused on risk management. Its property and casualty line has extended itself over the decades to include accident, agriculture, engineering, marine, motor, natural perils, nuclear energy, as well as more specialized sectors and services. At one point the company entered direct insuring but quickly retreated, an example of not just taking its brand promise too far, but potentially violating it because it put the company in competition with its customers.

Line extension is essentially a power move. It leverages existing category momentum and company momentum within a given category, creating further room for expansion without risking a new venture. The market wants to see more of you, and you are obliging. By the same token, it does not lend itself to categories or brands that are out of favor, where the market would just as soon you shrank your presence. In situations where you must rekindle favor, you are better served by applying value engineering to get to a better price supplemented with enhancement innovations to reawaken interest.

To execute a line extension, every function in your company must wean itself from practices established for product innovation, as follows:

- Research and development must accept that they are leveraging an existing platform and do not have permission to redesign it, flawed though it may be. Instead, they must work with marketing to focus on segment-specific attributes of the offer located closer to the surface than to the core.

- Product marketing for its part has to trade off scope for focus and therefore prune its wish lists to those elements pertinent to the target segment. Both groups are well guided by before/after usage scenarios in a day of the life of an idealized target customer.

- On the operations side, line extension sacrifices some of the efficiencies of mass standardization to get the benefits of mass customization. This requires reorchestrating the value chain end to end to locate the customizing activities as late in the chain as possible while still executing them reliably.

- Customer service, too, must be realigned to cope with increasing complexity. In most cases, this is not likely to be the only line extension they will be asked to absorb, so the reorchestration is in effect a redesign for extensibility to be done once and reused. The consequence of not pursuing this path is that you eat up the gains from the line extension in operational cost overruns.

- Finally, on the field marketing and sales side, teams must seek out novel communications channels and reformulate marketing messages to capture the attention of the target segment and to focus the sales channel appropriately. Again, putting in place a messaging architecture that can be repurposed for segment-specific uses allows line extension strategies to scale beyond the first segment.

Overall there is nothing in line extension per se that makes execution a high risk. There is one caveat, however, to keep in mind. The logic of line extensions will from time to time tempt you to cross the business-architecture divide. This is almost certain to be a bad idea. The increase in complexity cannot be paid back by the increase in business, for rather than getting better, the margins get worse. Thus, for example, American Express in 2005 is exiting brokerage and money-management service lines, where customers expect more of a complex-systems level of service, in order to focus on its volume-operations offerings.

With this caveat in mind, if your market and market position favor line extension, it is one of the most attractive innovation types, generating relatively high returns for relatively low risk. Thus, if your situation qualifies, this is probably the type you will pick.

SHOULD WE FOCUS ON ENHANCEMENT INNOVATION?

Unlike line-extension innovations that expand the market by bringing in new customers, enhancement innovations are focused primarily on earning more margin dollars from existing customers, either by keeping them as loyal customers or by upgrading them to premium offerings. Enhancement innovations are most familiar to us in their volume-operations guise in consumer markets, but complex-systems product managers in mature markets sift through hundreds of enhancement requests as well.

Here are some examples of volume-operations enterprises achieving competitive separation through enhancement innovation:

- **SWATCH WATCHES.** Swatch stands alone in the watch business by pricing watches low enough to be impulse buys and then using enhancement innovation to create buying impulses. The company has used this approach to appeal to a wide spectrum of demographics: Its 2005 spring/summer collection has more than 225 watches in 17 different categories, from fashion and fun scuba to pop and paparazzi. It has complemented this strategy with dedicated retail kiosks that vividly display its jazzy designs, thereby creating the foot traffic needed to fuel impulse buying. Meanwhile its competitors are stuck in department stores under glass cases with less traffic, higher prices, and bored sales reps.

- **PAMPERS AND HUGGIES.** The disposable diaper category is dominated by Procter & Gamble (Pampers, Luvs) and Kimberly Clark (Huggies). After the former company introduced the category in the 1960s, and it went through line extensions into older children as well as incontinent adults, competition has been driven by enhancement innovations. Pampers upped the ante by substituting tape for diaper pins in the early 1970s and a Z fold for more absorption. Huggies took the field by storm by adding elastic fit at the legs to prevent leaks. Between the two corporations, they have about 75 percent market share of the total category—all based on enhancements that add either convenience or good feelings.

- **MONTBLANC.** The luxury pen company has two series of collectible pens, one based on famous authors, the other on famous artists. Each pen in each series consists of a limited edition with a distinctive design in a distinctive package. They are just pens, but the ballpoints cost around $400 and the fountain pens around $700. There is no direct competition, although all collectibles compete for discretionary budget against all other collectibles. Distribution is restricted to further enhance the exclusivity of the brand. All series sell out within a year or two of release, without discounting.

- **BARBIE.** Barbie's line extensions into other dolls are not its primary economic engine. That would come from enhancement innovations that adapt Barbie to new fashion trends, new hot locations, new pop stars and styles, and the like. Enhancements go well beyond doll clothes into accessories like cars, homes, club scenes, and so on. As a consequence, the franchise's image is continually refreshed while its high-margin accessories provide extremely profitable returns.

Complex-systems offerings can also refresh themselves using enhancement innovations if they are distinctive enough. The goal is to complement long-cycle product innovation and medium-cycle line-extension innovation with short-cycle enhancement innovation, as the following examples illustrate:

- **BOEING.** The aircraft company's long-cycle product innovations are its 7X7 series, of which the 777 is the most recent. Its line extensions have been discussed relative to its workhorse 737 line. But that line itself is kept fresh with features like fuel-saving winglets that improve airfoil effectiveness and systems like Quiet Climb to meet noise abatement standards, Vertical Situation Display to improve the pilot's experience, and GPS Landing to increase safety in low-visibility situations. These enhancements reinforce the competitive separation achieved by product and line-extension innovations.

- **OTIS.** The elevator company's long-cycle product innovation is represented by its Gen2 system, which completely redesigned the subsystems to create an easier to deploy, easier to maintain system. Its line extensions cover everything from two-story apartment buildings to high-rises. Its enhancement innovations include its Elvonic software, which minimizes wait times, and its door-closing safety systems that avoid contact with people. Once again, the short-cycle innovations create customer and channel-partner interest in the current year's model, reinforcing competitive separation established by the longer-cycle modes.

- **CATERPILLAR.** The construction-equipment company introduced its first backhoe in 1985 and has had three long-cycle product innovations (Series B, C, and D). Series C introduced linkage architecture that allowed operators to quickly switch from one tool to another. Series D featured a higher-rotation linkage that allowed for digging deeper holes, but its marketing campaign emphasized user-oriented enhancements, including a move to joystick controls, more comfortable seats, and more glass for better visibility.

Enhancement innovations reinforce existing market positions, garnering a premium price for the vendor, factored by their overall status within the category. In the case of the market leader, all customers want is a good excuse to pay the price premium for what they are predisposed to think of as the safe buy. In the case of market challengers, the enhancement should be edgy enough that the market leader is not likely to copy it for fear of alienating their mainstream customer base. In the case of low-cost opportunists, where offering the lowest price is a condition of getting into distribution, a single enhancement can provide the entire marketing campaign. In all three of these cases, companies are gaining competitive differentiation through these investments.

That said, enhancement innovation is wasted if it is spent largely on catching up to other companies' previously introduced enhancements. Vendors get no credit for these, since the market has already assigned that value to the competing offer. All they do is help neutralize that competitive advantage, which has the effect of bringing the winner's price down, not the vendor's price up. It is critical, therefore, to make an original contribution in order to achieve an economic gain.

A useful model for systematically reviewing the universe of possibilities for making an original contribution is McGrath and MacMillan's consumption chain, which calls out fifteen different stages in the life cycle of a purchase transaction from beginning to end.* As an enhancement innovator, you should prioritize a single stage for treatment, interview customers and partners in depth about how it could best be reformed, and then design a program that distinctively differentiates your company's performance. Consider, for example, the many creative responses to waiting in line that have spawned differentiated offers, whether that be in queue management at Disneyland (you can make an appointment for a popular ride), waiting to pick up your burger at Taylor's Refresher (they give you a pager), or getting through the toll both on your local freeway (with an electronic Fast Pass).

There is always an opportunity to differentiate by enhancement. As long as the category is still in its indefinitely elastic middle state, this option should make the short list. Prioritizing it to the top of

---

*The Entrepreneurial Mindset: Strategies for Continuously Creating Opportunity in an Age of Uncertainty, Rita Gunther McGrath and Ian MacMillan, Harvard Business School Press (Boston, 2000), chapter 4.

the list, on the other hand, is largely a matter of how compelling the proposed enhancements are compared to the other options in play.

SHOULD WE FOCUS ON MARKETING INNOVATION?

Both line extensions and enhancement innovation modify the offering to make it more competitive for a more targeted set of customers. But one can also make the *same* offering more competitive by modifying other elements in the marketing mix. Companies in the volume-operations space who have gained sustainable competitive separation through marketing innovation include:

- **NIKE**. It began with Michael Jordan and moved on to Tiger Woods. In both cases, the company made major commitments to charismatic stars who have helped it define a unique brand image. It also was the first company in its category to build a showcase store, Niketown, a tactic that was subsequently copied by Sony and Apple. Its swoosh logo appears everywhere. And finally, its iconic saying, Just do it!, captured the imagination and values of a whole generation that had become increasing cynical of talk in any form. The net of all of the above is that the company has remarkable brand awareness and highly positive brand associations, the two elements of consumer marketing that drive economic success. It's not about the shoes anymore.

- **AVON**. It staked out a unique distribution idea for cosmetics—personal appointments at the consumer's home—and developed a sales channel with the skills and attitude required to compete economically with retail store fronts. Its "Avon calling" campaign in the 1950s emblazoned Avon ladies (currently five million worldwide) in the customer's mind.

Sales management and pink Cadillacs as sales incentives—not unique products—have established the company as a consistent performer in a category that is typically product driven. Today the company is migrating its direct sales model to the Web in developed economies, leveraging its strong brand recognition, while still counting on the commissioned representative in emerging economies.

- **AMERICAN GIRL.** Dolls are dolls, unless they are American Girls. The company launches each line with a book about a girl living in a particular era of history. The stories are both informative and compelling, leaving strong impressions that are food for much fantasy play thereafter. The dolls provide a focus for that play, but that is only the beginning. Each doll has its own doll house, doll furniture, doll accessories, and the like—all marketed by the story itself, reinforced by catalogs thereafter. Parents and grandparents can dish out hundreds of dollars without exhausting the inventory around even a single doll.

- **APPLE.** As the Macintosh was a testimony to disruptive innovation, the iPod is to marketing innovation. To begin with, the company had to negotiate a relationship with the music industry to get a full complement of songs online at iTunes. Then it had to design a device that was easy and elegant to use. Then it had to graphically capture the attention of its target market—who knew it would be the white wired ear pods standing out against a variety of silhouettes? Then it did line extensions both up and down to capture the premium user and defend the low end. Then it did enhancement innovations in the form of docking stations, iPod cases, and the like. Then it got Steve Jobs and Bono on the same stage. The end result is not just an iconic product, but the repositioning of an entire company from the computer sector into consumer electronics.

Overall, the tactics that go into marketing innovation for volume operations are well known and frequently emulated. But the ability to generate competitive separation is rare. This is a situation where it is critically important to go *far enough*. Most companies are unwilling to subordinate their other attributes to this cause. They advertise, they have brand campaigns, but at the end of the day they do not cross over the line that would break them free from their competitive set to become a unique part of their customers' world. Instead, they stay with the herd, maintaining an arm's-length relationship between vendor and purchaser—perfectly satisfactory, but not differentiating. This is fine as long as you collectively acknowledge as a management team that it is not your intent to differentiate in marketing, only to meet a market-acceptable standard. If that is your conclusion, then you will want to manage down the costs of marketing in service to good enough as opposed to making a big bet to become best in class.

In complex-systems business architecture, marketing is nowhere near as visible a function. Here the goal is to differentiate on reputation rather than brand, which requires a social rather than a psychographic focus. The fundamental objective is to establish intimacy with an exclusive community within which your company is the only vendor to penetrate the inner circle. Thus one of the keys to power in this mode is to operate invisibly, influencing outcomes behind the scenes, as the following examples will illustrate:

- **McKINSEY.** This company is highly differentiated not by its offers but by its access to senior executives in both the private and public sector. Its most visible marketing programs are the *McKinsey Quarterly* and the McKinsey Global Institute, both of which create forums for intellectual discussion and thought leadership. But much of its real marketing power comes from its alumni network, which carefully nurtures relationships with former employees to retain a connection to the firm. As these people rise in their new roles in business and government, they inevitably draw on the services of their prior colleagues, often without considering an alternative firm, and clearly with a preference for their alma mater even when they do. The firm is careful to maintain its mystique, never referring to specific clients in its published materials and never allowing another firm to position itself as a partner. It actively maintains the behind-the-scenes positioning that is key to complex-systems marketing.

- **GE HEALTHCARE.** GE destabilized a mature market in medical equipment by introducing a multivendor maintenance offer that gave customers a single relationship to manage ("one throat to choke") with a predictable budget number that included a price discount for volume. By doing so, it simultaneously froze out all its competitors from ongoing interaction with the customer. Now whether GE is providing system support and maintenance, technical training, continuing education, monitoring or diagnosis, management software, or performance-improvement consulting, it is monopolizing the attention of the customer, learning about the next generation of needs, and keeping the inside track for the next round of procurements.

- **BERKSHIRE HATHAWAY.** To be sure, the firm is primarily lionized for its investment performance, but Warren Buffett has been masterful at positioning himself as the "oracle of Omaha." His primary marketing instruments are the annual meeting and his annual letter to shareholders. What both do is impose onto the highly ambiguous world of investing a set of values and interpretative lenses that clarify and resolve challenging issues. Buffett's folksy tone becomes a vehicle for invoking common sense as an analytical platform, thereby inviting the rest of us to participate in his investment philosophy. In this way he creates an exclusive community that his competitors for investment capital can only envy.

Complex-systems marketing seeks to establish a unique and privileged position that is validated by a consensus of disinterested third parties. This means establishing and maintaining exclusive relationships with influential constituencies, people who typically value their privacy. For the most part, it is conducted behind closed doors or in one-on-one conversations. As such, it stands in direct contrast to the more public marketing techniques of volume-operations sectors. When a complex-systems enterprise seeks a new head of marketing, therefore, it is critically important to hire a leader with the right background.

Whether a complex-systems firm should prioritize marketing innovation is partly a function of the time horizon. Relationship marketing takes a long time to come to fruition. Early returns are not impressive because trust is something that builds exponentially over time, having no appreciable impact until you pass the knee in the curve. If you have the patience, however, and your firm keeps its commitments, you can generate very powerful and highly sustainable positions in the long term.

SHOULD WE FOCUS ON EXPERIENTIAL INNOVATION?

Experiential innovation differentiates offerings by focusing on the time interval customers spend in direct contact with the offer, the vendor, or the sales and services provider, and the quality of their interaction with the processes and products involved. The functional aspects of the offer, in other words, are treated as context; it is their experience that is core.

Companies in the volume operations arena that have successfully differentiated by using experiential innovation include:

- **DISNEYLAND**. Disney pioneered the theme park category. Today it differentiates by creating a family experience informed by the characters and story lines from its films. The experience begins with handling context extremely well, including cleanliness, safety, and convenience, thereby differentiating the parks from the more thrill-seeking, adolescent-optimized competition. Layered on top of this benign substrate is a host of rides and venues that reconstruct scenarios from the movies that allow families to engage in entertaining ways. These recapture experiences from the films and give life to what otherwise would be mechanical attractions. And because there is a consistency of theme across most Disney entertainments, the overall experience of the park is both highly structured and completely contained, both physically and emotionally, creating a predictable result that other parks cannot match.

- **CIRQUE DU SOLEIL.** This company's entertainments are in many ways the diametric opposite of Disney. It seeks to be edgy and unpredictable, to stretch rather than to reassure, staking out a territory at the intersection of visual spectacles and postmodern philosophies. It is a great example of a company's going so far that rational competitors either cannot or will not follow. As such it has completely redefined the category of circus in every dimension, virtually taken over Las Vegas as its private preserve, and by virtue of its differentiation is able to charge hefty price premiums for its displays.

- **AMERICA ONLINE.** AOL rose to prominence by creating a simpler e-mail experience targeted at consumers who were late adopters of technology but early adopters of new communication opportunities. It was the first company to use a progression of icons to reassure users that the log-on process was proceeding according to protocol, a period of great vulnerability for a late adopter. It's "You've got mail!" captured just the right tone to encourage this community not only to continue to use the service but to tell their friends about it. When the Internet came along, and later broadband communications, the company realized that their late-adopting customer base would continue to want a mediated experience and adapted its offers accordingly. Over time the brand will have to evolve, as adoption issues are inherently transitory, but for now it is highly differentiated and able to charge a premium for so being.

- **PROGRESSIVE INSURANCE.** The company has a highly differentiated economic performance that is derived from its exceptional focus on the customer experience. This begins with price quotations during the shopping process, which include competitors' rates for comparison; moves on to a 24–7 claims center that provides immediate response including, where needed, getting a claim representative to the trauma site; and culminates with a concierge service for vehicle repair, whereby the company handles the entire process on behalf of its customers, including paging them when it is done. By designing its processes from the customer back instead of from the operation out, it continues to create separation between itself and its direct competitors.

Experiential innovation's focus on the end user is effective in volume operations in consumer markets because the user and the buyer are either the same person or closely connected. That is not the case in the enterprise markets served by complex-systems vendors where the person with budget responsibility, the economic buyer, rarely actually touches the product or service. Nonetheless, such executives can be strongly influenced by experiential innovation if it focuses on their issues, which include networking with peers, motivating their organizations, consulting knowledgeable experts, and extracting from the information overload pertinent insights.

Companies that have been able to leverage experiential innovation to create competitive differentiation in a complex-systems business model include:

- **THE WORLD ECONOMIC FORUM.** The forum's annual meeting in Davos is renowned for its ability to attract the topmost leaders in business and government year after year. A priori concerns that unite this audience are their privacy and security, and the forum goes out of its way to ensure these by restricting invitees, controlling access, and investing in elaborate security systems and practices. Given these assurances, what its attendees truly value is the opportunity to connect and interact socially, creating both new perspectives and new opportunities to engage. The program itself each year is far reaching, expanding beyond business and economics to incorporate social issues and the arts, thereby leveraging the unique positions of it attendees to affect truly global outcomes. The tone of the event is one that invites attendees to engage in global actions with altruistic objectives while at the same time respecting the range of their other public and private commitments. Such a recipe cannot be constructed overnight—it builds on trust gained over time—but once in place, it is highly differentiating.

- **IBM.** In the 1970s and 1980s, as computers were becoming more mainstream in business, and the category was shifting from being called data processing to management information systems (MIS), IBM took the lead is educating an entire generation of business executives about what computing was and how it related to business. At the same time, it educated its own sales force and sales channel partners about business customers, focusing them on how each industry had unique needs and how those needs related to computing's capabilities. It also pioneered business-systems planning, where IBM executives sat down with MIS directors and helped them conceptualize, design, and implement their next generation of information systems. The overall experience was highly reassuring to the executives involved and helped give rise to the ultimate differentiator, "Nobody ever got fired for buying IBM."

- **THE GARTNER GROUP.** If ever there was a subject that attracted information overload, it is surely the IT industry and the myriad of vendor and product choices it offers across a bewildering array of categories. Gartner fundamentally changed the experience of economic buyers by introducing its Magic Quadrant, where all companies in a given category are arrayed across a two-by-two matrix ranking ability to execute and completeness of vision. This one intellectual construct has reduced the essence of the IT agenda to two persistent variables and allowed a generation of IT executives to wrap their minds around innumerable high-risk buying decisions. This gave it the market pull to differentiate itself in a highly competitive sector, acquiring rivals like Dataquest and Meta to form the market-leading conglomerate.

In each of these examples of experiential innovation, companies have looked closely at the customer experience end to end and mounted a concerted campaign to intervene proactively to reshape it to some significantly differentiated outcome. Customers appreciate these efforts and reward them with continued loyalty. Competitors, however, often copy the most visible one or two elements of these programs, and that does have a blunting effect on their differentiating capabilities. So the question arises, when would you invest in this form of innovation, and when not?

In the volume-operations domain, a key prerequisite for successful experiential innovation is for the underlying offer to be thoroughly commoditized. If it is not, then issues of features and functions are too likely to override experiential factors in the purchase decision. A second requirement is that the experience be replicable with sufficient frequency that it becomes part of the vendor's brand identity. Creating extraordinary customer experiences sporadically will not create the kind of loyalty effects needed to pay back experiential innovation. A third requirement is that it be scalable, which means, in effect, that it be embedded in the enabling practices and systems of the vendor.

On the complex-systems side, the first requirement is direct access to the economic buyer: Experiential differentiation cannot be delivered secondhand. The second is distinctive content that establishes true thought leadership: Participants have to feel they are learning something they genuinely did not know before. Finally, although not exactly a requirement, it is extremely helpful to have a charismatic impresario to orchestrate the experience and keep the network alive between events.

If your situation meets the above requirements, then you are likely to get great returns from experiential innovation—specifically, increases in revenues and margins with no appreciable changes to cost of goods, capital expenditures, or operating expenditures. Indeed, in the overall order in which they were presented, the innovation types in the Customer Intimacy Zone are characterized by increasing capital efficiency made possible by migrating the venue of value creation out of the physical world and into the customer's mind. Mature markets lend themselves to this discipline in large part because they have taken much of the variability out of the functional components of the offer, thereby freeing up everyone's attention to focus elsewhere.

A sustained attack on variability, in other words, is a necessary enabler of customer intimacy strategies. It is accomplished by the innovation types in the Operational Excellence Zone. Thus at minimum companies in mature markets have to minor in operational excellence. The question is, would you want to major in it? To answer that question, let us turn to the next section.

FOCUSING INNOVATION IN THE OPERATIONAL EXCELLENCE ZONE

We have said that to innovate in fractal markets one must add value at the customer-facing surface of offers while simultaneously extracting resources from the substrate. It is the second part of this formula that is the focus in the Operational Excellence Zone. We should acknowledge from the outset that mature-market competition mandates a fair amount of operational excellence just to keep up with the competition. We are not talking about that level of commitment

Innovation Types for Mature Markets

The Operational Excellence

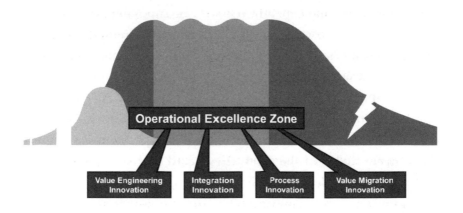

here. To warrant mention in the discussion that follows, companies must have so excelled at one or another of the innovation types in this zone as to achieve significant differentiation leading to sustainable competitive advantage.

In that context, we will look at the four innovation types diagrammed above, and again we can note a left-to-right progression from the one closest to the product itself, value engineering innovation, to the one most abstracted from it, value migration innovation. Implicit in this progression is an increasing commoditization in the base functionality of the product forcing differentiation efforts to seek out new venues for value creation.

SHOULD WE FOCUS ON VALUE-ENGINEERING INNOVATION?

Volume-operations companies differentiate with value engineering when they are able to capture the essence of an offer simply and cost-reduce every other element dramatically. Here are some examples:

- **BIC**. The leading pen manufacturer in the world, its original BIC pen is still in production and is an icon of value engineering. Consider its key features. It is a ballpoint pen, a major engineering accomplishment that has not been much improved upon in fifty years. It is disposable, so there are fewer SKUs for the supply chain to worry about. It is made of transparent plastic so you can see how much ink is left inside. It is hexagonal, so it does not roll off a table top. It has a cap, so there are no additional moving parts. And because it is so simple and has such a long production history, it can be made anywhere in the world in BIC superfactories that are optimized for mass production. Add to this major in operational excellence a minor in branding, and you have a formula for sustainably differentiating a commodity, one BIC has subsequently applied to lighters and shavers.

- **MOTEL 6**. The company established itself as the low-price leader with its original name, which referred to the initial price it charged for a night's stay. This price was made possible by selecting low-cost out-of-town locations, building standard motel designs optimized to facilitate cleaning and maintenance, and eliminating restaurant facilities. The company combined price-leadership value engineering with a compelling branding campaign featuring a folksy spokesperson and the tag line "We'll leave the light on for you." The down-home humor helped cut through the noise of other brand promises and connect with the listener on a message of basic value. The result is that it is the market leader in no-frills hospitality.

- **SOUTHWEST AIRLINES.** The company is a casebook example of how to redesign an offer from the ground up to design out costs. Build a fleet around a single standard plane, simplifying maintenance and reducing spares. Avoid airports that charge premium landing fees. Simplify pricing and seat selection to reduce bottlenecks at check-in. Focus on point-to-point round-trip itineraries to avoid the unused capacity of the hub-and-spoke model. Build a workforce around flexible work rules and reward productivity with employee stock ownership. Create an airline whose market capitalization exceeds the sum of all its competitors.

- **BUY.COM.** Initially an e-retail site where computer shoppers could compare specifications and prices and then buy, it has subsequently exploited its first-mover advantage to expand into an Internet superstore selling the gamut of consumer goods. Its value proposition remains the same classic retail formula—price, availability, and selection—with a perennial emphasis on great deals, especially promotions and close-outs. It is a pure value play that has scaled to be a major player in e-commerce.

There are a number of keys to a volume-operations implementation of a value-engineering strategy. The first is to have some abiding kernel of value that sustains competitive differentiation after all the cost reductions are done, be that product design, brand, business model, scale, or some other attribute. Without this kernel you will not be able to generate acceptable economic returns in competition with other low-cost competitors. The second is to be so

exceptionally thorough and persistent in your cost-reduction efforts that no future competitor can get in underneath your umbrella. And the third is to design every process to be able to scale,
ideally by embedding it in an automated system; and where that is
not possible, by designing around the process or designing it out -
altogether. The overall goal of all these tactics is to define each
transaction as atomically as possible to drive down each of its cost-
creating elements.

Value engineering in a complex-systems business model has a
different target. Here the focus is on the overall system, not just one
or another isolated component, and the goal is to radically reduce
the total cost of ownership over the lifetime of the system's use,
from initial procurement to final disposition. Value engineering is
first applied to disaggregating the system into a set of collaborating
modules—value *chain* engineering—then cost reducing each module in the chain. The key leverage comes from outsourcing and specialization, each element of the chain focusing its financial and
human capital on its core value-adding capability and leaving the
rest of the value-chain tasks to other companies.

Complex-systems enterprises that have innovated in this area
to achieve definitive separation from the competition include:

- **TSMC.** Founded in 1987 as the first outsourcer dedicated to
  fabricating semiconductor chips, the company is the leading
  third-party manufacturer in the sector. Its market is driven
  by the escalating costs of chip manufacturing equipment
  which require all but the largest companies to outsource.
  The company's specific success is based on orchestrating a
  value chain of partners, all the way from the leading design
  software houses to design services providers to mask makers
  to intellectual property licensors to assembly and test companies. By coordinating with these other industry players, the
  company can focus its own resources on advanced manufacturing process development and optimization, its specialty.

- **INFOSYS.** Founded in India in 1981, the company passed the $1 billion revenue mark in 2004 and competes favorably with far larger, more established consulting and outsourcing firms. Initially entrusted with the back end of IT projects—testing, documentation, and the like—it has worked its way forward to coding, then designing, and ultimately to managing entire IT systems. Subsequently, it has taken the next steps into business-process outsourcing, both for general enterprise services in finance and HR, as well as vertical-specific processes such as mortgage servicing. The key to the model is for Infosys to exploit its low-cost highly educated English-speaking workforce. To do so, it works with each client to modularize the overall activity in question, insert itself as a low-cost provider of modules that are not core to the client's strategy, and earn a relationship of trust that allows more and more work to cross over to its side of the ledger.

- **OPEN SOURCE MOVEMENT.** This movement is made up of a loose affiliation of organizations that support software like Linux that is put into the public domain and licensed for free. How can there be any economic advantage to that? Well, ask IBM and HP, both of which are major sponsors of the open source movement. Open source is a cost-reduction resource-sharing mechanism for managing technologies that are required for your business but not core to your differentiation. Total cost of ownership is amortized across many organizations that contribute to the maintenance of the technology, work that is supplemented with paid-for services to customize it to their company's specific needs. Long dismissed as suitable only for technology enthusiasts, the movement is now mainstream with a majority of Fortune 500 companies now using elements of open-systems software in their IT centers.

The key to value-engineering differentiation in a complex-systems model is developing or leveraging a modular view of the value chain that allows your company to specialize in one element, using scale, technology, and expertise to markedly differentiate on price from your competitors, while at the same time steering clear from supporting all the other elements the value chain requires but which are not your specialty. This implies establishing a reliable work flow connecting you with the other members of the chain and building a relationship of trust with the customer who is releasing direct control of the process to you. This creates the space to then differentiate as a low-cost provider within your element of the chain. But if the cost of establishing the relationships is too high, or the length of time it takes to do so is too long, then the strategy fails.

Overall, some of the most powerful positions in private enterprise are built on being the low-cost provider. If it is a fit with your industry, your value-creating focus, and your culture, and if your offer is in a mature market, value-engineering innovation should definitely be on your short list.

SHOULD WE FOCUS ON INTEGRATION INNOVATION?

Integration innovation pulls together a host of disparate, separately managed components and welds them into a single system. The primary benefits to a volume-operations customer are reduced hassle and greater ease of use. Thus, implicit in this value proposition is the absence of a compelling point-product feature that would cause one to prefer assembling a best-of-breed suite instead. Think, for example, of the audiophile assembling a sound system component by component while the rest of us buy the home equivalent of a boom box.

Markets look to the category leaders for integration innovation because they are the companies that have the largest installed base of disparate components and that set the standards for how those components interface with one another. (By contrast they look to category challengers to provide the point product innovations.)

Volume-operations companies that have created sustainable competitive advantage using integration innovation include:

- **MICROSOFT.** The company began as a challenger in desktop applications, first with Word versus Word Perfect, then with Excel versus Lotus 1-2-3. When the transition to Windows came, both Microsoft products became the market leaders in their categories. The company then produced the Office suite, anchored by these two lead products, but also included two much weaker products, the Access database and the PowerPoint presentation product. (At the time, Ashton-Tate was the market leader in databases; Aldus in presentation software.) The market went with the integrated offer over the point product, and now Office is the de facto desktop standard around the world, integrating more and more functions every year. Microsoft also used the same technique to counter Netscape's Navigator browser for the World Wide Web, integrating its Explorer browser into its Windows operating system, to such powerful effect that governments on both sides of the Atlantic have sued to gain competitor relief.

- **YAHOO.** Yahoo began life as the Web's primary search engine, which made it the first true portal to other sites. It leveraged that position into a destination site in its own right by integrating a host of information, shopping, entertainment, and communication offers into one personalized offering. You can pay bills; check your stocks; get directions to the ball; find a date, for that matter—all without leaving the site. Other sites may have better point-product features, but it is hard to find one more comprehensive. And that differentiation causes more users to spend more time on its site, making it one of the top advertising media properties on the Web.

- **SWISS ARMY KNIFE.** The company, actually, is Victorinox, but it is the knife that everyone knows. In its classic version it supplies the following: a small blade, scissors, a nail file that doubles as a screwdriver, a toothpick, tweezers, and a key ring. But that's just the beginning. How about a corkscrew? Bottle opener? Wire stripper? Saw? Magnifying glass? Altimeter? Now none of these are the *best* saw, altimeter, or magnifying glass you can find, but they are the most integrated. And that value proposition has made the product a standout for more than a century.

- **LEGOS.** The company only makes interlocking plastic bricks, but unlike most toy-brick makers, it was able to sell them at an unbelievable premium because it marketed them in kits that integrated into magnificent toys. You may think you are buying bricks but you are actually buying a Death Star, a police station, a mobile crane, or a working robot. The idea is simple yet so compelling that there are even Legoland theme parks on multiple continents. It's all a matter of integration.

Integration innovation in volume-operations markets implies some degree of ubiquity and commoditization at the atomic level. Without these, other factors will outweigh the value of integration, or the integration itself will require too much additional work to be worth the effort. It also implies an ability to create an experience at the higher level that is to some degree greater than the sum of its parts. The Swiss Army Knife is a good example—the value it has is in the options it provides more than in their actual functional utility.

When it comes to complex systems, integration innovation's value proposition is different. Here the concern is the ongoing cost of complexity of maintaining systems that are no longer differentiating. Customers long for simplifying architectures or relationships that can sweep all that complexity under a single rug. Once again, they look to market leaders to provide this service, in part because they installed the majority of the complexity in the first place, in part because they have the reputation and staying power that makes an ongoing relationship of interdependency acceptable.

Complex-systems enterprises that have successfully differentiated themselves using integration innovation include:

- **SAP.** The enterprise software company rose to international prominence during the transition in the early 1990s from the mainframe to the client-server era when it provided the most comprehensive and well-integrated set of functions for finance, human resources, order processing, and inventory management—or what ended up being called enterprise resource planning. Once established as the ERP market leader, it was then able to annex software categories that previously were beyond its reach. The first of these was supply chain management, where independent competitors could no longer sustain the point-product differentiation that overcomes the desire for integration. More recently, customer relationship management has fallen into the same state. Now the company is investing in architecture that makes it easy for future software to be built on top of its current legacy, creating a possibility of a business-process platform innovation opportunity in the future.

- **IBM.** The company is offering a different kind of integration, one based on taking end-to-end accountability for the entire IT function or any part thereof. This is essentially a service-based offer, with IBM acting as a kind of prime contractor, farming out the parts to its own product and service divisions or to third parties under its supervision. It is the ultimate in simplification and the essence of the strategy Lou Gerstner installed to revitalize the company. Its greatest appeal is to conservative customers who have been overwhelmed by the cost and complexity of modern technology. The company's global size and reach, its long-standing reputation, and its ubiquity as the mainframe market leader make it virtually the only candidate for supplying this kind of service offer.

- **AVNET.** The company's traditional business is volume-operations distribution of electronic components. But now about half its revenues come from advanced services that integrate those components into subsystems on behalf of manufacturers looking to outsource noncore work and speed time to market. The differentiation they have above a contract manufacturer is that they are already a part of their customers' supply chain, and by integrating the next module of value creation, they can help streamline the overall value chain, something that differentiates them from other distributors. As a result, they have become one half of a distribution duopoly that serves the electronics industry.

- **INTEL.** Again, the company's traditional business is a volume operation, but in this case it is based on proprietary product technology, making it very high margin indeed. That said, it needs to find growth and is seeking it through integration innovation, transforming itself from a component to a platform supplier. This involves integrating silicon, software, and reference designs that extend its anchor position in the PC platform to other venues. Initial successes are in the wireless area, where its Centrino technology has become standard on laptops and integrates with its PC base, and its XScale technology, which is powering handheld devices and integrates with Microsoft software targeting the same market.

What differentiates integration innovation in complex systems from that in volume operations is that the elements being integrated have not commoditized. Typically, switching costs are too high for that. But they have ceased to be active ingredients in the customer's value-creation efforts and are now perceived as burdensome costs. In such cases, customers do not seek to replace their vendors, but they cut back spending with them. Integration innovation, by reducing the cost burden and by creating a new platform that can play an active role in future value creation efforts, offers them a new lease on life.

There are several critical success factors at work here. First, the integration has to create a new level of interface, completely shielding the customer from the lower levels of complexity; partial integration does not get rewarded even though it does provide some value. Second, it has to be relatively low cost, a modest increment of the investments made to date, the sort of thing that can be justified by ongoing reduced total cost of ownership. Third, it needs to reopen the possibility for future interaction with the system in upcoming value-creation efforts. This in effect converts what was a product into what now is a platform, revitalizing the relationship between the vendor and the customer, and definitively differentiating the offer from all other alternatives that entail switching costs.

To sum up, integration innovation is an attractive alternative for companies that have a significant installed base of complex systems or a significant market share in a volume-operations category that has commoditized. If the success factor hurdles are ones you feel your company can overcome, this type should get further attention.

SHOULD WE FOCUS ON PROCESS INNOVATION?

In mature markets, as the offer itself becomes more and more standardized, the processes by which it is created, delivered, and supported become increasingly interesting as sources of differentiation opportunity. Once again, innovation for differentiation must be kept intellectually distinct from a normal ongoing commitment to improve productivity or to catch up to lower-cost or nimbler competitors. The latter is required just to stay in the game. What we will be talking about here is going much further down the process innovation vector, so far as to create an outcome competitors are either unable or unwilling to match.

In the volume-operations business architecture, process innovation of this sort typically accomplishes outcomes that conventional wisdom said could not be done. Obviously, when it is successful, this sort of thing is highly differentiating. Consider the following examples:

- **DELL**. The company changed PC retail forever by systematically questioning, deconstructing, and revamping the anchor processes in the retail model. It displaced selling in stores with selling over the phone and eventually over the Web, thereby forgoing paying one- and two-tier distribution fees and getting spotty value for so doing. It displaced building to stock with assembling to order, thereby cutting inventory holding costs to the bone. It displaced a 15 percent in-house R&D model with a 5 percent outsourced R&D model, effectively leveraging the R&D of its competitors. And it has so instrumented its supply chain that it too continues to financially outperform its competitors quarter after quarter selling the same products at roughly the same prices. Thus in a mature market, without the help of technology disruption, it has organically taken over an entire industry, acquiring its competitors, as Michael Dell has quipped, one customer at a time.

- **SALESFORCE.COM**. The company is leveraging the Internet to deliver enterprise software applications as a service rather than a product. In so doing it has effectively resituated the sector, moving it from a complex-systems to a volume-operations model. To bring this off, it has had to invent a whole infrastructure of processes to protect the customer's data, interface to legacy systems, adapt to customer needs without resorting to unscalable customization, and price the entire offering in a way that is acceptable to the market and makes money for the company. Still a relatively small company, its volume-operations approach is disrupting the entire software industry, sending much larger complex systems rivals like Siebel Systems into a tailspin, and putting Oracle and SAP on notice.

- **MCDONALD'S**. The company invented fast food as a scalable franchise, largely through rigorously engineering every process from procuring, preparing, cooking, staging, order taking, and cleanup to hiring, training, promoting, and terminating to real estate selection, store design, and facilities management. It ensured consistency and quality by enrolling all its franchisees at Hamburger U, its in-house management training program that instills this entire suite of process disciplines. The result was a franchise that took America and then the world by storm.

- **TOYOTA**. Automobile manufacture may be the single most complex volume-operations business there is, which means it provides great rewards for process innovation. Toyota helped lead Japan's rise to quality by focusing intensely on the quality control principles taught by Edward Deming and others and evolving them into the Toyota Production System. The cornerstones of its manufacturing process innovations—the kanban approach to just-in-time inventory management, the Autonamation approach to quality control—are now studied and copied worldwide. Yet still the company retains its advantage, in large part because its culture is so permeated with the values of process innovation that it continually comes up with novel improvements ahead of its competitors. Today it is the world's leading automobile company.

The key to process innovation in volume-operations businesses is a combination of original insight and execution discipline, with the emphasis on the latter. It requires a combination of what Tom Peters and Bob Waterman called in *In Search of Excellence* "loose/

tight" principles, where the looseness enables innovative suggestions to percolate up from below—think of quality circles and the like—while the tightness ensures rigorous consistency while executing the current process design. Changing processes in midstream, experimenting on the job, discovering as we go along—all these are bad ideas in a volume-operations environment.

It is a bit different in a complex-systems enterprise. While insight and execution discipline are still the key success factors, here the emphasis is more on the former than the latter. That is because each customer situation is inherently unique and evolving, so rather than having tight execution rules, what is required is tight alignment around key execution principles.

Consider the following examples of complex-systems companies that have achieved competitive differentiation through process innovation:

- **CELERA**. The company rose to prominence based on its contribution to accelerating the Human Genome Project. When the project was first proposed, its schedule was set based on sequentially decoding the gene, section by section, chromosome by chromosome, the way one might read a ticker tape. Craig Venter had a better idea. He proposed chopping up the genome more or less at random, sequencing all the chopped bits in parallel, and then using computation to figure out how to piece all the parts back together. Called shotgun sequencing, the approach evolved over time as tools got better and lessons were learned. All in all, however, it carved years off the schedule and catapulted the company to the forefront of genomic research.

- **BP**. One of the three largest energy companies in the world today, the company's claim to fame is its innovative use of technology to improve the success rates of its exploration and production. It was an early adopter of using graphic software to convert seismic data into 3D visualizations of oil fields, first in service to geophysicists at their workstations, later in service to the entire asset team as the company invested in huge aquariumlike visualization rooms with graphic images projected on the walls and manipulated in real time. More recently it has leveraged new sensor technologies at the drill site along with the Internet to capture drilling data, route it to wherever the analytical talent happens to be (often half a world away), update the earth model, and send corrected drilling coordinates back to the drill team—all in real time. By continuing to stay on the forefront of simulation, communication, and visualization technologies, the company has made its exploration and production processes highly differentiated, as most recently witnessed by its being the first to be able to locate oil under salt domes in the Gulf of Mexico.

- **BANDAG**. The company sells retread tires to the trucking industry through a network of a thousand franchisees worldwide. Founded on patented technology incorporated into its retread equipment, it built its worldwide franchise by capturing and refining process methodology to ensure high reliability output from its hundreds of dealers. Subsequently, it migrated its process orientation toward tire management solutions where it guarantees that its trucking customers will meet uptime goals and regulatory reporting oblications at a fixed cost per mile for all their tire needs. Such innovation has allowed it to retain its number one position in a brutally competitive environment.

- **NUCOR**. The largest steel company in America, its process innovation around minimills has been well documented by Clay Christensen and Michael Raynor in *The Innovator's Dilemma* and *The Innovator's Solution.* Essentially, by using recycled steel as its primary raw ingredient, the company was able to enter the steel business at the low end in the rebar market and then, as with other minimill competitors, leverage the price umbrella created by traditional manufacturers to move upstream. At each market transition, as the last traditional vendor was driven from the market, the low-cost minimill vendors faced only themselves as cutthroat competitors and were forced to innovate on process in order to break into the nearest higher-margin opportunity. Nucor achieved its current market position by leading the process transition to sheet steel.

Process innovations like these set companies apart from the others in their competitive set. They are distinct from the kind of day-to-day process innovation needed to maintain market-standard efficiency in a maturing category. So the key question management must ask itself as it looks to process innovation investments is, will they be differentiating? To believe so, you would have to think one or more of the following:

- Other companies have built-in barriers to adoption that will prevent them from adopting your approach.

- Your company can get there so much sooner than anyone else that it can gain an insurmountable market share lead or reap a windfall profit during the time it takes the others to catch on and catch up.

- You will implement so much better that you will consistently outexecute others with similar systems even if they are in the market with them at roughly the same time.

When conditions like these obtain, then majoring in process innovation should be very high on your list. When they do not, you are better off either minoring in it or investing elsewhere in the Operational Excellence Zone.

SHOULD WE FOCUS ON VALUE-MIGRATION INNOVATION?

We owe a debt of thanks to Adrian Slywotzky for drawing our attention to value migration as a phenomenon in category-maturity life cycles. The notion is a simple one. Over time, as solutions commoditize, the scarce element in the market migrates from one role to another in the value chain. Thus at the beginning of categories, technology providers and systems integrators are the scarce resources, but over time, as more and more of their expertise becomes embedded into standard products and services, the scarce elements become marketing expertise and customization capability. Later still it migrates to cost-reduction enablers, maintenance providers, and outsourcers. And it moves from the base system to accessories and consumables.

The key principles of value-migration innovation are, first, to sense the erosion in value in the established roles, second, to anticipate where the migration of value is headed, and third, to get there before your competition. Examples of companies in the volume-operations arena who have succeeded in value-migration innovation include:

- **GILLETTE**. The company was so successful with its value-migration strategy that the phrase *razor, razor blades* has become shorthand for referencing the value-migration concept itself. Kodak's migration from cameras to film and HP's migration from printers to ink-jet cartridges are other standard illustrations of the same phenomenon. In all three cases, the consumable moves from the status of an enabler to that of the primary revenue generator, while the device moves in the opposite direction. The shift to enabler status is made clear when you see it becoming price discounted in order to expand purchases of some other value chain element.

- **WAL-MART**. The company has engineered a fundamental shift in the retail value chain, migrating power from branded consumer packaged goods leaders like Procter & Gamble and Nestlé to the high-volume discount retailer. This is a function of buying power and distribution reach, with Wal-Mart providing as much as 40 percent of the revenues of even the most popular brands. As a result, it has been able to drive a series of far-reaching cost-reducing process reforms from industry-standard bar codes to vendor-managed inventory to the upcoming RFID-enabled inventory tracking—all of which reinforce its powerful role as the market-leading high-volume, low-cost distribution channel.

- **MARVEL COMICS**. The company came to fame as a next-generation comic book franchise, generating enough interest and appeal to spawn comic collecting as a cottage industry. More recently, however, the company has realized from the repeated successes of the *Spiderman* and *X-Men* movies that its value is migrating from print media to licensable intellectual property, its archive of comic-book characters providing seeds for film franchise bonanzas. The film medium is brand new, and the company was perhaps naive in its initial license agreements, but if the rest of its stable of characters can generate mass appeal as well, it still has the scarce element in the value chain to bargain with.

- **SABRE**. Originally an in-house air-travel reservations utility, the Sabre system was spun out from American Airlines to become a stand-alone entity, and then rapidly surpassed its parent company in market capitalization as value migrated from the carriers themselves to the information providers who broker passengers to them. This is an example of a larger value-migration trend, the information age, where information about an asset can be assigned more value than the asset itself. It is an age where mailing lists and data mining provide winning market segmentation strategies.

Each of these value-migration innovations called for a change in business model, either by the company currently leading the value chain or by a disrupter unencumbered by legacy issues. This has not been lost on business school graduates, and during the dot-com era the market was besieged by business-model innovations that were designed to introduce the next disruptive value migration. For the most part, these all fell flat on their faces. In retrospect, what we did not appreciate at the time was how most successful migrations are incubated over a prolonged period in a protected environment in which value is allowed to incrementally accumulate without competitive threat. In other words, they have to grow *unnoticed*. If instead you declare where you are headed, the marketplace, instinctively resistant to any entity gaining power at its expense, will self-organize to head you off before you get there.

So the key to volume-operations value migration is to discover the latent potential in undervalued resources, secure those resources while they are undervalued, and then capitalize on them downstream as the value migration becomes more obvious and more prevalent. This same pattern unfolds in complex-systems markets as well. In large part, however, it is unleashed by the migration of parts of the market from a complex-systems to a volume-operations model. In such a circumstance, the complex-systems vendor is unable to capitalize on it and must instead refocus its value-creating capabilities to some less commoditized emergent category. That said, there are still some examples of complex systems successfully capitalizing on value migration in categories where complexity persists and solutions have very high switching costs. Consider the following examples:

- **COMPUTER ASSOCIATES.** The company rose to prominence in the 1980s, first by acquiring systems software companies with vital franchises, later by acquiring ones with defunct ones. Why the latter? Management recognized that although these acquisitions had little potential for acquiring new customers, their current installed bases had very high switching costs. As a result, providing maintenance service to them would be highly profitable if operations were optimized to that end instead of being used as cash cows to fund increasingly improbable future growth plans. Value had migrated, in other words, from licensing new products to supporting existing ones. CA became expert at acquiring and eviscerating these companies, building for itself a farm of cash cows, which it used to fund its transition from mainframe to client-server systems software.

- **IBM.** The M in IBM standards for *machine,* but over the years the scarce value-creating element in enterprise systems has migrated from hardware to software and services, and IBM has restructured itself accordingly. Today the company's most valuable assets are its consulting group and its software franchises. Specifically, the company is focused on the technology and processes necessary to enable utility computing. On the software side, this implies a complete revamping of the systems software infrastructure called middleware, where IBM's entry is called WebSphere. On the services side, it implies a complete revamping of how companies manage their information technology, how they build their information systems, and how they maintain visibility and control over critical information processes in an outsourced model. Here is where the "other IBM," IBM Global Services, has come to the fore. Together, software and services are redefining a corporation that fifteen years ago was on the verge of dissolution.

- **GMAC.** Here *is* a corporation on the verge of breakup. That General Motors has been able to hold on as long as it has is in large part testament to a value migration in the automobile industry from product to service, and in particular, from manufacturing cars to financing and insuring them. GMAC, GM's independent financing arm, like its sister organization at Ford, contributes the bulk of the profitable revenue to the corporation as a whole.

- **AFFYMETRIX.** In the first wave of biotech, the key value-creating device was the gene sequencing equipment from Applied Biosystems. Now, however, value has migrated to the gene chip, where Affymetrix is the lead supplier. On each chip is an array of specified genes which, when exposed to test materials, allow researchers, doctors, and forensic analysts to learn about the contents of the substance in question based on which genes interact with it. While there is a still a growth market for devices that prepare and read the samples, the primary value creator, at several thousand dollars each, has become the gene chip.

Over all, value migration is an inevitable consequence of the category-maturity life cycle. The question is, when should it become a differentiation strategy for your company? The first determinant is your installed base. How much of your total asset value is tied up in these relationships as opposed to, say, a next-generation technology that would acquire a substantially new installed base? The greater the percentage, the more important that you keep up with value migration.

The second is simply market size. Consumables and maintenance models act like annuity streams: This earns them high marks for low volatility, which is fine if the absolute size of the revenue stream is large. But if it is not, then the models just do not work, and you need to focus on some other type of innovation, putting the current installed base under some kind of harvest-and-exit management.

A third issue to consider is category-maturity life cycle stage. If the mature product infrastructure upon which the value chain is resting is about to be disrupted, if it is moving out of the indefinitely elastic middle into decline, then you have to reevaluate the opportuity. Optimizing for services, content, and consumables requires significant fixed-cost investments that require some number of years to pay back. In mature markets where there is no threat of disruption, the risk factor in this investment decision is low, and the returns attractive. But as the threat of disruption increases, so must a corresponding discount for risk, and the risk/reward ratio can flip-flop in a hurry.

Finally, you have to ask yourself, do we have the moxie to pull this off? Each of these shifts implies a significant relocation of power among the various functions that make up your enterprise. There will be significant inertial resistance to overcome. Your CEO and top executives will be a key factor in this equation. It requires their total commitment to the shift to bring off a successful value migration.

WRAPPING UP

This has been quite a long chapter, so let us step back a minute to take stock. We have covered eight types of innovation, four in the Customer Intimacy Zone—line extension, enhancement, marketing, and experiential—and four in the Operational Excellence Zone—value engineering, integration, process, and value migration. We have suggested that all these types are best suited to creating differentiation in mature markets. Specifically, we have cited examples of each type in both volume-operations and complex-systems enterprises where they have created sustainable competitive advantage leading to significant market success. We have established, in other words, that each type does work, at least for some companies in some situations.

We did all this in service to the overall agenda of this book. That is, our focus throughout is to help you and your colleagues target an innovation type to which you can make an exceptional commitment, out of which you will generate differentiation sufficient to separate you from your direct competitors, and thereby gain you privileged treatment in sales cycles and premium pricing in contract negotiations. In short, we believe the fractal markets of Main Street can and should be hotbeds of innovation.

That said, the leaders of mature-market innovation strategies are not likely to be those who headed growth-market innovation. Growth markets are all about primary effects: new markets, new products, new processes, new customers. Fractal markets are all about secondary effects: existing markets, existing products, existing processes, existing customers. The people in charge this time around are most likely to be the ones closest to the day-to-day action: the people in marketing, supply chain, finance, and customer service. We do not normally think of such functions as incubators of innovation, but as this chapter has illustrated extensively, that is exactly what they must be for established enterprises to thrive on Main Street.

CISCO INNOVATING IN MATURE MARKETS

It is questionable whether any of Cisco's markets are mature in the classic sense of the term, but there is no question that its primary markets of wide-area-network routing and local-area-network switching are growing at a markedly different pace from only a few years ago. In particular, in the enterprise-systems sector, the source of half the company's revenues, growth rates just make it over the line into double digits—terrific from the point of a truly mature industry, but a far cry from what investors were accustomed to in prior years. It is not too early, therefore, for the company to embark on a mature-market innovation strategy, and the company has indeed done so.

The innovation-types model was not available to the company as it was making its management decisions, but it does reveal the logic behind them. Here's how that logic plays out following the vocabulary we have been developing:

1. Cisco is a complex-systems company. According to the model, that means that it and its competitors are likely to be similarly strong in customer intimacy; hence it will be more difficult to gain sustainable differentiation in the Customer Intimacy Zone. The company should look therefore to major in an innovation type from the Operational Excellence Zone.

2. Turning to the four innovation types in the Operational Excellence Zone, let us proceed by subtraction. We can feel most comfortable ruling out value-migration innovation. The market simply is not so mature that its initial sources of value creation have been exhausted. By a similar line of reasoning, solutions are not yet so commoditized that process innovation is the right focus.

3. As we look at value-engineering innovation, it turns out the company has already made significant strides in two arenas. In its complex-systems model businesses, it was the first to exploit outsourced manufacturing as a source of differentiation, and this helped it ramp faster and with less capital employed than its competition. More recently it has acquired Linksys to give it a volume-operations capability, with a management team that has shined at value engineering from the outset. That all said, one of its key competitors, Huawei, has very strong value engineering capabilities and is investing heavily to differentiate on this vector. That makes it unlikely that Cisco could gain definitive separation on the same vector.

4. All of the above leads us to look very seriously at integration innovation as the primary differentiation vector for the enterprise routing and switching businesses. Cisco has a lot of opportunity here because it grew substantially by acquisition during the 1990s, requiring it to lash together independently developed architectures, not always in the most elegant way. Moreover, as the market becomes increasingly dependent on the Internet, it is seeking to streamline its interactions with it. And finally, as the market leader Cisco is the best positioned for integration innovation, in no small part because it has the most stuff out there to integrate. For all these reasons this is where Cisco should focus.

It turns out that integration innovation is the natural differentiation vector for any complex-systems company that has achieved gorilla status in its sector. That's because the market has standardized on the market leader's offerings but is feeling increasingly burdened by the complexity of maintaining them. It wants to shift its high-value resources to greener pastures, but it cannot do so until the gorilla reduces the maintenance challenge.

Integration innovation provides the answer. Specifically, it offers customers and partners

- an increasingly coherent and more manageable environment that

- is familiar to the current generation of system maintainers,

- has proven reliability and probable longevity, and

- is predictable in its interactions with systems that interface with it.

These are compelling value propositions wherever a complex system has become foundational infrastructure upon which future development is planned.

In the case of Cisco, the focus of its integration innovation is its Internet Operating System, or IOS, that runs both its LAN switches and its WAN routers. Some twenty-four million lines of code, it is omnipresent throughout the company's product line. Everything that a Cisco product does is governed and managed by this software. However, since it grew like Topsy, having evolved to incorporate key innovations from each of Cisco's strategic acquisitions, it is a bear of a product to modify, and that poses a significant hurdle for the innovation team. Here's why.

The limiting factor in any integration strategy is the elasticity of the core technology that unifies the overall system. As that technology increases in size and complexity, it becomes harder and harder to incorporate innovations without breaking some other feature of the product. No matter how dedicated the attempts to document the system, there is inevitably a growing amount of undocumented features that maintainers simply have to know about. This leads to enclaves of expertise that do not scale well, and more important, they disappear with the retirement or defection of key employees. Regression testing becomes an ever-increasing burden, and introducing new teams to the system becomes a more and more daunting task. Left to their own devices, eventually such systems collapse under their own weight.

Under pressure to counteract these dynamics, it often occurs to engineering teams to rewrite the entire system from the ground up, this time "doing it right." This is actually a horrible idea, for it violates the one proposition the market wants held inviolable, namely, maintaining backward compatibility with previous versions of the system. If that is abandoned, an ungodly amount of cheese has to be moved, and no amount of product elegance can make up for the disruption caused. For that reason, forsaking backward compatibility, even in service to a far better product, is an unforgivable sin causing markets to dismiss incumbent vendors out of hand, as the PC software companies MicroPro and Lotus discovered when they revamped their respective flagship products, WordStar and Lotus 1-2-3.

Cisco actually launched an effort along these very lines in the late 1990s, but it headed it off in time, redirecting it to provide a special-purpose carrier-class "extra-reliable" version of IOS called IOS/XR. For the mainstream version of IOS, on the other hand, Cisco has opted to reengineer. Specifically, this means retroactively modularizing a legacy system so that it can be redesigned into an integrated suite of subsystems, with well-defined interfaces and strict intermodule communications rules. Such a reengineered architecture is inherently more manageable. When bugs emerge, they can be contained and tracked down methodically. When specific functions need to be modified, they can be torn down and rebuilt independently of the rest of the system. These are the benefits of integration innovation.

At Cisco the current phase of the reengineering effort is called IOS on Neutrino or ION. Neutrino is a next-generation, services-oriented architecture that is really slick. As IOS is decomposed into modular subsystems, various subsystems can be first emulated in the new environment and then actually rewritten to run in it. Software specialists call this process refactoring, and it can happen at a measured pace without pulling the legacy system out of service anywhere along the line. IOS, in other words, can migrate to a more elastic state, thereby giving Cisco's integration innovation a new lease on life.

That is how integration innovation must proceed at the foundational levels of a system architecture just to maintain backward compatibility. But as the modular interfaces are installed, they also enable integration at higher levels in the system. That means new functions can be added to the legacy cleanly because they are treated simply as another module. The integration clears a space, as it were, for the next generation of innovation.

In Cisco's case, its IOS-enabled routers and switches have become natural aggregation points for a wealth of network-related functions. No longer closed boxes, they can now act as chassis with slots to accommodate inserted cards containing the latest advanced technologies. Thus Cisco's fastest-growing product in 2005 was its integrated services router, which has slots to incorporate security,

VOIP, and video directly into its backplane. Similarly, the company's LAN switches have slots that actually incorporate routing capabilities, further integrating the overall network fabric and simplifying its management and maintenance.

All this integration creates an enormous separation between Cisco's offerings and those of its direct competitors. For while those competitors can and do surpass Cisco in point-product performance, they cannot match the overall value proposition of providing an integrated network fabric. Whenever a competitor steals a march on the company, Cisco engineers set out to catch up, and once their point products are close to parity, the integration-value proposition overshadows whatever feature distinctions may remain.

It is important to understand how much marketplaces collude in such outcomes. Customers are not alone in encouraging consolidation and standardization around integrated versions of the market leader's architecture; service partners and product partners do so as well, for it just makes their lives so much simpler. It is thus virtually impossible to compete against this value proposition head to head. One must instead dodge it by specializing in a niche application innovation for which the general-purpose infrastructure is unsuited, disrupt it by starting a wholly new category, or capitulate to it and become a partner helping to fill out its empty spaces.

For all these reasons, Cisco is majoring in integration innovation from the Operational Excellence Zone and having success at so doing. But what about the other half of the fractal market success equation? Does the company have a minor from the Customer Intimacy Zone? Indeed it does, and that is line-extension innovation.

Again, let us see why Cisco would not choose the other forms:

1. Enhancement innovation is simply premature. The underlying functionality of the network is not so commoditized that enhancements can win out over the next generation of functional improvements.

2. *Marketing* innovation seems like overkill. As the gorilla in the category, Cisco already has privileged access to virtually every customer. What more could marketing innovation accomplish?

3. *Experiential* innovation is way off the mark because there are simply too many other pressing issues to deal with first.

Line-extension innovation, we may recall, is used to create a second generation of growth after the first wave of adoption has crested. It focuses on segments that have bought into the category but still have unmet needs. In the case of Cisco, the most intriguing target is the small-to-medium business market, that large base of perpetually marginalized customers who have a need for complex systems but a budget more suited to mass-market products.

As we noted in our opening chapter, to serve this constituency vendors must either cheat down from the complex-systems design center or cheat up from volume operations. In the case of Cisco, given its complex-systems heritage and its acquisition of volume-operations Linksys, there is the opportunity to do both. Neither, however, comes without pain, and the company is still finding its way.

Cheating down from the top, the company has addressed the budget issues of the small business market by offering a low-end stackable switch. This has the same core functionality as its high-end products but does not have the modularity that would allow it to be upgraded. To add capacity, you simply add more switches to the stack. The next offer up in the line, by contrast, is a modular switch, which can be upgraded to incorporate the more advanced technologies. Transitioning from a stackable to modular switch is a little bit like coming of age: There is a conscious decision to step up to the next level of IT complexity. Once that step is taken, Cisco is back in its comfort zone. It is the zone just below that is a challenge for the company.

If we look at that same zone from the Linksys side of the house, it is also a challenge, but this time because it is a step too far up rather than too far down. Linksys has optimized its R&D and go-to-market approach around self-installed products sold through retail sales outlets like Best Buy and Office Depot. Small businesses love to shop these stores for bargains, and Linksys has established a strong brand reputation with this group. But when it comes to the sales and service complexity involved even with a stackable switch, the company's low-margin business model cannot accommodate it. Moreover, the company's lean R&D model is not consistent with the engineering investments required to maintain backward compatibility and architectural consistency across generations of product offers. In the Linksys model, when something becomes obsolete, you unplug it and throw it away (well, you recycle it). So for it, too, the small-to-medium business zone is a challenge.

Now it is possible to design a business model specifically optimized for the small-to-medium business (SMB) market. That is what competitors like HP and 3Com have done. You bolt complex-systems R&D onto volume-operations manufacturing and distribute through a local value-added reseller that provides sales and service at profit margins about halfway between a complex-systems and a volume-operations solution. The problem historically with this model is that it gets attacked from either side, the complex-systems companies cheating down to pick off the most lucrative customers and the volume-operations solutions cheating up to pick up the most cost-sensitive ones. Caught in between and unable to scale either up or down, VARs often saturate their local markets, causing them to flicker in and out of existence, rendering the model as a whole instable.

Given the unattractiveness of this model, and given that the company has effective offers at both ends of the spectrum, Cisco's best strategy is to extend its product lines toward the sweet spot of the SMB market but never to try to occupy it. This can prove frustrating to management teams who read reports about how much money small to medium businesses spend, and who want to replicate their enterprise and consumer market share successes here as well. But at the end of the day, the company is better served focusing on its own opportunities rather than envying those of others.

CHAPTER SEVEN

MANAGING INNOVATION IN DECLINING MARKETS

This is the third and final chapter in our survey of innovation types and their relationship to the category-maturity life cycle. As we have already noted, when a category is on the rise, management's job is to grow the company by leveraging that category's growth dynamics. When it is relatively flat, management's job is to outperform the category as a whole by outinnovating the other companies within it. In this chapter, however, the category is in decline, and here management's job is to exit the category, repositioning the company into greener pastures.

In a declining category, management must recognize that the problem is not one of company performance, although it may be exacerbated by it. This concept is often difficult to grasp for execution-oriented management teams who are used to succeeding through outperforming the competition. Just remember, you are now in a lemmings race, and the goal is not to come in first, it is to get out of the race before you drive your company off a cliff.

The fundamental options in a declining market are to renew or to harvest and exit. Renewal represents a category shift, meaning new target customers, new market needs, new products, and a new value chain, potentially a new sales channel, new pricing, new competitors. It is not, therefore, something you can execute under the heading of business as usual. Instead, you must mobilize the entire enterprise on a life-or-death journey that gets no second chance.

Innovation Types for Declining Markets
Leveraging Category Renewal

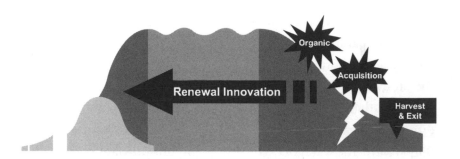

You cannot iterate your way to renewal. You have to get it right the first time.

Given the size of this bet, the rewards must be commensurate. Most successful renewal efforts, therefore, reposition the company from a declining category into a growth category and not into a maturing category. This means a return to the product leadership zone, and reengaging with the various forms of innovation there. This time around, however, your options are fewer. You do not have the luxury of sponsoring a disruptive innovation because it takes too long to gestate, and the risk that it might fail is too great. In addition, you do not have the opportunity for platform innovation, because you are a newcomer to the category without the assets required. This means your options are restricted to two: application innovation and product innovation.

Large companies, whether complex systems or volume operations in orientation, will likely choose product innovation. The reason is that they need relatively large markets from the outset to generate enough revenue to keep their lights on. They can afford in the short term to sacrifice the margin power that application innovation would create in order to establish a broader initial footprint in the market. In subsequent rounds, after they are convinced they have fixed their category power problem, they will worry about their company power.

Smaller enterprises, by contrast, are better served targeting application innovation. Think of this as a return to the bowling alley. These companies need the protection of niche markets and highly committed customers to reincubate themselves. They do not have the kind of balance sheets that can afford to give up pricing power. In short, they must solve for both category power and company power in the same move. This means they must shrink to fit the niche market that gives them the best chance of revitalizing their franchise.

Once the target of renewal has been chosen, there are two paths to take to reach it. Organic renewal generates offers for the new target category internally. Acquisition renewal acquires them from the outside. The choice depends on time and the current state of your core competences. Organic renewal implies there is time to bring along the new category, and it implies that the organization has retained the product leadership skills required to do so. Acquisition renewal implies the opposite. Indeed, if you expand acquisition renewal to include selling the company as well as acquiring another company—as we believe you should—it is by far the more flexible option in a declining market. That said, if neither of the renewal options plays out, there is a remaining alternative: Harvest and exit the business. We don't treat this as a type of innovation, but like everything else in business, it rewards taking an innovative approach.

ORGANIC RENEWAL

If your company retains a vital product-leadership capability, the challenge of organic renewal is not to come up with compelling innovations in a new category but rather to manage through your enterprise's natural tendency to reject them. We will have a lot to say about this challenge in the next section, where we dig into the power of inertia and how it must be co-opted to serve next-generation initiatives. For now, let us just register that renewal requires exceptionally decisive management, as the following examples will indicate.

Let's begin with volume-operations enterprises. Each of the following companies was able to transition from a leadership position in a waning category to one in a growing one, leveraging technology it developed in house:

- **INTEL.** The company invented DRAMs (dynamic random access memory) and rose to power riding the adoption wave that displaced magnetic core memory in computers with silicon-based chips. By 1985, however, commoditization was well under way and the Japanese competition in the category was fierce, so the company chose to exit the category to focus on its microprocessor business. There it was able to establish itself as essentially the sole-source provider to the personal computer industry.

- **ADOBE.** In collaboration with Apple and Aldus (which it subsequently acquired), the company helped invent the desktop publishing industry, contributing its PostScript printer language to enable the elegant bit-mapped fonts we take for granted today. With the rise of global networking, however, it became clear that the practice of print-and-distribute would be displaced by distribute-and-print. This meant that the printing language could no longer reside with the printer but had instead to be carried within the document. To serve that paradigm, Adobe refocused itself on Acrobat technology, which it has subsequently made the de facto standard for the Internet age. But this required confronting new target customers with a new value proposition and a new whole product supported by a new value chain. It is a testimony to Adobe's decisive management that today Acrobat is one of the few proprietary technologies that can rival Microsoft for desktop ubiquity.

- **APPLE**. The company rose to prominence with Macintosh technology that redefined the user interface to personal computers. But the IBM PC was too broadly adopted for Macintosh to displace, and so it was left to Microsoft Windows to take the graphical user interface paradigm forward in that sector. By the time Steve Jobs returned as CEO, Apple's share of the PC market was hovering around 3 percent, with few prospects. Jobs stopped the bleeding with a series of enhancement and marketing innovations, most notably adding translucent colored cases to the iMac. But he has subsequently really turned the corner by catching the wave of digitized music and images, first with Apple's notorious Rip/ Mix/Burn campaign for the Macintosh, then with the launch of the iPod and Apple iTunes. By so doing he has repositioned the company from a marginalized PC manufacturer to a leading consumer electronics provider that worries more about taking share from Sony than from Dell or HP.

- **WESTERN UNION**. The company rose to power as a communications utility, first with telegrams, later with telexes. Subsequently, however, long-distance calls, faxes, and eventually e-mail displaced its proprietary network, causing its category to decline. In response it has repositioned itself into financial services, focusing on a money-transfer business that had always been part of its operations. Today the company has one hundred thousand money-transfer agents worldwide and is a key enabler of remittance payments across international boundaries.

The challenge for volume-operations companies in organic renewal is that they must beat the clock. It takes time to generate the kind of volume needed to offset the fixed costs of category participation. In the examples above, all four companies were able to extract enough from the outgoing category to sustain them during the transition. This is a critical success factor inherent to this innovation type. It holds for complex-systems enterprises as well, as the following examples show:

- **IBM**. The company rose to power based on a proprietary mainframe business with a vertically integrated business model, producing everything from chips to networks to software to services. To leverage its extensive infrastructure, it subsequently diversified into minicomputers and PCs, but it fell on very hard times in the early 1990s when its growing cost structure collided with a precipitous category decline in the mainframe business. Most analysts at the time concluded that the company had overreached itself and should be broken up. Instead, it repositioned itself as the e-commerce-enabling company for global enterprises, shifting its core differentiation from hardware to software and services. This included the forced migration of a horde of executives from internal-facing to field-facing positions and an explicit shift in investment focus away from the cash-cow businesses. Management throughout was decisive, and today IBM is the leading services-led vendor in the IT industry.

- **NOKIA**. For most of the twentieth century Nokia was known as a diversified corporation in paper and pulp products, rubber manufacturing, and cable. It was through the cable side of the house, first with coaxial cable for computer networks, that it entered the electronics sector. In the 1990s, it entered the mobile-phone business and, well, the rest is history. The company invested heavily in building handset manufacturing capability, drawing on the cash cows of paper and pulp and rubber products. Once the transition was complete, Nokia divested itself of these other businesses, and today it is the leading mobile-phone supplier in the world. This is a remarkable example of organic renewal going from the many to the one.

• **CORNING**. This company is a remarkable example of how to recover from a failed transition from the many to the one. It rose to prominence as a diversified-materials company based on glass manufacturing technology with products in multiple industries as well as a consumer line of kitchenware. Under the influence of the telecommunications boom, it divested itself of its consumer lines and heavily invested in its fiber-optics cable business. When the bubble burst, fiber-optic capacity was hugely oversupplied, financial performance plummeted, and the company came very close to going under. It rescued itself by returning to its diversified roots, reinvesting in categories that had been revitalized by the change in economic sector power, and today it is a leading supplier of LCD screens to the entertainment and mobile-electronics sectors, environmental technology subsystems to the automotive sector, and sample-handling materials to the life-sciences industry. Again, it took decisive management intervention to navigate this twisting path to renewal.

• **KIMBERLY CLARK**. The company has been celebrated in Jim Collins's *Good to Great* for its extraordinary self-transformation from a sleepy underperforming player in the coated-paper business to an extraordinary competitor in the paper-based segment of the consumer products business. The key act of transformation was to sell all its paper mills and funnel that money into its consumer brands like Huggies and Kleenex. This is organic renewal with a major twist, for it required the company to shift from a complex-systems architecture appropriate to an industry supplier to the volume-operations architecture required for a CPG manufacturer.

If we look back over these examples, there are some key principles for success. The first is that the leadership supervising the change is more likely to come from within than without (Lou Gerstner being a remarkable exception). Andy Grove, John Warnock, Steve Jobs (on his second time around), Jorma Ollila, Wendell Weeks, and Darwin Smith were all deeply versed in and well trusted by the company cultures they led through the transformation process. By contrast, when the board turns to an outsider, it is much more likely that renewal strategy will be tied to acquisition renewal because it takes too long for a new CEO to establish the kind of trust organic renewal requires.

Second, while the transformation does not always require the dramatic exits that were engineered at Intel, Nokia, and Kimberly Clark, it does require management to invest heavily and at great risk in a fledgling business at a time when its mature businesses are its cash cows. Thus even when iPod was less than 10 percent of Apple's revenues, it was already getting the lion's share of its advertising budget. When you are moving the center of gravity of an organization, bold gestures are required to communicate to all involved management's depth of commitment to the change. General Colin Powell makes this point when he says it is not enough to move the troops to a new position; you have to redeploy the generals as well. John Thompson, the vice chairman of IBM who developed the software and life-sciences businesses there, calls this "hiving off the new business," including giving it separate accounting so that neither its expenses nor revenues can get hidden within larger, more established lines. Absent such broad and decisive gestures, it is too easy for cash-cow businesses to reassert their privileges and derail the change.

Third, and finally, it requires a mature organization to outperform younger and often nimbler start-ups in a zone of innovation that typically favors the unencumbered entrant. Product innovation demands great R&D. This is typically part of the heritage of any established enterprise, but the company may have lost touch with it during the years on Main Street when customer intimacy and operational excellence took pride of place: If that is the case, then everyone is better off following the acquisition path to renewal.

ACQUISITION RENEWAL

Although the decline of categories can be perceived as inevitable, particularly in hindsight, they often catch management by surprise, either by arriving earlier or by declining faster than anticipated. In both such instances, the chances for organic renewal are diminished as that innovation type needs runway to get up to speed. Companies in this predicament, therefore, are better served by acquisition renewal.

Acquisition renewal, to be clear, does not require a crisis to precipitate it. It is the one form of innovation that can be pursued in parallel with all the others without disturbing them—until the M & A switch is actually thrown. Diversified enterprises, in general, specialize in this approach, as witnessed by General Electric's superior performance, which over time has migrated with the corporation from a heavily industrialized portfolio reflecting economic advantages of the mid- to late twentieth century to one weighted in financial services and media, reflecting the economic leverage of the information age. GE is, in effect, perpetually renewing itself though acquisition and divestiture and is a role model for this practice.

To execute GE's model requires a depth of management expertise that is not found in most corporations. For the majority of companies, therefore, structural innovation is used sparingly, typically only when a prior innovation strategy has faltered. Consider the following examples from complex-systems enterprises:

- **BEA**. The company began life in 1995 with the goal of creating for the Unix community the kind of reliable systems software that IBM provided for its mainframes, building itself initially around the acquisition of proven software. It was a strategy focused on the data center and on client-server computing. But several years into the effort, with the Internet swirling around it, the company realized that the focus of IT investment was shifting to the World Wide Web. To capitalize on this shift, it bought WebLogic and through it became the dominant application-server provider for the World Wide Web. Moreover, management allowed the culture of WebLogic to become the reigning culture within BEA, letting a group of faster-moving dot-com executives displace the more deliberate style of their predecessors. The end result was that the company reached $1 billion in revenues less than ten years after its founding.

- **DOCUMENTUM/EMC**. This is structural innovation with a different twist—the company became acquired rather than being the acquirer. The situation was as follows: In 2003, after considerable effort, Documentum had won the competition for leadership in the enterprise-document management category. At that point, it perceived that its future competition would come from companies ten or more times its size, including Microsoft, Oracle, and IBM. It was not in a declining category, but it was faced with an unmanageable competitive disadvantage. At this point, it elected to accept an offer from EMC. Now it enjoys a larger footprint and has access to deeper pockets to help navigate its future.

For its part, EMC saw itself as the market leader in enterprise storage, but it could foresee that category becoming commoditized because it had already become so in the low end of the market. Further, it recognized that such commoditization was the result of a value migration under way from hardware to system software. Therefore it set about a software acquisition strategy around the theme of information life-cycle management. Documentum is now part of EMC's ILM suite of products and services and a key element in repositioning the company from a hardware to a systems and software provider.

- **MONSANTO.** Monsanto's history is intermingled with the impact of genetic research on both the agricultural and pharmaceutical sectors. The company rose to prominence in agricultural chemicals, its most notable product being the herbicide Roundup. It branched out into molecular biology and genetic modification of plants in the 1980s and 1990s, in part to create Roundup-resistant crops. Its research generated breakthrough products in agriculture, but unfortunately these spawned a storm of protest in Europe, which labeled them Frankenfoods. At the same time, its pharmaceutical arm was struggling to compete in a consolidating industry where megamergers were the order of the day. In response, the company took three structural actions. It spun off its industrial chemical and fiber capabilities. It merged with Searle and eventually with Pfizer to be part of an industry-leading pharmaceutical corporation. Then it spun back out the agricultural division as the new Monsanto. Today it is a stand-alone company with market-leading products facing a world that is gradually accepting genetically modified foods as a legitimate tool to fight world hunger and increase agricultural yields. Two weakening franchises were thus transformed into two strong franchises, freed from slow-growth industries and positioned in high-growth sectors.

- **APPLERA**. The company began life as PerkinElmer, a company not unlike HP spinout Agilent in its diversity of measurement instruments and industrial equipment. As the computer sector took off and PerkinElmer's entry did not, the company repositioned itself to focus on its life-sciences division, which hosted a disruptive technology for genetic sequencing. This was the same Applied Biosystems we discussed in our discussion of disruptive innovation. It was spun out, along with a genetic-applications business called Celera, while the original PerkinElmer was sold to EG&G, a consortium focused on serving the power generation utility industries. Subsequently, Applied Biosystems remerged with its sister division Celera to form the current corporation, Applera. The key act of leadership in all this was the ability to commit to life sciences and drive all subsequent structural decisions to further that commitment.

In complex-systems enterprises, acquisition innovation helps respond to shifts in industry structure. Management uses category mutation as a way to slip out of a tight spot and into a better one. In volume operations, it is more frequently the case that the problem is one of brand performance. Here are some examples of how volume-operations enterprises have used acquisition innovation to work around brand problems:

- **GATEWAY**. Gateway grew to prominence as a low-cost personal computer, beating out competition from the likes of Packard Bell while pricing itself under the umbrellas of IBM, HP, and Compaq. In part its success was owed to its innovative "cowhide" branding, which gave Gateway packages a distinctive look and set its media ads apart. When Dell took the industry by storm, however, the company found itself not in a declining category but in an unsustainable competitive advantage position. Its innovation in branding was not sufficient to overcome its deficit in operational excellence, and the company's performance declined badly. It addressed this problem by acquiring eMachines, the low-cost leader in retail PCs, and then by allowing that management team to take control of the company and dramatically improve its operating efficiency. Today the company is the third largest PC maker in the United States, focused primarily on retail sales, where its two brands can compete effectively against Dell's online approach.

- **LOTUS/IBM.** We have already discussed how Lotus was unable to capitalize on the disruptive innovation of Lotus Notes. This was a failure of organic renewal to succeed in displacing a well-entrenched cash cow, the Lotus 1-2-3 spreadsheet. Notes had established a strong brand, but it could not overcome the fact that 1-2-3 was a volume-operations business, whereas Notes required a complex-systems architecture. The company turned to acquisition innovation to solve this problem by getting itself acquired by IBM. IBM left the Lotus management structure largely intact. For the first time, the Notes team got access to the complex-systems support resources necessary to give it its best chance, and it was subsequently able to place over one hundred million licenses, making it a strong second to Microsoft in collaboration-software installations. This is another example of the bidirectional nature of acquisition: It does not matter who the acquirer or acquired parties are; it only matters that the combination is more powerful than either entity standing alone.

- **ALTRIA.** As public sentiment and then public policy in the United States was turning against the tobacco industry, Philip Morris found itself in a declining category in that market. It undertook a structural transformation to migrate to more life-supporting sectors of the consumer products group sector. It began by restructuring and rebranding itself as the Altria Group, and under that name it acquired first General Foods, then later Kraft Foods and Nabisco. In 2004, more than half its domestic revenues, and more than 60 percent of its domestic profits, came from food products.

What all these examples illustrate is that brands given new homes, or homes given new brands, can entertain a new lease on life. Acquisition innovation gives management the opportunity to jettison the baggage that was holding performance back and capitalize on assets that are still vital.

One critical success factor for acquisition innovation in either a complex-systems or a volume-operations environment is executive leadership that is dispassionate and decisive. Everyone in the organization is under a high level of stress, so the goal is to get things done quickly and fairly, so that people can find the new normal as soon as possible. This is not a time to get close to the troops, or a time to worry about being liked. It is a time to set a firm course and stay on it unwaveringly through to completion.

A second key to acquisition innovation is postmerger integration. Mergers of equals are extremely difficult to execute, so this is best handled as a merger of "unequals," where one team is clearly in charge and the other is adapting to the new agenda. Best practices require management to clearly discriminate between core and context assets, making sure to preserve the integrity of the acquired core, the truly differentiating capability that was the spur that led to acquisition, and making equally sure to disband, shed, or absorb the acquired context, the remainder of the acquired company's assets. The sooner this is done, the better for all involved.

A third success factor is to focus an exceptional amount of executive attention not on the process of integration but on the new market outcome that integration will enable. From the CEO on down, there should be monthly meetings driving the migration to the new category position forward. Managers should be so obsessed with this outcome that they do not have time to worry about political infighting. Nothing unites a new organization as much as a common enemy. The sooner you can get it focused on its new competitors, the better.

Finally, as we noted at the beginning of the chapter, renewal innovation in either form, organic or acquisition, is a high-risk endeavor. That means there is a good probability it will fail. If it does, management can and should adopt a harvest-and-exit strategy, typically reaching out to a leveraged-buyout firm for assistance. This is not as gloomy an outcome as it is frequently portrayed to be. People find other jobs, technologies find other homes, customers have already made clear they have found other vendors, shareholders get something out of it, and LBO limited partners get even more. Nothing under the sun is immortal, so there is no need to pretend that enterprises have to be.

WRAPPING UP

This concludes not only our discussion of innovation types appropriate to a declining category but also our overall discussion of innovation types in total. Over the past three chapters we have examined some fourteen types of innovation illustrated by more than one hundred examples of companies that have used them to achieve competitive separation within their chosen category and target markets. This is what we meant by innovation that creates differentiation for economic success. All our exemplary companies demonstrated the insight, courage, and perseverance *to go far enough.*

So just remember one thing in your day-to-day dealings with Darwin, as you struggle to gain the kind of competitive separation that creates attractive returns: *If one hundred other companies can do this, so can you.*

CISCO INNOVATING IN DECLINING MARKETS

Since Cisco has focused on the Internet for the bulk of its history, its major markets have yet to decline. But the company uses both innovation types associated with a declining market to guard against getting caught up in a market decline. This is not quite the same thing, because it does not require quite the same level of decisive intervention, but there are still plenty of opportunities to learn best practices nonetheless.

CISCO AND ORGANIC RENEWAL

Organic innovation in a declining market refers to making in-house R&D bets on catching the next great wave, thereby rescuing the franchise from the downward spiral of a declining category or sector. Although Cisco has yet to face this situation, it is actually conducting a variant of this exercise because it foresees a future in which the network, as currently understood, could become marginalized. Given that every market trend is toward increased networking rather than the opposite, how in the world could the network become marginalized in any time frame that is meaningful for present-day decision making? The answer lies in a sea change that is about to hit enterprise computing.

For the past decade, enterprise computing has been constructed around an architecture called client-server. In this architecture, Microsoft and Intel rose to power dominating the client side of the ledger, the desktops at which you and I sit, and more recently the devices we take in hand when we become mobile. Meanwhile Cisco, along with SAP, Oracle, IBM, EMC, and others, rose to power on the server or back-end data center side. The architecture that links the two poles aligns as a stack of functionality with the end user at the top and electricity at the bottom. Each of the companies named above has staked out a strong position in one or another layer of this stack, with Cisco dominating the network layer, SAP the application layer, Oracle the database layer, and so forth. As long as client-server architecture is the prevailing paradigm, each of these positions is virtually unassailable.

For two key reasons, however, client-server architecture is running out of gas. First, it was designed and optimized for intraenterprise computing, but now we are entering an era of increasing dependence on interenterprise outsourcing. And second, it is too monolithic to absorb and adapt the next generation of technologies while still maintaining backward compatibility with legacy systems. This is slowing enterprise-computing investment to a snail's pace at the time of this writing and creating an opening for what most experts believe will be the next architectural paradigm, services-oriented architecture, sometime just known as Web services.

In this new architecture, every function performed by every device is conceived of as a stand-alone service that can be called upon as wanted and dropped when no longer needed. Computation, storage, video, voice, games, transmission, you name it, it's a service. All this begs a number of questions. Where will all these services be hoteled? Who will host them? Who will decide what protocols and standards govern their invocation? Who will be able to charge rent for using them? And who will have to pay those rents?

These are the questions that keep Cisco and every other leading company in enterprise computing up at night. Each of the current leaders can make a case for why their layer of the client-server stack is the natural center of gravity for this next-generation web of services. But to actually perform that role they must convert what today is a relatively proprietary and closed set of products into a still proprietary but now relatively open set of services. In short they must convert their products into platforms.

Platform innovation, as readers may recall, is an innovation type for growth markets. What is it doing back here in declining markets? It is standing here as the candidate destination for what may well be one of the great renewal migrations of all time.

To be the leader in a platform play requires only one thing: followers. Specifically, the other major players in the ecosystem must voluntarily embrace your platform. Knowing how much power this confers onto another company, why would these other companies ever do this? The answer is threefold:

1. They get enormous productivity gains from leveraging your services

2. They get access to a much broader marketplace

3. They do not perceive the power you gain coming at their expense

Cisco's plan is to deliver on all three points.

The network, in Cisco's view, is a natural host for called services because all calls that travel from A to B must be carried over the network. This gives it an advantage similar to the old adage about the three most important success factors in retail: location, location, location. Cisco seeks to leverage its own location advantage by providing services that are noncore to its major partners. Security and data backup are two examples jeopardizing Symantec's position in the client-server stack, especially now that it has acquired Veritas. But perhaps Cisco will license technology from Symantec to round out this function. In that case, it may be threatening to Legato, who competes with Symantec, and who was recently acquired by EMC. EMC is a key partner of Cisco's, one the company does not want to alienate, and thus begins the long and delicate dance of a paradigm shift. Move too fast, and you force people to attack you in self-defense. Move too slowly, and someone steals a march on you.

So here is the question: How much attention should the executive team at Cisco give to this opportunity? Realize that it calls for the best engineering minds to solve the technical issues and the best of market-facing talents to navigate and orchestrate the value chain responses. This same pool of talent is much in demand to develop more immediate opportunities and respond to more immediate threats. How would you organize to ensure that whatever talent you committed to this outcome stayed focused on it? How would you keep that team from becoming too isolated, too ivory tower?

Right now Cisco would be the first to admit it does not have the answer to these questions. So rather than simply act, which is, frankly, its natural tendency, it is finding itself talking more than it is used to, leveraging the market councils on outward-facing issues, leveraging the engineering councils on inward-facing ones. From an outsider's perspective, the organization is migrating toward alignment. It is evolving a common perspective. This is the very opposite of the decisive actions that organic renewal normally calls for, but companies have this luxury when they are not under the gun. There is always the risk, of course, that they will substitute talking for acting altogether, an anxiety that is never far from the surface in discussions with Cisco management. But there is also the opposite risk, which is to embark on a bold undertaking without alignment, ensuring an ongoing internal resistance that will dog the entire journey. It is the right balance of these risks that Cisco is teetering to find.

CISCO AND ACQUISITION RENEWAL

During the 1990s, Cisco was probably best known for its extraordinarily active M&A strategy. Here is the number of acquisitions per year from 1993 to 2004:

1993	1994	1995	1996	1997	1998	1999	2000	2001	2002	2003	2004
1	3	4	7	6	9	18	23	2	5	4	12

The differences in shading of the various years represent different M&A strategies at work, as follows:

- *1993–1997: Portfolio Building.* The company entered the category of LAN switches and bolstered its presence in incumbent legacy technologies, including ATM/Frame Relay and SNA.

- *1998–2000: Optionality.* The company navigated the bubble by using its highly valued stock price to buy companies in a host of markets and technology sectors. No one strategy could ever have integrated all these purchases. Instead, the company was buying a set of options to hedge against a set of possible future developments.

- *2001–2002: Purchased R&D.* In the downturn, the company's stock was drastically devalued, and management restricted its acquisition strategy to simply paying up for technology and components.

- *2003–present: Portfolio Building.* The company returned to its roots, dramatically bolstering its presence in the categories of SAN switches, consumer networking, and wireless.

Portfolio building represents the normal strategy for replenishing corporate capabilities to escape being swept up in a category decline. Many companies fail here because they believe they can develop more competitive alternatives themselves and are loath to share their equity with another company whose offers are perceived to be inferior. This is the classic NOT INVENTED HERE syndrome. It fails to assign value to time, both in the negative, representing the time it will take the company to get a product to market plus the time it will take to establish a market position of value, and in the positive, representing the time in market that the established company already has plus the time they will have while your company is getting into position.

Cisco has two views of portfolio building. For critical technologies that align directly with its Ethernet and Internet trajectory, it will do anything it can to get to the head of the class. Assuming they are culturally and geographically compatible, the best companies are bought for top dollar, and the management teams are integrated directly into the fabric of the company. These are the flagship acquisitions, and they are in the minority. The majority of acquisitions are what might be called gap fillers—products that fill in gaps where the Internet has yet to penetrate. They are critical to offering end-to-end network capability, but from the perspective that eventually the Internet will become the all-purpose net, they are inherently short lived. Here Cisco shops for a pragmatic purchase that fills a short- to midterm need. Cultural and geographic compatibility are less critical, and often the management teams move on to enjoy the results of their "liquidity event" elsewhere.

What gives coherence to this strategy is the overarching vision that Internet protocol networking is destined to become the single dominant standard for all networking everywhere, from bits moving back and forth on a chip to data streams traveling between planets and everything in between. Is this vision correct? Who knows? But pragmatically it doesn't matter because the coherence this vision creates is valuable in and of itself—not just for shaping M&A strategy, but for shaping the priorities of the company as a whole

So what, then, are we to make of the boom-and-bust years of the Internet bubble? During this period Cisco's M&A strategy adapted to circumstances in ways that seem bizarre now but were appropriate for the time. During the bubble it went on a buying spree unprecedented in the technology sector. There was no way that any company could integrate all those purchases, so what could the company possibly have been thinking? In a word, they were stockpiling options.

In the past ten years there has been a lot learned about real options—how they allow companies to invest in high-risk commitments in manageable stages or to hedge their exposure to low-probability, high-consequence outcomes. In the case of Cisco's bubble strategy, the low-probability, high-consequence outcome was that one or another of the zanily valued start-ups bursting on the scene might actually be the true next big thing. Normally, one simply has to take one's chances in this arena, but if your own stock is also zanily valued, you have the opportunity to buy an option on that future at virtually no cost. That is, as long as the market adds their zany value to your zany value, you get a free ticket.

Obviously, this is not a stable idea, but until it was proved to be unstable—until all stock currencies were revalued in the light of achieved revenue and earnings performance—it was actually riskier to shun this path than to take it. Here's why. Companies who stayed sane during the bubble found their stocks devalued because they did not "get it." This made them acquisition candidates for companies whose stocks were overvalued because they did get it. Thus America Online acquires Time Warner. Thus Quest acquires U.S. West. Thus any number of dot-coms acquired any number of real businesses, only to sink them under the collapse of their own stocks.

But let us leave these surrealistic times. They were displaced by a well-deserved downturn. But don't forget what people were saying then. Do you remember people asking each other whether the recovery would be a "V" or a "U"? No one had yet figured out that it was going to be a big "L." But Cisco pulled in its horns regardless, as the acquisition numbers for 2001 and 2002 witness. And if you added up the price of those acquisitions, you would see how much further it had pulled in its horns.

Now the company was buying tangibles, not options, and was more likely to pay cash for them rather than stock. This is the least innovative type of acquisition innovation there is and the one that has the least impact. There is nothing wrong with it, but one should not look to create sustainable differentiation for competitive advantage by pursuing this course. Rather, in Cisco's case, it was simply good therapy after a prolonged binge.

Stepping back from Cisco's history of acquisition innovation, the best practice that is most important to note is how the company assimilates acquisitions. Here it applies the model of core/context analysis to great effect. Core represents the differentiating capabilities of the acquired company that attracted Cisco to pursue it in the first place. In virtually all cases this has consisted of engineering- and product-marketing talent focused on product innovation. These parts of the organization Cisco has left intact, with an ongoing focus on differentiating for competitive advantage. The remainder of the company—the line functions of sales, outbound marketing, services, finance, and the like—is context. These functions have expertise of great value, but it is not their role to be differentiating elements. These parts of the organization Cisco absorbs into its existing fabric of line functions, with an ongoing focus on productivity.

During the height of the bubble, when acquisitions were fast and furious, the company institutionalized the processes needed to execute this kind of integration. In this way it ensured that the decisiveness so needed in merger integration was baked into the very processes that implemented it. There was little time lost to negotiating, for the majority of the issues had already been decided going in. This truly is a best practice, one well worth emulating. At its heart is the notion that there is no such thing as a merger of equals, or rather if there is, it is a perilous undertaking that extends the integration period far too long with far too few returns to show for the exposure and risks entailed. Far better are the mergers of unequals, where the acquiring entity sets the ground rules, like them or not, allowing those who do to stay and those who don't to move on.

The one exception to this rule at Cisco has been the integration of Linksys, the company's sole foray into a volume-operations designed business. Here the company has to tread carefully, for it is not certain what is core and what is context. As a stopgap, it has isolated the division to protect its integrity, assigned one of its top executives to sponsor it, and allowed it to continue its operations undisturbed. But this is only by way of a prolonged experiment, a period of observation. Eventually the company must seek a closer integration because the future of networking calls for coordination between the consumer products at the edge and the complex systems at the center. At the end of the day, this, too, is not a merger of equals. It is, however, a marriage of opposite architectures, and Cisco is still working through the protocols of that relationship.

CHAPTER EIGHT

MANAGING INNOVATION IN YOUR ENTERPRISE

O n balance, it is a very good thing that there are many types of innovation. It allows management teams to be reasonably optimistic about their chances to differentiate successfully from competition, and it permits companies with very different gifts to make a place for themselves in the same economy. But it does make for a somewhat complicated framework of ideas, all in all some fourteen types ranged across the category-maturity life cycle, with no guarantee that we have exhausted all the types. So how exactly does one go about getting from this broad universe of choices to focusing alignment around a single innovation vector? And how does one translate that alignment into go-to-market programs that actually change the competitive landscape and secure returns above the cost of capital?

That is the subject of this chapter. Its goal is to help your management team choose an innovation vector and build a portfolio of programs around it so broad and deep as to defeat even the most tenacious competitor. We see this as a seven-step process, as follows:

1. Socialize the Idea

Management teams have little enough time to strategize, so the opportunity cost of embracing a novel methodology is high. They should be rightfully cautious about adopting the next new thing. The innovation-types model may or may not be the most useful lens through which to view your current situation. For such reasons, we encourage you to introduce the fundamental ideas and foundational models in a get-acquainted session prior to committing to any major undertaking. It is usually better if this talk is given by an outsider so that people can listen without bias. After the talk, the management team should caucus to make the call as to whether this methodology is worth pursuing at this point in the company's history.

2. Analyze the Portfolio

Assuming there is support to pursue the project, the next step is to submit your company's portfolio of offerings to a category-maturity life cycle analysis. The kinds of questions you are seeking to answer include:

- Where are each of our primary product lines in the category-maturity life cycle?

- How are they performing relative to the competition?

- What forms of innovation are competitors using to differentiate from us?

- What forms of innovation underlie our differentiation efforts to date?

- How successful have they been?

- Is there a reason for us to change our focus?

Out of this discussion, teams would normally choose one or more categories to target for an innovation project.

3. Analyze the Target Category

Here the goal is to get a clear view of the target category's current dynamics and the nature of the company's opportunity to change the competitive landscape. Questions to answer at this stage include:

- How is the category as a whole performing?

- Where is the boundary between complex-systems and volume-operations offers?

- Which business architecture is having the greater success?

- Which business architecture is more appropriate to our company?

- Are we able to keep the opposing architecture at bay?

- Which of our competitors operate on the same architecture as us?

- What do we believe their innovation strategy to be?

- How successful are they at executing it?

- What do we believe has been our innovation strategy to date?

- How successful have we been at executing it?

- How successful has the competition been at neutralizing it?

- Do we think it is time for a change?

At this point, you and the rest of the team may not be sure if changing innovation strategies is a good idea or not. Proceed as if you are sure it is. That is, commit yourself to the possibility that there may be a better innovation strategy than the one you are pursuing now. However, do not eliminate your current strategy from consideration unless and until you have good reason to do so. It may be you have the right strategy but have simply not gone far enough down the innovation vector to create competitive separation. You should keep your current strategy in contention—in other words, as long as you think it is still a viable alternative.

4. Reduce the Number of Innovation Types Under Consideration

Begin with all fourteen types under consideration. After reviewing each type in the abstract, citing examples from the text and other experience in the room, invite the team to propose candidates for elimination. There are three primary reasons an innovation type would be excluded from further consideration:

- It is inconsistent with the category's current state of maturity.
- It has been preempted by a competitor, so achieving competitive separation on its vector would be extremely challenging.
- It is a poor fit with your organization's core competencies.

The goal at this stage is to get the candidate innovation types down to a manageable number. To help in getting to this goal, complement the process of elimination with a process of preference. Reasons an innovation type would be preferred are simply the opposite of the reasons for elimination:

- It is consistent with the category's state of maturity.
- It has not been deeply exploited by any direct competitor.
- It is a good fit with your core competencies.

Continue to work the processes of elimination and preference until you have a minimum of one and a maximum of three innovation types to take forward as strong candidates for creating market-winning competitive differentiation.

During this process do not be surprised if you make changes to the innovation-types model itself. You may add types, for example, or divide one type in two, or push two types into one. There is nothing sacred about fourteen types. What is critical is that each type be considered as a vector and that the group appreciates the need to go down that vector sufficiently far enough to leave competition behind. Only that outcome generates the kind of market preference needed to secure the margin advantages that are key to dealing with Darwin.

5. Develop Attractive Options

This is the fulcrum of the entire exercise. To drive it, form a coalition of executive sponsors, one for each of the innovation types still under consideration. These executives will support cross-functional teams—we call them Darwin teams—drawn from leaders and high-potential performers who have some affinity for the innovation type in question. Each of these teams is then taken through the following process:

Begin by reviewing the material on the innovation type in focus. Discuss the examples in the text of companies that were successful in using it to gain competitive separation. Come up with additional examples from the group's own experience. Time and circumstance permitting, engage with one or more outside experts who have demonstrated success in this arena. Build a list of the defining attributes of this type of innovation, going beyond the text to incorporate the experience in the room. In short, saturate yourselves in the ideas that make up this type of innovation.

Then brainstorm all the potential ways your company could leverage this type of innovation to create distinctive competitive differentiation. The goal is to generate a list so long that, were you to implement it in total, customers would be astounded and competitors would be overwhelmed. To spur the process, ask each member of the group to consider the following questions:

- What are the first things you would change about our offer to make it more innovative in this dimension? (Get people to answer this question individually first, noting their ideas on paper in private, before sharing them with the group. This ensures that you do not lose the shyer people's thinking.)

- Suppose we did all these things. What is one more thing we could do to our offer that would really put our offer out of reach from any competitive alternative?

Once you have built as deep and broad a wish list as you can, rate and rank the ideas on it in terms of the following criteria:

- Will it attract the type of target customer we would like to have?

- Does it give that customer a compelling reason to buy?

- Is it feasible for us to execute, given our core competences and those of our current go-to-market partners?

- Is it differentiated from what our most successful competitors are doing today, and would it be difficult for them to copy?

- Is it consistent with and reinforcing to the other tactics we are considering?

Ask each team member to rank each item on each criterion, scoring it from one to five, five being best, and then add up the results and prioritize by total score. This creates a rank-ordered list of tactics, typically with a cluster of high-scoring ones at the top. Draw a cut line just after the last of these, and focus the team on the tactics above the cut line.

Now focus the team on brainstorming programs that would bring these tactics to life. Begin by listing all the functions in your company's organization that could touch the offer in some way—R&D, marketing, sales, services, logistics, sourcing, finance, and any others that come to mind. Take the prioritized list of tactics, and for each item, brainstorm what each function would change in order to make the innovative offer a reality. Basically, you are building a large table, where the columns are the functions and the rows are the tactics and the cells are the changes each function would make to implement the tactic.

After you are done, step back from the table you have built and synthesize its ideas into a suite of program proposals. Each is defined by the differentiated in-market outcome it seeks to create. One program might focus on revamping a product, another on changing the marketing, another on customizing the services, and so forth. Imagine yourself announcing these offers one after another to your sales force at a big sales meeting. Don't stop adding programs until you can imagine them all standing on their feet cheering.

As a final step, submit your program ideas to a financial analysis. Estimate how much investment in time, talent, and working capital it would take to make them a reality. What kind of market success would it take to justify that kind of investment? How confident are you that the programs you are proposing would have that kind of market success? How valuable would such a success be to the company as a whole? Seek out the right balance of aggressive targets for in-market performance with realistic requests for investment, and adapt your final proposal accordingly.

6. Select a Prime Innovation Vector

Each of the Darwin teams reports out to the coalition of sponsors on its proposed set of programs. The coalition may accept reports as is or send them back for more work if they feel they have overlooked key opportunities or incorporated inappropriate assumptions. Once all final recommendations are in, then the executive sponsors select one innovation program to be the corporate priority for the category in question.

At this point, it is critical to put all the other innovation types on the shelf. Remember, the goal is to create sustainable competitive differentiation by overdelivering on a single innovation vector. To choose a potpourri of attractive programs from multiple vectors—a bouquet of the best of the best, as it were—actually makes it easier for competitors to neutralize your differentiation. It is far better to take any extra innovation energy you have and make yet another addition to the prime vector to put your offers that much further out of reach.

7. Engage the Entire Organization

As the columns in the tables that were used in program brainstorming make clear, once an innovation vector has been chosen, every function in the organization, from reception to the CEO's office, should be asked to rethink its role and its processes in light of the choice. Why? Because you have just declared your core.

The goal of this entire process is to extract resources from context to repurpose for core. That's what makes innovation fundable. The way you do that is to take your existing resources and redirect them to accentuate the innovation vector your programs are bringing to market. Some functions will be directly involved in creating the most visible parts of the innovation. Their path is clear. But every function has a chance to reinforce the new value proposition.

To engage the entire organization, marketing can begin by restating the brand promise in terms of the new innovation. Development can describe the new product, and services can describe the new services. In this context, the remaining functions should caucus to answer the following questions:

- What has become more important in our work because of this new commitment?

- What has become less important?

- What can we do differently in the day-to-day exercise of our responsibilities to reinforce the value proposition we are making to our customers?

- What can we stop doing, or stop doing so much of, in order to get the resources to focus on our reinforcement agenda?

- How can we show the world by our actions that our company truly does have a differentiated approach to the market?

At the end of the day, it is the most senior executive's responsibility to engage every person in the organization in this journey. This is what we mean by alignment. This is what creates the focus that will set your company's execution apart from that of your competition. This is what creates the customer outcomes that are so compelling. This is what makes your company the best place in the world to work.

PART THREE

MANAGING
INERTIA

You have just crafted a superb innovation strategy, one that gives every promise of creating the separation you need from your direct competitors, earning the customer preference your profit margins require. Now you face one more hurdle to realizing its vision. You must overcome the inertia of your own organization that fosters resistance to making the changes necessary to implement it.

Executives faced with this challenge tend to demonize inertia. They see it as a passive-aggressive response to their dynamic leadership agenda. It is no such thing. Inertia is the property of an object in motion to stay in motion. As such it is an ally of the current strategy, helping it to stay its course. It is the legacy of the last innovation. If your innovation is successful, in the future inertia will help it to stay its course. Without inertia our efforts would wobble and fall over, and innovation would be wasted.

Inertia, in short, is not the enemy of innovation, but it does resist it at the point of change. Therefore, at that very point, management must learn to deconstruct inertia in order to reconstitute it elsewhere. This is the significance of the mantra. Extract resources from context in order to repurpose them for core.

CORE AND CONTEXT

Core, in our parlance, is that which differentiates your company to create sustainable competitive advantage. It is grounded in the innovation type upon which you have based your strategy. Core stands in contrast to context, which is everything else you do. Context includes most of the things you do to meet commitments to your key stakeholders—investors, employees, customers, and partners—and to comply with the laws of your nation and the standards of your industry. It also includes all the things you do just to keep pace with your competitors and thereby meet what has become the market's standard of performance. In short, there is a great deal of context in your life, and managing context is where you spend the bulk of your time.

That said, if you do not create core, if you do not renew core, if you allow your competitive differentiation to erode, then your offers cannot earn the margins you need to fund the enterprise you are helping to manage. That is why, although context outweighs core by bulk volume, core outweighs context in terms of strategic importance. At the margin you would like to spend more time on core and less on context than you do today.

Now nothing in business is inherently either core or context. The distinction comes into being only after you have declared your strategy for differentiation. That establishes core. Only by declaring core does context come into existence. The key property of core is that it creates competitive advantage. The key property of context is that it does not. This has fateful implications for managing context.

If you perform context tasks badly, the market will punish you for not meeting its standards. But if you do them brilliantly, the market will give you no extra credit. Thus, for example, if an airline loses your luggage, you will be furious and consider switching carriers. But if it does not lose your luggage, you do not deem it worthy of a reward. Same for overnight packages arriving on schedule, for customer service lines that do not keep you on hold, for milk that has not turned sour, and for cars that do not need to be recalled.

But it goes further than this. Context is anything and everything that you have not specifically declared to be core. For example, when Domino's Pizza delivers in less than thirty minutes, it gets credit from its customers because they consider on-time delivery part of its core. When Round Table delivers in less than thirty minutes, however, it gets no such credit. That is not part of its declared core. So while it will be punished for a late delivery, it will not be rewarded for an early one.

Given all this, you can see why management's focus should be on minimizing the enterprise's engagement with context. But why does it build up in the first place? Where does it come from? For the most part, present context is the legacy of past core. That is, at one time or another virtually every process we now take for granted, that we now treat as context, was new, and companies were able to leverage it for competitive advantage. It was core then, creating differentiation that led to competitive advantage. This stimulated competitors to find ways either to emulate it or to neutralize it, thereby restoring a competitive equilibrium. As more and more competitors mastered the new technology, it no longer differentiated. Core became context. This is the property of all Darwinian systems, including free-market economies. What is currently core eventually becomes context, which in turn forces competitive participants to invent new core. Each cycle raises the bar. That is where evolution comes from.

From the point of view of any one participant, it can feel like you are trying to climb up a down escalator:

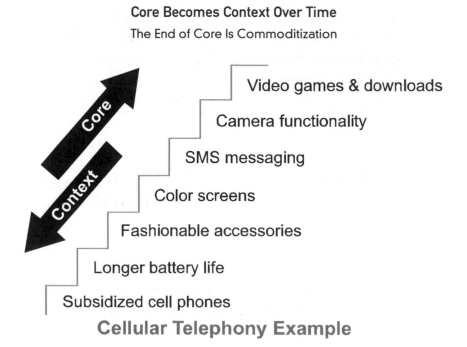

Core Becomes Context Over Time
The End of Core Is Commoditization

Video games & downloads

Camera functionality

SMS messaging

Color screens

Fashionable accessories

Longer battery life

Subsidized cell phones

Cellular Telephony Example

Consider the example of the cell phone industry. Handset competitors introduce differentiated offerings at the top of the escalator, but as other firms copy them, they are driven inexorably to the bottom. This leads to still other innovations being introduced, and as they drift down, still more after that. All this, of course, is great for consumers—it's what we mean when we say evolution raises the bar. But it is increasingly challenging for the economic models of the vendor companies involved. For not only do they need to continue to compete at the top of the escalator, they also have to maintain all the programs that have drifted to the bottom.

The resulting buildup of context in relationship to core is a management dilemma, illustrated by the following figure:

Context Buildup

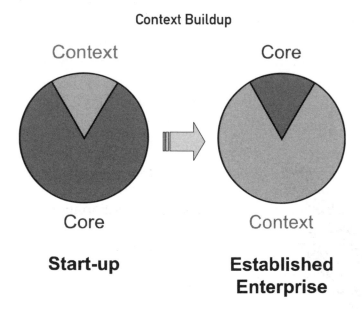

Start-up   **Established Enterprise**

The two pie charts represent the percentage of organizational resources committed to core. When an enterprise is starting up, its core/context ratio is heavily weighted to core. As such, it is remarkably differentiated for a company its size and surprisingly effective at competing with much larger vendors in its space. As it grows and thrives, of course, it attracts competitor emulation, causing its original core to convert to context, but it keeps ahead of the game by adding new core. What is not envisioned and typically not well managed, however, is the disposal of old core, now become context. The company simply grows by adding resources to do the new work, retaining responsibility for the old.

Over time, therefore, the ratio of core to context inevitably shifts. Understand that in terms of absolute numbers, an established enterprise has far more resources devoted to core than does a start-up. But in terms of relative allocation of resources, its core/context ratio is the inverse. Why does this matter? *Because context is the breeding ground of inertia.*

It is not hard to see why. As we have just made clear, context work only permits two outcomes: neutral and bad. There is no upside reward for excellence, although there are plenty of penalties for failure. As a result, managers in charge of such processes become increasingly risk averse—*because that is the only intelligent response.* This risk aversion in itself is not bad. When you put someone in charge of a nuclear power plant, you are actually glad they are risk averse. But over time, as more and more processes in an established enterprise become context, the total population of risk-averse managers begins to exceed that of risk-taking management. Now the ability of the organization to change strategy by embracing the next set of changes becomes seriously impaired.

As a result, established organizations with unfavorable core/context ratios, even though they are funding core projects with a budget that dwarfs the entire resources of a start-up, often find themselves struggling to compete. The inertia of context becomes so great that the investment in core cannot overcome it, and innovations are unable to get to market.

Note that these pie charts reflect the distribution of core, not of core competence. Core competences are the things you are exceptionally good at, and the mature organization has no shortage of them.

In a commoditizing world, as competition catches up, established enterprises do not lose their core competence, they lose their differentiation. In short, they discover *their core competence is no longer core.*

This is indeed a sobering experience. On the one hand, a perennial asset for creating competitive advantage has lost efficacy even though the company is still heavily invested in the capability. On the other hand, finding new core means setting off into untested waters with no track record to reassure you or your customers and partners. Anxiety on both sides of this equation leads organizations to cling to core competence even though it no longer differentiates, thereby increasing inertia and blocking deployment of the next generation of core.

Understandable as this clinging behavior is, it is disastrous from a competitive point of view. Offers that once were differentiated are now commoditized. Customers continue to buy—indeed, unit growth in the market increases—but at ever-diminishing price premiums. Thus revenues flatten, profits sink, and investors defect. This is the Darwinian stimulus that drives management to create the next round of core. But if all your resources are stuck in context, and if investors are no longer engaged, how can you fund the next round of core? And how will you overcome the growing inertia that blocks its path to market?

The answer is you must learn to kill two birds with one stone.

Two Birds, One Stone

Extract resources from context to
repurpose for core.

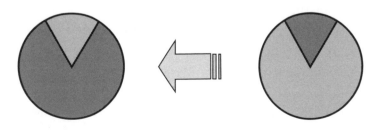

Extracting resources from context to repurpose for core accomplishes three key objectives:

1. It solves your balance sheet problem. You do not have to seek additional investment if you can fund your future from your current asset base.

2. It solves your income statement problem. You do not have to initiate a cost-reduction program if you can increase the revenues and margins earned by your current asset base.

3. Most important, it solves your inertia problem. By taking mass out of context, you reduce its inertial resistance to core. The more mass you move from context to core, the more powerful this change dynamic will be.

Two parallel efforts are required to create a context-to-core resource migration. First, to extract resources from context, you must reengineer the current workload so that it consumes fewer resources and makes fewer demands on scarce talent. And second, to repurpose those freed-up resources for core, you must recycle your current workforce in a way that is consistent with its talents and meets the needs of the next generation of core.

Both these challenges have defeated many a management team in the past. The purpose of this section is to ensure that they do not defeat you in the future.

CHAPTER NINE

EXTRACTING RESOURCES FROM CONTEXT

T o understand the dynamics that resist extracting resources from context, consider the following framework:

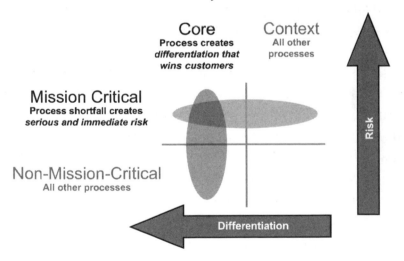

Core-Context Analysis Framework

We know that we want to prioritize resource allocation for core. That is the meaning of the arrow driving to the left and of the vertical oval in the left two quadrants. But our decision is complicated by the presence of mission-critical risk. As managers we must allocate resources to guard against this downside. That is the meaning of the vertical arrow and the horizontal oval in the top two quadrants. It does not take too much reflection to realize that the upper right-hand quadrant is going to pose a problem. Mission-critical context is laying claim to the very resources we need to deploy to the next generation of core, but we dare not release them from their current assignments.

What specifically do we mean by mission-critical context? Every product shipment, every financial transaction, every Sarbanes-Oxley attestation, every employment agreement; our computer security, our inventory supply, our investor reports, our e-mail system. Few if any enterprises have a strategy to differentiate on any of these things—hence they are not core—but woe to the manager responsible when one of them fails—hence their mission criticality.

So to ensure that they do not fail, we assign experienced employees to these tasks and experienced managers to supervise their work. We build systems that track this work and escalate problems should they arise. We have backup systems that engage in the event the primary system goes down. In short, today we tie up a lot of valuable resources to guard against the downside of a mission-critical failure.

Now let us look toward a desired future state, one in which those resources are being extracted and repurposed. In this world, innovation cycles through the domains of core and context as shown on page 209.

Innovation begins in the lower left-hand quadrant, where the focus is on core, but the project is contained to minimize risk. This is the domain of nonmission-critical core, a world of laboratory experiments, incubation efforts, skunk-works organizations, and pilot projects. Risk is encouraged in the quest for differentiation, and the rest of the enterprise is protected by restricting the scope of consequence.

When the innovation is judged ready for prime time, it moves from the lower to the upper left-hand quadrant. Now we are in the domain of mission-critical core. This is a time when we release the next generation product line, launch the next new marketing campaign,

The Cycle of Innovation

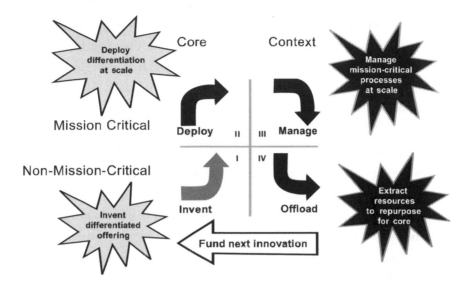

enter the next new market category, open sales offices in the next new geography. It is where enterprises expect to make their highest returns because they have distinctive competitive advantage, and they are exploiting it at maximum scale. There are risks, to be sure, but there is reward commensurate with them.

Innovations stay in the upper left-hand quadrant for as long as competitive differentiation is sustained, the longer the better. But eventually Darwinism has its day, and competitors find a way to neutralize the advantages being exploited at their expense. When this happens, the work migrates from the upper left to the upper right. Now we are in the domain of mission-critical context.

Once management realizes that a class of work no longer contributes to competitive advantage, its attitude toward it must change. The work must still be done, and done well, but the focus now shifts from differentiation to productivity. Standardization replaces differentiation as the primary focus, the target shifts from outperforming competitors to simply meeting market standard, and management attention shifts to systems and automation and any other tool that will free up talented people for other tasks.

To maximize resource extraction, however, one must move the work from the upper right-hand quadrant down to the lower one, systematically wringing out the risks that lay claim to high-value resources. We must convert mission-critical context, in other words, into non-mission-critical context. This is the world of six-sigma optimization and DMAIC analysis, of quality circles, statistical process control, service-level agreements, and eventually of outsourcing the work altogether. Organizations will still retain a thin veneer of management to oversee these relationships, but the bulk of the scarce resources once committed can now be released. Those released resources, in turn, are used to fund the next cycle of innovation.

The cycle of innovation diagram represents the world we seek to create. There are two major barriers that block our way: one to do with our failure to reengineer the work properly, the other with our inability to recycle our workforce properly. We'll address the first of these in the remainder of this chapter, and save the second for the chapter that follows.

If we look at the world we live in today, we can readily see opposite how the pattern we seek to create gets thwarted.

Start reading this diagram from quadrant III. That's where the resources are getting stuck, and for good reason. There are genuine risks involved, and therefore people and systems must be deployed to manage them. Once they get good at this work, it is not only risky to turn it over to people less familiar with it, it is less productive to do so because they will be less efficient. Intensifying this sensitivity to change is the natural risk aversion of the managers in charge. With no upside and plenty of downside, can you fault these folks for wanting to sandbag a few of their best people and stock up on extra resources just in case? And finally the people themselves are in their comfort zone. This is their core competence, after all, and they take pride in the skill with which they execute it.

Clinging to Context
How Resources Get Blocked

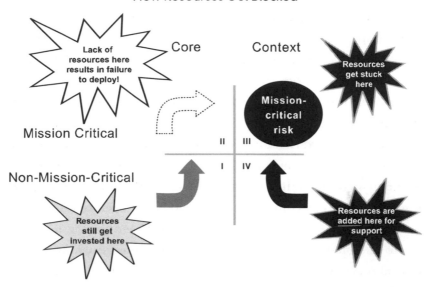

For all these reasons, the team in place does not manage down the resource commitment to mission-critical context; it actually manages it up. That is the significance of the upward arrow in quadrant IV. Because every year more and more context work appears, and because there is no mechanism in place for disposing of it, the workforce becomes more and more overloaded. To give it some relief, management adds supporting resources to take some of the load off its shoulders. This further increases the resource commitment to context and adds inertial resistance to the next round of core.

Nonetheless, management continues to fund the next round of innovation. It understands it must invest in the future, and invest it does, so actually nothing changes in quadrant I. This is an important point. People argue that established organizations lose their way because they fail to innovate. That is not true. Established organizations innovate like mad. Look at their labs, look at their pilot projects, look at how much they spend quarter after quarter on R&D. And it is not that they are incompetent in the work they produce. Many of the great innovations that venture capital has funded were in fact projects that were started in corporate labs or division-sponsored skunk works.

So let's be clear: The problem is *not* that established enterprises cannot innovate. The problem is they *cannot deploy the innovations once they are hatched!* Look at quadrant II and what do you see? Nothing! There's nobody there to take the handoff, nobody to deploy the next generation of innovations. And why not? Because they are all over in quadrant III tied up in mission-critical context.

But surely once this is seen, management takes corrective action. Not so. It persists in its current allocation because of a fundamental error in management thinking at work here that goes all the way to the top of the organization. Management is mistaking mission criticality for core!

Here's how it happens. Management teams are appropriately focused on making the quarterly number. That's about as mission critical an objective as you can get. So do they embrace the next new innovation to get it done? Of course not. They go to their tried-and-true offers instead, selling them to their most supportive go-to customers, albeit at more of a discount than they would like. And by so doing, they make the quarter. But also by so doing they fall back another quarter in the race to enter and win the next market, and they leave the fringes of their current markets even more exposed than they were before. In other words, to meet their mission-critical obligations, they are actually sacrificing core.

For make no mistake: Although meeting a revenue forecast is absolutely mission critical—CEOs get fired if they miss more than a few—it is not core. Core is the engine that drives your competitive differentiation. It is what helps you make *future* quarterly financial targets, not present ones. When you sacrifice your commitments to core in order to make the current quarter, you are in effect liquidating your company, one quarter at a time, by underinvesting in the future in order to pay off your present debts. You are doing just the opposite of what you ought to be doing: You are actually extracting resources from core to repurpose for context.

"But we have no choice," an anguished voice blurts out. That is not true. You are, to be sure, in a pickle, but you do have a way out. You must find a way not only to meet your mission-critical obligations but also free up resources to deploy the next generation of core. You must, in short, find a way to become *radically* more productive.

The key to becoming radically more productive is not to work harder. That can make you incrementally more productive in the short term, but it does not lead to a stable outcome. It does not address the fact that next year there is another load of context coming in, and you still have done nothing to rid yourself of your current load. The only way to become radically more productive is to attack the workload itself. And that is the function of something we call the five levers model.

THE FIVE LEVERS

The five levers represent a sequence of management actions that systematically reengineers mission-critical workloads to first extract risk so that one can then extract resources. Each step is characterized by an enabling activity, see page 216.

Here's how the model plays out:

1. *Centralize.* Once a process is understood to be context, once the desired outcome has shifted from differentiation to productivity, the first opportunity to extract resources comes from centralization. This eliminates the management overhead of maintaining multiple instances of the same process in multiple organizations, thereby freeing a modest number of resources for reassignment. Centralization also loosens the hold of vested interests on the process maintainers. These interests typically invoke a legacy of entitlement to re-

The Five-Levers Model

Extracting Resources from Mission-Critical Context

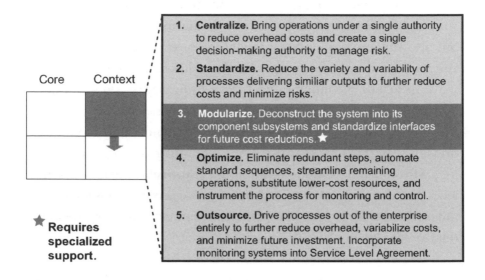

quest ongoing enhancements in work output that go beyond the minimum required. In a radically productive
world, there is no room to accommodate such requests. The
current task team, however, is often beholden to these interests for past favors. Centralization breaks the link of that
obligation and frees management to be much more frugal
in its subsequent commitments.

2. *Standardize.* Once similar processes have been put under a
single point of control, the next resource-extraction opportunity is to migrate from multiple instances of the process to
a single instance. Such standardization further reduces the
resource consumption, since each act of maintenance need
not be replicated or reproduced. At the same time, reducing
differentiation also reduces risk. The less variability in any
system, the less chance of failure and the fewer resources

required to manage it. This is a cornerstone of radical productivity. Of course, people on the receiving end of these changes are not likely be happy about having to accommodate them. Nonetheless, since the process is context not core, the opportunity to extract resources must take precedence over currying to their preferences, *even when the process is funded out of their budget*. Everyone has to keep in mind that the money in their budgets actually belongs to the company, not to their organization or to them personally, and the company's first priority is to invest that money in core.

The combination of levers 1 and 2 effectively migrates a workload to a shared services model. It has the effect of reducing innovation relative to the tasks under management, which is precisely what you want because you intend to spend those innovation resources on core not context. But if you stop here, you will not have solved the problem of the next workload coming in. That means sooner or later the shared services organization itself will begin to bloat, and you will be in the soup again.

To make further progress, each of the process models under shared-service management needs to be deconstructed in order that it can be further optimized. This is the role of the third lever in our sequence, and normally it requires specialized support:

3. *Modularize.* Modularization consists of deconstructing a product or process into its component elements so that it can be reengineered for radical gains in productivity. The reason this typically requires specialized support is that it involves exercising a bifocal vision. One eye looks at the process as it is currently being executed. The other eye looks at a library of templates that come from the best practices of radically productive companies. This is normally best done by importing expert consultants, whether they be from an external agency or an in-house six-sigma team. The goal of

their modularization effort is to come up with the simplest representation of the process that meets the input and output criteria for quality results. Such simplification alone can reduce risk and free up valuable resources.

4. *Optimize*. Once a process has been modularized, it can then be optimized. During this phase, redundant and superfluous tasks can simply be eliminated. Others can be automated, and the remainder streamlined. All this simplifies the management and execution of the work, reducing complexity and risk, allowing you to substitute less expensive resources and free up your most experienced people. As a final step in the optimization, teams instrument the process with metrics and monitors to further reduce variation, extract risk, and maintain control.

5. *Outsource*. The ultimate goal of radical productivity is to so thoroughly "de-risk" context, one can safely get rid of it by outsourcing. In some cases, this involves an intermediate stage called outtasking. That is used whenever one portion of the overall process still bears too much uncontrolled risk to outsource but another part is ready to go. It also permits keeping some part of the process in-house in cases where you suspect that what today looks like context has the potential to resurrect itself as core in the future. Just do not become too enamored of outtasking over all. In the end it is a stopgap measure. You cannot outtask your way to radical productivity.

RADICAL PRODUCTIVITY ULTIMATELY MEANS OUTSOURCING

Outsourcing is like nuclear power. It can be used for good or bad, and it has a reputation to match. Indeed, I would argue that outsourcing as currently practiced has a fatal flaw, namely, the alienation of the current workforce and its social allies. We are going to address that issue head on in the final chapter of this section. For now, let us agree to set it aside for the moment and review the reasons why outsourcing, despite its issues, is still so compelling.

- **LABOR COST REDUCTION.** Reductions in the cost of direct labor are common with outsourcing, particularly when it is combined with offshoring. As long as there are dramatic differences in the standards of living between countries, such savings will be available. No global corporation can compete if it cedes these sorts of advantages to its competitors and does not participate in them itself. That said, onshore outsourcing can also produce lower labor costs because outsourcers, who see the work as core, are willing to invest more in productivity improvements than those of us who see it as context. Moreover, they can amortize such investments across multiple-client engagements, thereby giving them a better overall return on capital. And companies who treat a given task as core can also invest more in their people, allowing them to recruit superior talent and grow its capabilities over time. At the same time, by asking outsourcers to compete with one another, your company can drive down your effective cost of labor over time in ways that you could never negotiate with an in-house workforce. And finally, whether on- or offshore, outsourcing frees you from the cost of all the context work entailed in managing the workers involved.

- **IMPROVED RETURNS ON INVESTED CAPITAL.** This is a key metric for investors who optimize their allocation of capital to achieve the highest risk-adjusted returns they can. They want their capital to go to core, not context, for it is only through improved competitive performance in the future that they are rewarded. They like outsourcing for two reasons: In the company where the work is context, it frees up capital so that it can be repurposed for core; meanwhile, in the company to which the work is going, that same work is defined as core, and investment will contribute to increased returns This is the economic magic of outsourcing—that one company's context can be another company's core, and by transferring the work from one to the other, both companies and their investors come out ahead.

- **MINIMIZATION OF FIXED COSTS.** A third benefit of outsourcing is that it allows companies to transform a fixed cost into a variable cost. Even when a company pays a modest premium over its in-house cost of performing the same task—and one should scrutinize these cost comparisons as in-house teams often understate their fully loaded costs—outsourcing can buffer companies against cyclicality in their business sector. That is, with a variable resource pool to draw upon, one can staff up in good times and downsize in bad times without bearing the cost and pain of a hiring/firing cycle in-house. This not only avoids the direct expense of recruiting fees and severance packages but also the emotional exhaustion that saps much needed energy away from competitive performance.

- **ABSORPTION OF RISK.** A fourth benefit of outsourcing is that companies can transfer responsibility for risk to the outsourcer, making it their responsibility to insure for liability and ensure against failure. Low-probability, high-consequence outcomes, such as data center failures or security violations, force companies to encumber significant resources at considerable expense. Outsourcers must pay this tax just like anyone else, but they can amortize it across multiple clients, thereby eliminating redundant capital expenditure for the rest of us.

- **REDUCTION IN INERTIAL MASS.** The more context work a company keeps in-house, the more risk averse a management agenda it must embrace. By releasing its workforce from context work, huge chunks of inertial mass are removed, and resources are freed up either to optimize the next load of incoming context or to be repurposed for core.

- **FOCUS ON CORE.** In times of change, the scarcest resources are time, talent, and management attention. Context processes tax all three. Until the process is completely off your books, management must continually balance the interests of context teams with those of core. Outsourcing frees everyone's calendars to focus more on core.

For all these reasons it is critical to drive as much context work as possible out of the enterprise completely. This is how we clear away the current year's load in order to make room for the next year's. Outsourcing is the ultimate tool in extracting resources from context and is a key enabler of radical productivity.

WHERE TO FOCUS THE MODELS

The core/context and five-levers models are normally applied within each function of the organization. The function begins by discovering its relationship to core and from there declaring which of its activities are core enabling and which are context managing. They then incorporate the dimension of mission criticality, thereby distributing their total workload across each of the four quadrants. Once so distributed, they then bring this template to their resource allocation decisions. How this plays out varies by function, so it is worthwhile to look into the process in a bit more detail.

Begin with sales and marketing. Here the dialogue opens with a rather peculiar question: Which of our markets are core, and which are context? This is not exactly the sense in which we have been developing these two terms, but it turns out to be a very fruitful application of the distinction.

A market is core when it is in play, meaning that market share is in flux, and market leadership is up for grabs. Gaining a market leadership position in a growing market is perhaps the single most sustainable form of competitive advantage, and one that garners just the kind of privileged margins we are seeking. By contrast, when a market is not in play, we mean its market-share pattern has been established for some time and is not likely to change more than a point or two unless something truly disruptive is introduced. Resources invested here are less likely to affect whatever margin advantage we may already have. Such a market is context, not core.

A simple way to discriminate markets in play from the rest is to examine cumulative annual growth rates (CAGRs). High CAGR markets are adding many new customers every quarter. Those customers have yet to select their preferred vendor. That's what puts them in play. By contrast, low CAGR markets typically are saturated, meaning most sales are made to existing customers. These companies have already identified their preferred vendor and resist change. That is what makes market-share changes more difficult to engineer and why we say the market is less likely to be in play.

Continuing with this thought process, a market is mission critical when the revenues we seek from it are material to the current financial performance of the company, and nonmission critical when they are not. Thus markets under incubation are nonmission critical as are markets that supply the odd opportunistic sale. By contrast, wherever we have significant revenues at stake, core or context, the markets are mission critical for sure.

If we put the two notions together, we typically see the majority of a company's revenues coming from markets that are mission critical but not core, meaning they come from established markets where our market position is relatively well established and not particularly fluid. By the logic of our models, sales and marketing teams are encouraged to treat such markets as mission-critical context and to apply the five levers to extract resources from them. Resources they free up are reallocated to mission-critical-core markets as a first priority, then to non-mission critical core. Any time, talent, or management attention applied to non-mission-critical context markets is thoroughly discouraged.

All this makes perfect sense, but it goes against the grain of traditional management practice. In most operations, both sales and marketing resources are allocated by revenue, the assumption being that all markets should be put on more or less the same diet, with some leeway allowed for incubating new ones. But this practice is all wrong. It ensures that established cash-cow businesses drink too much of their own milk, while cash-hungry rising stars fail to maximize their market share gains for lack of funding. Correct management practice is to insist that established businesses improve their productivity annually, producing more and more revenues using fewer and fewer resources. Such practices, however, are often neglected, either because vested interests derail them in pursuit of feathering their own compensation programs or because fear of mission-critical failure leads management to overresource the zone.

Now let's be clear. There is always a risk in applying the five levers. Any time you touch any mission-critical process, there is the possibility you will send it spinning out of control. But there is even greater risk in not touching mission-critical processes, in leaving resources to languish in context instead of being repurposed for core. Cynical managers may point out that the first risk is immediate and personal and the second, deferred and diffused, using that logic to excuse their inaction. But if you let them get away with that, understand you are the one who will be left holding the bag after they skip town. Better to face this issue squarely now, and enforce the practices outlined above.

When we turn from those who market and sell the offers to those who make them, specifically the line functions of R&D and professional services, there is a similar core/context question to answer: Which of our offerings are core, and which are context? Once again, the answer is: When a category of offering is in play, meaning market share is up for grabs, it is core; and when it is not, it is context. Similarly, when a category's revenues are material contribution to quarterly performance, it is mission critical, and when they are not, it is not.

This leads to the same resource-allocation dynamics we saw in sales and marketing. Most of the enterprise's revenue comes from product categories where market-share positions have already been staked out, meaning they are in the mission-critical context quadrant and warrant the application of the five levers. Once again, traditional management practices resist this notion, defaulting to a resource allocation that tracks to revenue contribution. This results in bad outcomes. The company's flagship offers become painfully overfeatured over time, since the resources assigned to them have to find something to do to earn their keep. This in turn leads to unsustainable cost profiles and creates an opening for disruptive innovation from below as described by Christensen in *The Innovator's Dilemma.* And when even this amount of overdelivery cannot soak up all the extra resources allocated, a host of secondary projects also get funded, and even some pet projects as well, none of which are likely to be aligned with core. So overfunding context breeds more context, accelerating the decline into inertial stasis.

Again, we should not be cavalier. Mission-critical offers are always under attack by someone, and neglecting them completely will undoubtedly result in revenue shortfalls eventually. Therefore, an appropriate level of attention must be maintained. But they do not need to be overmaintained. In particular, established enterprises competing in established categories do not need to be first to market with every new feature. That is a product-leadership innovation strategy that is warranted for growth markets or for marginalized competitors who need to find some claim to the customer's attention. Nor do established enterprises need to continually cater to the whims of their most sophisticated users, dedicated customers though they may be. Their list of enhancement requests should have to compete with every other possible use of company resources, and in particular, they should be given lower priority relative to the resource needs of mission-critical core offers, and even non-mission-critical core offers in many cases.

Finally, for all those line functions that neither make nor sell the offers their company lives by, core and context take on a third and distinctly different set of meanings. Here the functions may be tempted to think that all their work is context, none core, but that is, in fact, rarely the case. Instead, the question they must first ask themselves is this: Given the markets and product categories our company has declared to be core, and given the innovation vector we are seeking to maximize to the point that our competitors throw up their hands in despair, what can we do in our function that would further accentuate our differentiation in those domains?

What can finance do to further experiential innovation? What can human relations do to enhance value engineering? What can logistics do to support marketing innovation? What can manufacturing do to support process innovation? The answer in every case is, quite a lot. Simply by focusing on the differentiated end being sought, every one of these functions can reengineer its processes in ways that will ultimately affect the customer. In fact, it is secondary alignments like these that create the kind of overall competitive advantage position competitors are unable to emulate. For although a competing product division may be able to get a knockoff offer to market or throw a sales team into your target market, there is no way it can enlist the rest of its organization to support reinforcing such a tactical response.

Once these functions determine what they can do to reinforce core, then they, too, can fill out their four quadrants, overlaying the dimension of mission criticality onto their work. As they do so, they can then apply the five levers to mission-critical context processes in order to extract resources to repurpose for core. At the end of the day, just as there is no job that is 100 percent core, there is no job that is 100 percent context. We all need to be reengineering our work all the time to increase our relative contribution to core.

NEXT STEP

This chapter provides the tools necessary to determine where and how to extract resources from context. But that alone is not enough.

To actually implement this approach to radical productivity, you must enlist the entire workforce to participate. Historically, however, any strategy that ended in outsourcing has implied abandoning the interests of at least some workers. No workforce can align around such a strategy.

So before we can move forward with these ideas, we need to complete the circle and describe how we intend to repurpose our workforce for core. That will be the subject of our next and final chapter.

CISCO AND CORE/CONTEXT ANALYSIS

The first step in managing context is to explicitly declare core. At the highest level this is done by isolating one or more innovation types as zones of competitive differentiation. In the case of Cisco, these zones are product innovation in advanced technologies linked to line-extension innovation and integration innovation with its established routing and switching product platforms.

Just by this simple declaration, management has dramatically simplified the playing field. It has said that in growth markets, Cisco is not pursuing disruptive, application, or platform innovation as a source of sustainable differentiation for competitive advantage at the present time. It has said the same about enhancement, marketing, experiential, value engineering, process, and value-migration innovation for mature markets. This does not mean that there are not groups within the company engaged in these forms of innovation, but only that they do so acknowledging their lower priority relative to the declared innovation zones.

In particular, if a direct competitor has made deep inroads leveraging a noncore form of innovation, then Cisco is warranted in counterattacking to neutralize that competitive advantage. Also, if a modest investment in a noncore form of innovation would enhance the effectiveness of our declared core, or improve the productivity of our context efforts, it is also warranted. What is not warranted is a private messianic commitment to create a whole new foundation for competitive differentiation. One might think this to be an unlikely turn of affairs, but you would be surprised what goes through people's minds when working past midnight.

To make this direction more tangible to the enterprise at large, the next step is to translate it into specific declarations about markets, offers, and operational processes. Here the executive team at Cisco has taken a number of strong steps, as outlined below.

CORE/CONTEXT ANALYSIS OF MARKETS

To begin with, here is how Cisco assesses its markets at a macro level, first in terms of geography, then in terms of customer segments:

Cisco's Markets
Geographic Focus

	Core	Context
Mission-Critical	India Eastern Europe China Russia II	III U.S. Canada Japan Western Europe ANZ
Non-Mission-Critical	Brazil I Middle East Southeast Asia	IV Africa Latin America

As we should expect from the prior chapter, the overwhelming majority of Cisco's revenues come from the developed economies that occupy quadrant III. The point of this placement is that Cisco's position in these markets is not significantly in play. Therefore, from the point of view of competitive advantage strategy, they are relatively inert and do not require the kind of market-development investment they previously called for. Instead, sales and marketing teams are being managed to higher and higher goals of productivity because market inertia is now working in their favor.

By contrast, on the core side, again not surprisingly, the major geographic markets that are in play are the developing economies. Recent wins in India and Eastern Europe have raised those two markets to mission-critical status. That's because once a company's position begins to form, there is a window of opportunity in which to stake out its claims. At the end of that window, the market coalesces around the positions in place, and from then on it is much more difficult to move market share. In this light, Cisco's biggest exposure is China. It, too, is in play, but here it is a key competitor to Cisco, Huawei, that has put it in play. That company has the inside track, and given the importance of this industry to China and the active role that public policy plays in the country's economy, it is hard to see how Cisco can prevail. Nonetheless, until the final positions have coalesced, it must do everything it can to stake out the best market status role for itself it can.

The markets in the lower left-hand quadrant are coming into play, or what Cisco likes to call markets in transition. The company is a strong proponent of investing at market transitions, so even if each of these situations has problematic elements, they should be high on the team's radar. By contrast, the markets in the lower right-hand corner should not. They are not in play at this time, nor are they sufficiently robust to be material in a mission-critical sense. They should be treated opportunistically and not be targeted for investment in the foreseeable future.

Turning to customer segmentation, the company's current situation maps out as follows:

Cisco's Markets

Customer Segment Focus

	Core	**Context**
Mission-Critical	Service Providers Small to Medium Business	Enterprise
	II | III	
	—Customer—	
	I | IV	
Non-Mission-Critical	Networked Home Data-Center Virtualization	Small Office

Again, focusing on quadrant III first, Cisco's strongest customer segment, enterprise networking, accounts for approximately 50 percent of its revenues. It is certainly mission critical. At the same time, the company already has dominant market share, and although it would never take that for granted, nobody believes it is currently in play. As a result, the market is not core. Once again, this means inertia is on Cisco's side, and so it can expect to increase productivity in this segment without sacrificing competitive advantage.

Two major customer segments that are in play, on the other hand, are the telecommunications service providers and small-to-medium business. Each has posed significant challenges for the company in the past—hence, in part, the reason they are still in play—but additionally each has recently been put in play by an external forcing function.

In the case of the telecommunications service providers, the forcing function is the long-expected migration from traditional circuit-switched networks to full dependence on Internet protocol. Voice, data, or video, whether they be delivered by wire, cable, or wireless, will all be treated as streams of zeroes and ones running across an Internet protocol network. To be sure, telecommunications service-provider networks will be loaded with advanced capabilities, but they will be capabilities built on top of IP, not in competition with it. And that is what gives Cisco a new lease on life in a market it has traditionally stumbled in.

Cisco is the challenger, not the favorite, in this race. As such, it must target niche markets where it can stake out local gorilla status. Cable operators in the United States are one such customer segment, and bringing voice services to them is a key initiative in the company's service-provider market strategy. Outside the United States, however, cable providers are much weaker, and it is wireless that offers the best possibilities. In cellular, the incumbents own the field, so Cisco must seek out Wi-Fi partners to challenge for market share in wireless traffic. Unfortunately for Cisco, in order to win as a chimp as opposed to as a gorilla, it must commit deeply to application innovation and services-led offerings. This runs directly counter to the primary innovation vector, which is product innovation, so the Service Provider Council must try to hive off its efforts in order to create segment-specific focus.

This challenge is at the heart of Cisco's problems with prioritization and organizational alignment relative to the telecommunications sector. The entire team is frustrated with the status quo, and there are multiple points of view about how best to go forward. CEO John Chambers is clear that he does not want to replicate an unprofitable business model in telecommunications, but he and his team have yet to crack the code for what the right approach should be. In the meantime, a high-end router designed specifically for this segment's greatest traffic needs has given the company something to help keep customers occupied for the short term.

Turning to small-to-medium business, the forcing function is recent weakness in traditionally strong competitors like HP and 3Com. Combined with next-generation engineering that allows Cisco to field far more cost-competitive offers than in the past, this is putting the small-to-medium business networking market in play. The company has rallied around its Commercial Council to drive a cross-functional attack aimed at winning over indirect channel partners. Every line function represented on the council has stepped forward to align its processes with the objective of winning dominant share with this constituency.

Once again, the innovation vector is not Cisco's primary focus. The biggest concerns of this customer segment and the channel partners who serve it are too much product complexity, too onerous business processes, and too high a base price. These call for a whole suite of next-generation go-to-market programs centered around the innovation vector of value engineering. This is particularly challenging for the engineering organization to support, given its commitment to integration innovation, so it is largely the channel management organization and the supporting line functions that are taking the most dramatic and creative steps.

Of the remaining core markets, consumer is crossing the line to $1 billion in 2005 and thus is being graduated to mission critical. It has long been understood as core, hence not only the acquisition of Linksys but also its special treatment within the overall organization. The challenge the division faces at present is to install mission-critical systems that scale. In earlier years the direct engagement of the founding entrepreneurs allowed Linksys to adopt highly competitive tactics leveraging their industry relationships and personal experience and judgment. In particular, on the innovation side, it has thrived on a unique combination of product innovation and value engineering that let it be a very fast follower in markets that were just taking off. As a result, it has been able to capture market-share leadership without having to incur heavy R&D costs or risks. But founders are not scalable, so going forward, the company needs to find a way to institutionalize its competitive advantage, perhaps through process innovations that can replicate some of their best practices, particularly in the operational excellence zone.

Looking down into quadrant I, Cisco is clear about two long-term market-redefining trends—data center virtualization and the networked home. Both of these are core as each puts an entire sector of the marketplace in play. Each, therefore, has the downside potential to disrupt Cisco's market-leading position. At the same time, if they can be co-opted, each has the upside potential of dramatically extending the reach and impact of network technology. At present, however, neither market has enough traction to be material to the current quarter's results. Cisco addresses opportunities of this type through a combination of R&D and business transformation projects, where it engages with early adopter customers to help them use advanced technology to create disruptive outcomes in their marketplaces.

And finally, on the lower right, Cisco acknowledges that small businesses are right at the midpoint between the company's complex-systems sweet spot and its Linksys division's volume-operations capabilities. Rather than attack this marketplace directly, therefore, its strategy is opportunistic: letting Linksys sell in the first generation of offers with a view toward enabling an upgrade to Cisco's low-end line extensions at a later date.

CORE/CONTEXT ANALYSIS OF PRODUCTS

Beginning again in quadrant III, note that routers and switches, which account for more than 80 percent of Cisco's current revenues, are labeled mission-critical context. As before, this is because neither product category is in play. Cisco's market position in both is strongly held, particularly in the enterprise, and particularly in

Cisco's Markets
Product Category Focus

	Core	**Context**
Mission-Critical	Security VOIP Wireless II	Routers Switches Optical III
Non-Mission-Critical	I SAN Switches Application- Oriented Networks	IV Legacy Protocols

the developed economies. Further investments in product leadership in these categories are subject to diminishing returns. That is why the company has turned its focus to integration innovation, converting these products into closely held platforms for hosting its advanced technologies in quadrant II.

Those advanced technologies are all labeled core because market share in each of the categories is currently in flux. Security, voice-over IP, and wireless are all very fast-growing markets where market-share ratios are still subject to significant shifts. Each either has met or is about to meet the $1 billion revenue mark that John Chambers uses as a proxy for materiality, and thus mission criticality.

SAN switches represent a different case. The first generation of the market has largely already played out, although Cisco continues to take some share from conventional SAN-switch vendors. The total revenues, however, are just barely material, and if there was nothing more at stake, the company would move the category to quadrant IV. But in Cisco's view, SAN switches are an early card in the long-range game of data center virtualization, and as such they have strategic value beyond their immediate category. And closer in, when SAN switches transition to IP protocol, Cisco expects its technology lead to give it significant advantage even within the category's traditional boundaries.

Finally, just now peeking its head out into the marketplace is a next-generation offering called Application Oriented Networks. This is a family of devices that networks messages, not just bits and bytes. They live right at the boundary between what traditional computers and traditional networking devices do, and they represent a disruptive architecture that has the potential to redefine that boundary. This is about as core as you can get, but there is no revenue to speak of in the category at present, so it has yet to become mission critical.

There is one persistent irritant for Cisco recorded in this diagram, and that is optical devices. Even after Cisco trimmed its commitment to the category, it still absorbs a substantial portion of R&D resources with little chance of generating a satisfactory economic return as the category is presently not in play. The case for keeping it depends upon the service-provider market eventually converting to IP networks and becoming a major conduit for video. In that future, Cisco's high-speed CSR router can be optically enabled to route huge amounts of data to consumer neighborhoods. At present, however, the optical product line is not well differentiated and is overkill for all but the most high-volume applications. It represents a mission-critical context tax on current performance that makes meeting Cisco's ambitious performance goals that much more challenging. As such, it causes a fair amount of grumbling among the executive team, something Chambers is very much aware of but is unwilling to resolve.

CHAPTER TEN

REPURPOSING RESOURCES FOR CORE

This chapter represents the last step in our journey to create competitive advantage in a commoditizing world. Our path has been lit by the mantra Extract resources from context to repurpose for core. The issue this chapter addresses is aligning our workforces with that mission.

In the move toward a global economy, workforces in all the developed economies have been profoundly threatened by offshore outsourcers leveraging low-cost labor. This trend shows no signs of subsiding, and companies who do not avail themselves of this opportunity are severely challenged to price their goods and services competitively. In the public sector, politicians are divided between those who favor protectionist responses to mitigate the impact on their fellow citizens and those who believe the twin forces of consumer benefit and natural selection should prevail. Alignment, in short, does not characterize the current state.

In our view, this problem must be solved by the corporations themselves—management and labor collaborating with each other for the collective good of customers, employees, and investors. Together they must build a solution that actively embraces both outsourcing and offshoring while at the same time building a stronger in-house domestic workforce compensated commensurately with its local standard of living. We grant that this is a tall order, but we think it not only can but must be filled. This chapter outlines an approach we think can prove successful.

The essence of the problem with outsourcing is highlighted in the diagram below:

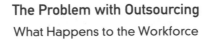

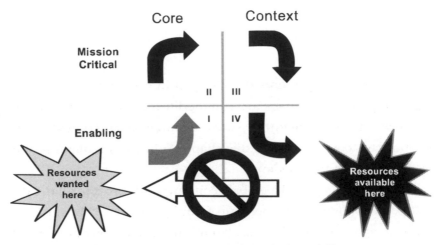

In the prior chapter, we showed how using the five-levers model management could systematically simplify, streamline, and de-risk mission-critical context work so that it could eventually be out-sourced. The goal was to extract resources from context to repur-pose for core. On the balance sheet, this works fine because money is what economists call a fungible asset—it is the most repurposable substance known to man. People, on the other hand, are not.

The human resources that are freed up in quadrant IV do not generally have the skill sets required to be repurposed in quadrant I. The possibility that they could somehow be retrained to gain such skills has been explored numerous times with little success. Thus the actual way in which this model has been implemented has been to lay people off on the right and hire them in on the left.

This is Darwinism at its meanest and most parochial, eroding culture and values, devaluing experience, and dismissing loyalty. It adds recruiting fees, hiring risk, and training costs to the front end, and severance packages, knowledge loss, and trade-secret leakage risk to the back end. It sends recurrent shock waves through the entire workforce, diminishing productivity everywhere. In short, this is a very bad model indeed.

But what else can we do? People in quadrant IV are simply not likely to be suited to fill openings in quadrant I. True. But they are quite likely to be suited to fill openings in quadrant III. And that in turn can allow people in quadrant III to be freed up to fill openings in quadrant II. And that in turn frees people in quadrant II to fill openings in quadrant I. We call this Tinkers-to-Evers-to-Chance movement resource recycling:

Resource Recycling

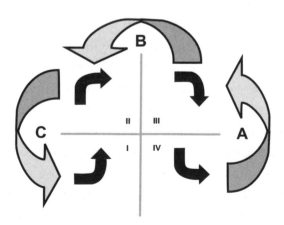

Work circulates clockwise
People recycle counterclockwise

Here's how it works. What people in quadrant IV bring to jobs in quadrant III is experience and expertise in managing context. All those tasks that fall to the bottom of the escalator, all that obsolete core that each year adds yet more weight to the pile of context—that's what these people understand. So if we do free someone up in quadrant IV, we can reasonably expect they have the aptitude for work in quadrant III. To be sure, they still need to be retrained to work on a new set of tasks, but they do not need a personality transplant.

Following the counterclockwise recycling path, what people in quadrant III bring to tasks in quadrant II is experience and expertise in managing mission criticality. Whether the work is core or context, if it is mission critical, it has to be done on time, on spec, and on budget. It requires maintaining visibility into all pertinent risk factors, implementing control systems that alert appropriately when those factors are drifting out of specification, installing intervention practices to head off problems before they escalate, and preparing contingency plans for the times when they go awry anyway. The class of people who thrive under this kind of pressure are the ones that were getting stuck in quadrant III managing mission-critical context and thus were not available in quadrant II to help deploy the next generation of mission-critical core. By recycling people from quadrant IV back into quadrant III to pick up their current workload, we free these people up to get over to quadrant II to bring out the next generation of innovation. Of course they, too, will need to be trained on a new generation of tasks, but they will not need to change their essential aptitude or orientation.

Finally, what people in quadrant II can bring to tasks in quadrant I is experience and expertise in managing core. Core work is always in some sense unprecedented, or else it would not be differentiating. That typically requires thinking outside the box. It also implies ongoing iterative experimentation—unprecedented processes never work right the first time; they almost always require tinkering. It takes a special person not only to tolerate but also to thrive in the ambiguity and uncertainty of original development. These folks love to go back to quadrant I, and the good news is that this time you don't have to train them because what they do precedes what trainers would know.

Stepping back from these various local movements, what we see in aggregate is that as work moves from core to context, it passes through three zones:

Resource-Recycling Zones

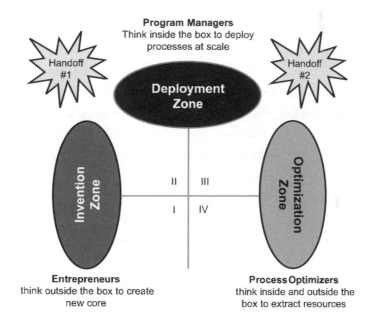

Each of these zones has its defining contribution to value creation. Different value propositions will spend more or less time in different zones, but each will touch all three to some extent. In the invention zone the focus is on creating core. Once the innovation strategy has been selected, this is where it goes first. All the program development, all the test marketing, all the initial customer acquisition, all the pilot projects and specialized customer support—everything it takes to create and validate differentiated offers happens here.

Note that this zone does *not* equate to a department. That is, do not think of invention as being owned by a single function such as R&D or product management. To be sure, if the selected innovation strategy is disruptive innovation, it may well be *led* by R&D. But if the choice is marketing innovation, it will be led by marketing, and if it is process innovation, it will likely be led by operations. Note, too, it does not equate to a phase of the category-maturity life cycle. You have to invent every time you change your innovation vector, then deploy, and eventually optimize. And finally, note we are saying *led* here. The invention zone, like the other two zones as well, is staffed by cross-functional teams who draw from the entire portfolio of corporate resources the skills and support needed to fulfill the zone's mission. No one function dictates to the other. This is an inherently collaborative effort.

What all successful invention zones do have in common are leaders who are gifted entrepreneurs. These are people who make things happen regardless. They are driven by an idealistic vision but are exceedingly pragmatic about how it gets realized. They are typically very quick, highly self-confident, and very focused. They often are horrible managers, but they are terrific motivators. They know where they want to go, and their enthusiasm is contagious. And although they may not know the route, and can often be found charging down blind alleys, they do manage to get there eventually. At the end of the day, people are all about making an impact, and once it is clear they really have, they are ready to move on to the next thing. That is why they like to cycle between quadrants I and II.

When an innovation has proved its viability and demonstrated the kind of market impact that makes companies want to deploy it at scale, it is ready to transition into the deployment zone. The fundamental contributions this zone makes are to harden the programs so they can meet the tests of mission-critical use and be deployed at scale. Again we are talking about a cross-functional team. Every part of the offer—its marketing, its sale, its delivery, its servicing, even its financing—has to be made reliable and scalable. Failure at any link creates a breakdown in deployment that can be potentially catastrophic. Competitive markets rarely give second chances. You do not want to lose a race because of an unscheduled pit stop.

Leaders in the deployment zone are typically gifted program managers. Unlike entrepreneurs who pride themselves on thinking outside the box, these people take pride in thinking *inside* the box. They understand the discipline of getting things done on time, on spec, and on budget. They are typically terrific managers from the point of view of setting expectations, defining deliverables, establishing accountability, installing metrics, securing commitments, and monitoring progress. They communicate accurately and frequently and are good at keeping discussions on topic and to the point. It does not matter to them whether the train is carrying core or context. It only matters that it arrive on time, safely, with its cargo.

They are also overkill for context work. Nonetheless, as long as that work is still mission critical, they are reluctant to let go of it, and management is loath to see them reassigned. That is how they get stuck in quadrant III and end up being missed when needed in quadrant II. To free them up, we need to transition the work once again, this time into the optimization zone.

The optimization zone is focused on continuous improvement in quality and productivity. The two are closely related, for improvements in quality lead to lower costs of support, and improvements in productivity reduce the opportunities for error—a virtuous relationship that was captured in Phil Crosby's influential book, *Quality Is Free*. As in the other zones, work on optimization is inherently cross-functional, much of it here targeting the transaction costs entailed wherever a process transitions from one line function's domain to another's. Early efforts focus on doing these "processes as usual" more efficiently—that's the inside-the-box part of the job.

Later efforts focus on process reengineering, outside-the-box thinking that modularizes and then streamlines processes, reducing risk and even eliminating whole classes of tasks.

Optimization zone efforts are led by process optimizers. These are people who have expertise in industrial engineering, process modeling, quality control systems, and the like. They are able to step back from the specific details of everyday work to see the underlying systems that shape that work and to reshape those systems to reduce friction, improve quality, and lower cost. They also are gifted at evangelizing the cause of process improvement and at converting rank-and-file members of a workforce into everyday process optimizers. Indeed, their goal is that everyone on the workforce who is not actively engaged in the role of inventor or deployer should by default be functioning as an optimizer.

A focus on optimization is commonplace among all companies that are striving to differentiate in commoditizing markets. What is novel in our approach is its focus on freeing up deployment resources to recycle back to core tasks. Companies who omit this dimension fail to field next-generation offers that can stand up to commodity price competition. They make productivity gains through optimization, but their lack of differentiation means they end up having to pass them on to the customer in the form of lower prices. In so doing, they lose the ability to create attractive returns for their investors and initiate the very downward spiral of workforce reductions and increasingly commoditized offerings they were seeking to avoid.

Finally, in addition to three zones, note that the model also calls attention to two handoffs. Transitioning work between zones, it turns out, is something of an unnatural act, in large part because the styles of each zone are so different. In the case of Handoff #1, between the invention and deployment zones, the problem is that entrepreneurs want to transition their offers much earlier than program managers are willing to accept them. That's because in the entrepreneur's mind, the offer is "essentially done," while to the program manager's critical eye, it is trailing loose ends in every direction. The result is that many an innovation falls into a chasm between early adopters, who ignore loose ends, and mainstream pragmatists, who inspect for them relentlessly.

The correct response to this problem is for the executive sponsor of the innovation to directly intervene to manage the handoff phase. This person must keep the entrepreneurs engaged longer than they want and hold them accountable for working with program managers to construct appropriate acceptance criteria for the transitioned product. At the same time, they have to work with the program managers to make sure they have freed up the quality resources needed to bring a next-generation innovation to scale. Since this requires a cross-functional team, the executive sponsor needs to have enough clout to drive support from sales, marketing, engineering, and services. That means, in turn, that they should report to the CEO and be held personally accountable for completing the transition in a timely manner.

When we turn to the second handoff, we see what amounts to a mirror image of the same challenge. That is, whereas the entrepreneur wanted to let go of the offer too soon, the program manager tends to cling to it too long. Ingrained sensitivity to mission-critical risk and its consequences makes program managers reluctant to entrust their offers to an optimization team. Once again, executive intervention is required, but here it is the executive sponsor for optimization who must intercede. This person must ensure that the program manager and process optimizer establish an aggressive time line and clear criteria that allow for accelerating the handoff and recycling the resources. Once again, the cross-functional nature of the program requires cooperation from multiple functions, any one of which is liable to sandbag to retain resources. Optimization executive sponsors, therefore, must have the same kind of clout as their innovation sponsor counterparts and the same kind of direct accountability to the CEO.

Companies that follow this approach to resource recycling are able to embrace outsourcing without jeopardizing the security of their workforces. Instead, they continually renew and refresh the skill sets, and thus the economic value, of every member of the workforce by cycling them through new and different tasks while keeping them within the same value-creation zone. This allows them to build on a common base of experience and best practices while continually reestablishing the relevance of that base to the next generation of offerings.

How this plays out is illustrated by the following diagram:

Resource Recycling Meets Outsourcing

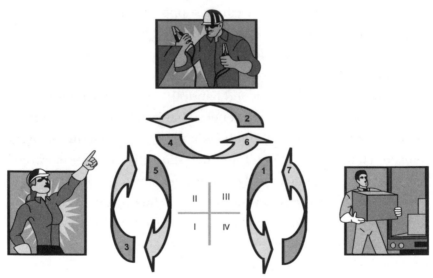

Zone rotations drive perpetual innovation

As we have stated, in this model, work flow and resource allocation circulate through the three zones in a way that combines ongoing innovation with ongoing workforce development and renewal. Let us intercept the process in quadrant III at the time of

Handoff #2 and follow the arrows through one complete cycle to see how it all unfolds:

1. Process optimizers take responsibility for work being done by program managers and begin to apply the five-levers model to reduce risk and extract valuable resources, beginning with the program managers themselves, followed by other deployment resources as the process becomes further de-risked and streamlined.

2. Deployers are now freed to be reallocated into quadrant II, where they can participate in the handoff for a next-generation innovation.

3. Inventors of that next-generation innovation complete their work, meeting the criteria set by the program manager and the executive sponsor.

4. After the handoff, deployers proliferate the offer at scale, allowing the organization to reap the rewards of its investment in innovation. In particular, this is the time to lock in the market-share gains that secure long-term competitive advantage.

5. In the meantime, inventors return to quadrant I to get to work on the next next-generation innovation.

6. Eventually the marketplace catches up with the innovation, and core becomes context. As a primary source of revenue, however, the offer is still mission critical, and therefore it still remains under the control of a deployment-zone program manager and team.

7. Having those resources tied to mission-critical context creates the need for the next wave of process optimization, calling for process optimizers. In order to free up these optimizers from quadrant IV to return to quadrant III, outsourcing the prior wave of optimization is a must.

Thus outsourcing, far from undermining the integrity of the workforce, actually provides a much-needed exhaust vent for work that no longer warrants its attention. The work flow of the five-levers model, in other words, has been completed. Optimizers have squeezed out as much cost and risk as possible, have put in place visibility and control systems to manage what is left, and can now feel comfortable about transitioning the work to another company. Meanwhile, with the next load of mission-critical context arriving in quadrant III, the experience and expertise they have gained through this cycle are in high demand.

Overall, the model asks you to think of work as riding a conveyor belt through the four quadrants and to think of the three zones as gears that continually circulate to keep the work moving. Management is continually increasing shareholder value as it extrudes resource-intensive low-margin work and replaces it with invention-intensive high-margin work. Labor is continually renewing its value by gaining expertise in the next wave of differentiating work, whether it be in the invention, deployment, or optimization zone. Companies as a whole are refreshing their competitive advantage without depleting their financial capital or exploiting their human capital. Indeed, they are creating surpluses in both areas that increase their investment opportunities in the next round of marketplace competition.

Companies who fail to embrace resource recycling, by contrast, sacrifice the future to gain a one-time boost in productivity. They sidestep investing in the next learning curve and thereby reap the benefit of continuing to use a fully trained workforce, but at the cost of trapping themselves in a downward spiral of commoditization. In the future, as differentiation diminishes and margins narrow, their only choice is to continue to exploit the productivity advantages of using experienced labor. By not investing in their workforce's next-generation skills, they render it increasingly incompetent to compete for the next generation of work. In effect, management is liquidating the asset value of its workforce experience in order to meet its operating income targets. It is like selling off the company a piece at a time and declaring the proceeds as operating income. Performance looks great right up until the time you have to shut the doors.

By contrast, companies that do commit to resource recycling can look forward to an ongoing renewal of competitive advantage. This is the mechanism by which companies *can* innovate forever. Each new learning curve is funded by the higher margins that the last learning curve enabled. The one losing behavior in this system is to try to stop the flow. Clinging to work anywhere along the line results in bottlenecks that will bring the gears to a halt and put the person doing the clinging at risk. As Bob Dylan put it in *The Times They Are A-Changin'*, "He who gets hurt will be he who has stalled."

Such wisdom runs counter to the traditional behavior of labor negotiators who seek to preserve jobs that, in reality, everyone would be better off not to preserve. We cannot support the high cost of living of a developed economy by retaining low-value work. We must transition that work to a lower-cost economy where it can still create a good profit margin. In the meantime, we must reach out for the next generation of work that can create the high returns our standard of living requires.

There is an implicit level of faith and trust required to bring this off. Adversarial relationships between labor and management undermine the foundations needed to succeed—as a number of our most mature industries have sadly demonstrated. The lesson we must all learn is that whatever time, talent, and management attention it takes to establish the required level of faith and trust, that is what must be spent.

Dealing with Darwin requires patience and empathy, but it must also maintain an unsentimental realism. There is a time for protectionist actions, but only in service to a transition plan. There is a time for layoffs, but only in service to clearing away past logjams that cannot be worked out through more organic means. Mostly, however, there is the opportunity to create vital and vibrant organizations that thrive in competitive markets and raise the bar for all of us. That is what we must all work together to grasp.

CISCO AND RESOURCE RECYCLING

The function at Cisco that best exemplifies good practices for resource recycling is services. Accounting for roughly 20 percent of the company's $20 billion in 2005 revenues, the services organization consistently delivers high margins and gets high ratings on customer satisfaction. It does so by an exceptionally creative approach to managing core and context through resource recycling.

Before we dig into the details, understand how challenging it is to be a professional services arm of a complex-systems company focused primarily on products. The range of tasks you are asked to take on is extraordinary. At the high end, you are asked to help invent architectures and collaborate with customers on first-of-their-kind systems. At the low end, you are asked to make sure that spare parts are available worldwide to support a 24–7 service commitment to customers and partners. And in between, depending on the time of day, you may be asked to design a network, calm an anxious prospect, fly out to an irate customer, install a major network hub, troubleshoot an erratically performing product, or teach a training class.

In short, services is a high-margin, low-margin, medium-margin, medium-high margin, medium-low margin business. So how in the world do you design an organization that can respond to these demands and still generate high-margin returns?

Cisco begins with a construct it calls Prepare-Plan-Design-Implement-Operate-Optimize. The more you get toward the front end of this sequence, the closer you are to core and the more the services organization wants to engage with the customer directly. By contrast, the more you get to the right, the closer you are to context and the more the services organization wants to engage with customers indirectly through service partners.

Implementation projects lie right in the middle of this spectrum. Classically, systems companies cushion their revenue exposures by taking a large share of these revenues. There are two problems with this tactic. The first is that it alienates potential service partners who are competing for the same work. The second is that over time, as systems standardize, implementation services commoditize, and service organizations find themselves saddled with expensive resources that they cannot bill out at attractive margins.

Both of these problems are widely known, but still the majority of companies fall prey to them because they cannot resist the siren lure of revenue. Cisco can. It is extremely clear that it wants partners to do as much of the implementation work as they possibly can and the customer is willing to allow. In short, Cisco classifies implementation projects as mission-critical context in their strategy along with the downstream processes of operating and optimizing networks. By contrast, it classifies the preparation, planning, and designing processes upstream as mission-critical core, doubly so for customers in their core markets. Thus Cisco Service's resource recycling goal is to extract resources from implementation, operation, and optimization, to repurpose for preparation, planning, and design.

To do this it divides its operations across two groups, Technology Support Services and Advanced Services, the former taking the lead on context, the latter taking the lead on core. The workflow thread that binds the two together is a common focus on the life cycle of intellectual property that pertains to services best practices. Here's how it all plays out.

Services practices have their birth in quadrant I projects where early-adopter customers work with a special unit of the Advanced Services organization on what Cisco calls business transformation projects. These are the most advanced form of services R&D the company engages in, very much an effort from the invention zone. Project leaders have two key deliverables. First they must satisfy the customer and the application requirements of the project itself. Second, they must capture best practices and key learnings from the project and convert them into reusable intellectual property to serve subsequent project teams that engage as these applications become more prevalent. In this way, Cisco can leverage the scarce resources of Advanced Services architects and implementers across a broader population of less experienced consultants, both in-house and among partners.

When growth in demand for a given class of advanced service drives a transition to mission-critical status in quadrant II, Cisco formalizes and standarizes the offering to ensure it can scale. A good example here is network design. Cisco offers design development, design review, and design validation services, customized to the needs of cable and DSL service providers as well as enterprises deploying advanced technologies like wireless or voice-over IP. This exercise in packaging corresponds to Handoff #1 between the invention zone and the deployment zone. The teams that work on business transformation projects are thus freed up to go find additional next-generation projects while the work products are reformulated for broader deployment.

As these deployments are launched at scale, Cisco Services works with the customers across the entire P-P-D-I-O-O life cycle in order to ensure a quality outcome end to end and to secure a superior customer reference to help grow demand for the new service and preference for Cisco. As more and more projects get done, the context nature of the back half of this cycle, the Implement-Operate-Optimize end, comes to the fore. Now is the time for the team to extract resources from context to repurpose for core.

The key again is to capture intellectual property that can enable less scarce resources to perform the work that is encumbering the more scarce ones. In this case, packaging up design templates and training implementation partners in their use allows the scarce resource of network architects to be redeployed on more core tasks. At the same time, it creates business for partners and improves both the quality and the productivity of their delivery. Customers benefit from having readier access to resources at lower cost, partners benefit by getting a steady stream of business that fits their margin model, and Cisco benefits by recycling its resources to the higher-margin work that fits its business model.

As markets scale even further, the focus shifts to quadrant III, and the leadership baton is passed to the technical support organization. Here the goal is to transform what has heretofore been an interaction into a transaction, whether that be an online self-service request or a download of a software tool. This requires even tighter packaging of intellectual property, and that is this organization's specialty.

When customers or partners are confused or stuck, however, they still need interactive support, even if that is not what fits the margin model. Cisco Technical Assistance Centers are 24–7 operations in order to provide such support over the Web, over the phone, or thanks to VOIP, both at the same time. Because this is low-margin business, however, Cisco works hard to outsource it to partners with lower-margin business models. To support these partners, Cisco licenses its proprietary intellectual property and software tools, getting high margins for these deliverables. Once again, the outcome is a win-win-win, with Cisco and the partner both gaining revenue streams that fit their margin models, and the customer getting higher-quality lower-cost service in the process.

If you turn to the executives involved in managing this virtuous cycle, you see something of a poster-child gallery for our three zone profiles. The invention zone is well represented by Sue Bostrom, who was recruited from McKinsey in the 1990s to create the Internet Business Solutions Group, Cisco's original business transformation arm. Sue is a great outside-the-box thinker who likes to break new ground but is happy to pass the baton once an offer has crossed the chasm and is ready to scale. Gary Moore, who heads Advanced Services, has a terrific deployment orientation, having spent much of his career at EDS and prior to that in U.S. Army security. He has brought a strong level of discipline to the services function, expanding its revenues, reinforcing its high-margin model. When his team has run its leg of the race, it hands the baton off to Technical Support, run by Joe Pinto. Joe is an optimizer's optimizer whose first act upon joining Cisco was to convert its technical support operations from a phone to a Web orientation. Today more than four out of every five support requests are solved online at roughly an order of magnitude in cost savings per call. Meanwhile, Pinto is focused on shortening cycle times and packaging IP for partner reuse. Finally, the interactions among these three zones and the teams that populate them is orchestrated by Wim Elfrink. Like Bostrom, he is most comfortable in an invention zone role, which may be why Cisco Services has led the company in adopting the business practices around core/context management and resource recycling.

But services is not the only place where these disciplines are practiced. Actually, an early version was first ushered in by Carl Redfield and Randy Pond, who pioneered and then optimized the outsourcing move to contract manufacturing in the 1990s. In so doing, they solved the dilemma of context buildup by excluding context work from the outset. How they did so and maintained visibility and control at the same time is an interesting story.

Just before Cisco's fortunes took off, the company manufactured its own products and was at the time struggling with a build-to-order model that was more complex than the operations team could reliably manage. Customers were ordering precisely what they wanted, but too often the company would ship something else. The manufacturing team set about solving this problem by installing a preship test system that would automatically download the customer order, test the product to be shipped to confirm compliance with all its elements, and only print the shipping documents if total compliance was achieved.

At the time this system was being rolled out, demand forecasts for Cisco routers were going through the roof. The capital required to build out manufacturing capacity was going to be immense, and so outsourcing came under consideration. Since this was mission critical, however, many were loath to outsource and thereby lose visibility and control over the supply. It was the manufacturing team that had the bright idea of simply installing their test system at the outsourcer. In this way they could maintain the necessary visibility and control without actually managing the process itself, and the company was able to build a worldwide supply chain without creating a legacy of inertia.

Today the manufacturing and logistics functions at Cisco are entering a new era and must once again reinvent their processes. Their earlier solution to the problem has over time become bogged down in context itself. It is too centralized and too standardized to meet the present demands for flexibility and responsiveness. Thus the company is engaged in a new round of reengineering, focusing on modularization, lever number three of the five levers. As it revisits its processes, tags them as core-enabling or context-enabling, cross-tags them as either mission critical or not, Cisco is determining on a more selective basis which ones to outtask and which ones to keep in-house.

Over on the sales side, core/context analysis of markets led to a field operations reorganization in the summer of 2005 to get better execution focus on invention versus deployment. In the past sales had organized by global geographic theater, thereby lumping together all the various types of markets, regardless of where they fit in a core/context analysis. This meant every theater leader had to sort out the mix and be good at managing in each of the three zones. The result of this type of organization is bound to be mixed because it does not allow people to play to their personal strengths.

In the new approach to geographic theaters, the company aggregated its two most established markets—the United States and Canada and Western Europe—and put them under two of its strongest deployment-oriented leaders, Rob Lloyd and Chris Delicoat. This represents a focus on mission-critical context to improve execution efficiencies where the consequences of subpar execution are high. It is leaving its management of India and China under the current regime. This represents continuity in its mission-critical core markets. At the same time, it has aggregated a number of emerging markets in Latin America and the Caribbean, the Middle East and Africa, Russia and the Commonwealth of Independent States (CIS), and Eastern Europe, and put them all under one of its strongest invention-oriented leaders, Paul Mountford, who had just demonstrated his creativity by leading the revitalization of the small-to-medium business market. This represents an investment in a series of non-mission-critical core markets to accelerate their transition to $1 billion mission-critical materiality. Overall, by pulling the emerging markets out from under the established markets, each type of market will get better execution focus, and different types of leader will be able to perform at their peak.

Finally, on the engineering side, Cisco is still finding its way toward resource recycling. Management clearly understands the core/context dynamics at work, but it is blocked by the depth of task expertise required to take on the next generation of technology. Repurposing for core implies that your current talent can step up to that transition in a timely manner. But if the transition is to a whole new discipline—say, from optoelectronics to services-oriented software design—there is too big a gap to cross.

My own view is that such gaps are the exception, not the rule, and that management needs to get more aggressive with resource recycling, in part to ensure that the cash cows don't hoard key deployment resources. But in the meantime, the company is taking a different approach to the core/context challenge. It is still extracting resources from context, but instead of repurposing them for engineering the next generation of core, it is transferring them to field-facing roles in pre- and postsales support to help deploy that next generation. This transition has its own challenges, essentially those of a changing profession, but in the high-tech sector, there is enough commonality across these roles to make that transition a practical alternative.

Overall, under Chambers's leadership, there has been continued emphasis at Cisco on the need to address the issues of core/context dynamics and resource recycling. But he is not prescriptive about how. The ideas and practices outlined in this chapter are competing for management attention with other alternatives. What is not in question is the end goal. Chambers is adamant about transforming Cisco into a company that can innovate forever and anchoring that transformation in a culture that uses job assignments creatively to increase the asset value of its people every year.

CHAPTER ELEVEN

MANAGING INERTIA
IN YOUR ENTERPRISE

T o close our discussion of managing inertia, let us look at how you might go about applying its lessons within your own enterprise. As with our earlier discussion of managing innovation, this is an unabashedly how-to chapter. Unlike that earlier chapter, however, this one needs to start out with a warning.

The undertakings of core/context analysis and resource recycling are both politically charged. In the case of the former, there are powerful interests vested in context that may well take offense at any attempt to curtail their access to prime resources. Personal compensation and promotion are both either actually at stake or perceived to be, and such rewards are always contested. Similarly, when it comes to outsourcing and resource recycling, whenever job security is either actually threatened or perceived to be, that threat extends beyond the individuals involved to the welfare of the families they support. When our families are threatened, even the most peaceable among us will counterattack.

In short, dealing with Darwin asks us to engage with some of the most volatile issues in our workplace. And engage with them we should. We just need to be thoughtful about how. Volatile issues need to be aired multiple times before they can be directly addressed. People need a chance to put things in perspective before they are asked to make commitments. Doubt, anxiety, suspicion, and cynicism need to float to the surface, be aired, and be dispelled before an organization can move on.

All this is the job of leadership and management. The role of the frameworks we have been developing in this section is to give shape to these discussions. They should be introduced early on in the process to provide a common vocabulary for working through the challenges of extracting resources from context to repurpose for core. They should not, however, be expected to win people's hearts and minds all by themselves. Only patient dialogue can do that.

With these caveats in mind, we can now lay out an aggressive agenda for redirecting the inertial momentum of your enterprise from context to core. The essential steps of that agenda are as follows:

1. *Conduct a core/context analysis of your current business.*

Begin with categorizing your various market segments in terms of the four quadrants. In the case of complex systems enterprises, these will typically consist of multiple grids to represent how core and context play out by product category, customer industry, and geography. In volume-operations businesses, one is likely to develop views by product category, consumer demographics (which include geography), and sales channel.

Take time to debate these placements because they help guide resource-allocation decisions downstream. Because these issues are subjective, you can expect a diversity of views. At the end of the day, however, everyone needs to be on the same page in order to go further.

2. *Conduct a resource-allocation analysis to complement your core/context analysis.*

Do not get distracted by budgets here. Focus on head count, specifically on identifying and locating your top performers in each of the three zone disciplines: invention, deployment, and optimization. These are individuals whose leadership or functional expertise can change the outcome of a project, and you want to make sure you are leveraging their skills to the maximum.

3. *Set a more ambitious agenda.*

Now that you have mapped out how things are, turn to determining how you want them to be. The reason you are doing this exercise is that you are not satisfied with your enterprise's current performance. The question is, how would you improve it?

Essentially your effort consists of:

- targeting one or more core opportunities for intensified attention

- determining the top performers who can best drive the programs (this may identify the need for one or two key hires)

- targeting one or more context opportunities for resource extraction, again with particular reference to top performers

You want this process to take managers outside their comfort zone. If it goes smoothly, you probably aren't being ambitious enough.

4. *Plan out your moves as a team.*

Extracting resources from context to repurpose for core is a collaborative effort. Withholding even one key resource in an act of self-serving suboptimization can put the entire effort at risk. Moreover, getting the timing right is critical as well, for it does no good to free up resources if the work they are meant to do is not yet ready to be done. Sorting these issues out begins with collaborating within each line function and ends with collaborating across functions, all with a view toward reaching a common coordinated plan.

5. *Focus on time to market.*

To create a necessary and proper sense of urgency, make a direct assault on the scheduling assumptions of your plan of record. These assumptions were made in response to a given set of resource constraints, and the goal of this process is to use aggressive resource recycling to remove those constraints as much as possible.

6. *Get the gears moving.*

Focus initial efforts on freeing up top-performing deployers from their current mission-critical context assignments. Assign optimizers to attack their workloads with a five-levers approach, and set a date for their last day in their current roles. Meanwhile, manage inventors more closely than usual to accelerate the readiness of the next-generation innovations for mission-critical deployment. Drive the entire organization to earlier achievement of Handoffs #1 and #2.

7. *Keep the gears moving.*

Once resource recycling has begun, you must not let it stop. Remember that each new learning curve is paid for by the margins created by the last curve and in turn is expected to generate high-margin returns to fund the next one. If any gear stops rotating, the other gears either have to stop—which starts the downward spiral of commoditization—or continue to turn—which will create gaps and shortages elsewhere in the system. You have to maintain the entire operation in a continuing ongoing act of replenishment.

In sum, these steps outline a new strategy for managing inertia. It is based on keeping all parts of the organization in perpetual motion, continually refreshing the offer portfolio for the marketplace and the skill sets of the workforce. It does not see inertial momentum as the enemy of innovation but rather as its legacy. It does not seek to stop it or jettison it but rather to redirect it. Extracting resources from context to repurpose for core is a formula for the incremental redirection of inertial mass. That is what we are doing here.

Both management and labor must be vigilant to make this strategy succeed. Management must not succumb to the temptation to harvest the current skills of the workforce a bit longer, gaining a short-term productivity gain at the expense of long-term viability. Labor must not succumb to the temptation to go along with this strategy and coast for a bit on its past accomplishments. And both must resist the siren lure of entitlement, the notion that at some point we get to stop producing competitively but still get to be compensated as if we were. That's not the way Darwin works.

Natural selection is a game with no time-outs. It does, however allow for unlimited substitutions. Resource recycling not only delivers efficiency; it also provides refreshment. There is respite for the weary as long as it is followed by an energized willingness to reengage. What we cannot afford is to carry nonperformers. That is why a no-layoff policy does not serve. There are times in some people's lives when they are simply unable to commit the necessary energy to work. We must respect those times, but we cannot allow that behavior to encumber the greater good of the enterprise.

So sometimes resource recycling does mean firing people. Just as it sometimes means that new people are hired. The notions that companies should provide lifetime employment or that individuals should give lifetime loyalty are not consistent with the nature of modern economics or modern life. What is consistent is to make better use of our collective creative intelligence to increase the returns on our mutual efforts and to share the rewards thereof equitably with all our stakeholders.

Communities need abiding sources of employment. Customers need stable sources of supply. Governments need a vital tax base. Investors need opportunities to create attractive risk-adjusted returns. We are all more or less strategically aligned. We are just being asked to execute at a new level of competitiveness.

That's what evolution is all about, a continual raising of the bar. It's how countries raise their standard of living. It's why new companies get formed every year. It's why each of us must learn new skills throughout our careers. We may get tired, but we are not likely to get bored. Mostly we just have to perform.

Welcome to the race.

GLOSSARY

- **acquisition innovation**. See *innovation types*. Creating differentiation through acquisition and divestiture, regardless of whether you are the acquiring or acquired party.
- **application innovation**. See *innovation types*. Creating differentiation by finding and exploiting a new application or use for an existing technology. The cornerstone of solution-oriented marketing.
- **bowling alley**. See *technology-adoption life cycle*. A stage in the technology adoption life cycle during which technology is being adopted for niche markets but not yet for broad horizontal usage.
- **brand**. The mental associations aroused by the name of a company or product. A key tool for the volume operations model to gain customer preference in consumer markets. In the complex systems model, a frequent source of management confusion (see *reputation*).
- **business architecture**. Organizational structure based on prioritizing one of two business models (see *complex-systems model* and *volume-operations model*). Innovation types are understood and executed in completely different ways depending on which model an enterprise adopts.
- **CAP,** or **Competitive Advantage Period**. See *managing for shareholder value*. A term used in investment analysis to estimate the length of time an investor believes a company can maintain a differentiated position that creates competitive separation.
- **category.** A term used by customers to classify what they are buying and distinguish it from other purchasing choices. Emerging

categories are typically defined by naming one or more reference competitors. Established categories help analysts follow a market and investors determine their asset-allocation strategies.

- **category maturity life cycle**. A model that describes the rise, duration, and decline of a category of product or service.
- **category power**. See *hierarchy of powers*. Competitive advantage gained by participating in a given category and thereby inheriting its ability to compete with other categories of purchase for budget. Growth markets increase category power, declining markets diminish it.
- **chasm**. See *technology-adoption life cycle*. A stage in the technology-adoption life cycle during which the market stagnates for lack of a natural customer constituency to sponsor it. Visionaries who used to sponsor the category have moved on to other interests. Pragmatists are now the desired sponsors, but they do not see enough adoption activity by their peers to be comfortable supporting the new paradigm.
- **chimp**. See *market-share hierarchies*. A market-share position that is subordinate to the market leader, or gorilla, in a market where both vendors have proprietary technology that is incompatible with the other's. To survive, chimps must typically create strongholds in niche markets where they are the local market leader, or "gorilla in the niche."
- **collaboration culture**. See *corporate culture*. One of four business cultures, it is rooted in the need for affiliation and characterized by team-level accountability to subjectively understood determined values. For example, the original HP.
- **commoditization**. The natural result of free-market competition over time as vendors neutralize more and more of one another's differentiation. It enables customers to swap one vendor for another, thereby engendering price competitions that eliminate profit margins for all but the most operationally excellent firms.
- **company power**. See *hierarchy of powers*. Competitive advantage gained by virtue of a company's market-share status in within a

given product category. Characteristically the market share leader has the most power, with a significant drop-off to vendor #2, and an even more drastic drop-off for vendor #3. Hence Jack Welch's strategic intent to be number one or two in a market or else exit.

- **competence culture**. See *corporate culture*. One of four business cultures, it is rooted in the need for achievement and characterized by individual-level accountability to objectively defined metrics. For example, Microsoft.

- **competitive advantage grid**. A model for analyzing competitive advantage strategies within a given category based on a matrix of type of power sought (category, company, market, and offer), cross-referenced by value-discipline focus to create differentiation (operational excellence, customer intimacy, product leadership, disruptive innovation).

- **competitive separation**. Differentiation that causes customers to perceive a given company's offers differently from those of the other companies in its competitive set, thereby reducing the threat of substitution and increasing its ability to command a premium price or greater volume in its target markets.

- **complex-systems model**. See *business architecture*. One of two business architectures, it is optimized for business-to-business commerce with large institutional buyers making substantial purchases after careful consideration of the alternatives and characterized by consultative sales relationships and a high proportion of customization in the development of each customer's offer.

- **conservative**. See *technology-adoption life cycle*. An adoption strategy that embraces new technologies only when they threaten to completely displace older established alternatives.

- **context**. See *core/context analysis*. Any activity that does not differentiate the company from the customer's viewpoint in the target market. Context management seeks to meet (but not exceed) appropriate accepted standards in as productive a manner as possible.

- **control culture**. See *corporate culture*. One of four business cultures, it is rooted in the need for order and security and characterized by team-level accountability to objectively defined metrics. For example, General Electric.

- **core**. See *core/context analysis*. Any activity that creates sustainable differentiation in the target market resulting in premium prices or increased volume. Core management seeks to dramatically outperform all competitors within the domain of core. (Note this use of the term is unrelated to either *core competence,* which describes differentiated capability, or *core business,* which describes categories accounting for a high percentage of overall revenues.)

- **core/context analysis**. A resource prioritization framework that discriminated differentiating processes from all other work. Core/context management advocates funding differentiating initiatives in growth markets by extracting resources (carefully) from mission-critical context initiatives in mature markets.

- **corporate culture**. A set of implicit rules that shapes communication, motivation, and decision-making. In the TCG Advisors' model, there are four archetypal cultures cultures—cultivation, competence, control, and collaboration—based on privileging one or another layer of Maslow's hierarchy of needs.

- **crossing the chasm**. See *technology-adoption life cycle*. The transition in a technology-adoption life cycle that represents the first penetration of the mainstream market, typically achieved by targeting a beachhead segment of pragmatist customers who are under pressure to address a problem that current technologies cannot solve.

- **cultivation culture**. See *corporate culture*. One of four business cultures, it is rooted in the need for self-actualization and characterized by individual accountability to subjectively defined values. For example, Google.

- **customer intimacy**. See *value disciplines*. One of three value disciplines, it invests heavily in customer information gathering in order to differentiate offerings by aligning them more precisely with target customers' needs and values.

- **Darwinian.** An adjective to describe the ongoing raising-the-bar effects of free-market competition for the scarce resources of customer revenue and investor capital, which forces established competitive advantage positions to either evolve or else become commoditized.

- **declining market.** See *category maturity life cycle*. A period in the maturity of a market when, setting aside cyclical fluctuations, growth rates are negative. Strategically, a time to either reinvigorate the category or to harvest and exit.

- **delighter.** A novel attribute of a mature-market offer that creates customer preference without increasing cost or introducing risk.

- **demographic segmentation.** A method of analyzing markets in terms of customer communities based on shared demographic characteristics such as age, income, gender, or ethnicity; typically used to focus consumer offers in volume-operations markets.

- **deployers.** See *resource recycling*. People who excel at managing mission-critical programs on time, on spec, and on budget, deployers are key to ramping business processes to scale.

- **deployment zone.** See *resource recycling*. The upper two quadrants in the core/context analysis model that share the attribute of being mission critical, the zone most scrutinized by securities analysts and growth investors. The natural zone in which to recycle deployers.

- **discontinuous technology.** See *disruptive innovation*. One of two types of disruptive innovation, discontinuous technology is incompatible with currently prevailing standards, forcing those who adopt it to displace their existing systems, thereby initiating a technology-adoption life cycle.

- **disruptive innovation**. See *innovation types*. An innovation type that initiates a growth market by creating a new category through one of two mechanisms: discontinuous technology or value-chain discontinuity.

- **dissatisfier.** An attribute of a mature-market offer that, poorly handled, can cause customers to reject the offer, but which, if brilliantly handled, would not lead to customer preference.

- **early market.** See *technology-adoption life cycle*. A stage in the technology-adoption life cycle during which technology enthusiasts and visionaries sponsor new technologies while the mainstream marketplace watches but does not participate.
- **enhancement innovation.** See *innovation types*. An innovation type in the customer intimacy zone that differentiates a mature market position by leveraging a modest R&D investment to create a large increase in the perceived value of an established offer to re-stimulate customer interest.
- **experiential innovation**. See *innovation types*. An innovation type in the customer intimacy zone that differentiates an otherwise commoditized offer in a mature market by modifying the customer's end-to-end experience from initial encounter to ultimate disposition.
- **fault line.** See *category maturity life cycle*. A transition very late in the category maturity life cycle when a category becomes obsolete by virtue of a discontinuous technology or disruptive innovation entering the tornado.
- **GAP, or Competitive Advantage Gap.** See *managing for shareholder value*. A term used in investment analysis that interprets a company's current reported revenue and margin performance as a gauge of the competitive separation it currently enjoys in its target markets.
- **gorilla.** See *market-share hierarchies*. A market-share leader whose position is sustained by proprietary technology that has high switching costs, leading to both high GAP and long CAP, the marks of exceptional shareholder value.
- **growth market.** See *category maturity life cycle*. A period in the development of a market when growth rates are significantly in excess of 10 percent. Strategically, a time when gains in market share create more shareholder value than maximizing profits.
- **hierarchy of powers**. A model organizing type of business power from most strategic to most tactical, as follows: category power, company power, market power, offer power, program power.

- **horizons 1, 2, and 3.** A strategy management model outlined by Merhdad Baghai, Stephen Coley, and David White in *The Alchemy of Growth*, it segments strategic initiatives into three time zones—1) the current fiscal year, 2) the twelve-to eighteen-month period just beyond the current year, and 3) developments further out in time than that.
- **indefinitely elastic middle.** See *category maturity life cycle*. The duration of a mature market, commencing with the end of the growth market phase, ending with the onset of the declining market phase.
- **industry segmentation.** A method of analyzing markets in terms of customer communities based on participating in a common industry sector. In business-to-business marketing, the primary organizing principle of vertical marketing and the key to crossing-the-chasm and bowling-alley strategy.
- **inertia.** A risk-averse characteristic of established enterprises that privileges allocating resources to current lines of business and resists redeploying them into emerging ones.
- **innovation for differentiation.** See *innovation outcomes*. Innovation initiatives that succeed in creating competitive separation from reference competitors in target markets.
- **innovation for neutralization.** See *innovation outcomes*. Innovation initiatives that succeed in reducing or eliminating a competitive separation achieved by a reference competitor in a target market.
- **innovation outcomes.** The economic results of an investment in innovation, of which there are four: differentiation, productivity, neutralization of a competitive differentiator, or waste.
- **innovation for productivity.** See *innovation outcomes*. Innovation initiatives that improve the return on resources deployed by increasing their yield.
- **innovation strategy.** Intensely focusing on one or two innovation vectors to create competitive separation. Specifically, fielding highly differentiated offerings that dramatically outperform competitive alternatives in the dimensions targeted.

- **innovation that is wasted.** See *innovation outcomes*. Innovation that does not result in differentiation, neutralization, or productivity. Specifically, innovation that seeks to differentiate for competitive advantage but fails to generate privileged treatment from customers in their purchase behavior.
- **innovation types.** A model of innovation that compares and contrasts fourteen different approaches to creating differentiation for competitive advantage.
- **innovation vector.** The idea that each type of innovation can be thought of as a strategic direction for investment that competes for resources with alternative vectors. An enterprise's overall differentiation is the sum of its performance along all vectors that, were resources allocated equally, would equate to zero—hence the need for innovation strategy.
- **integration innovation.** See *innovation types*. An innovation type in the operational excellence zone that differentiates a mature-market position by integrating a set of established products and services into a single more easily managed offering.
- **invention zone.** See *resource recycling*. The left two quadrants in the core/context analysis model that share the attribute of being core, the zone most scrutinized by industry analysts and venture investors. The natural zone in which to recycle inventors.
- **inventors.** See *resource recycling*. People who excel at developing core, inventors are key to ensuring a continuous supply of innovations that create sustainable competitive advantage.
- **investable category.** An existing product or service category in which market shares are tracked by securities analysts seeking to help investors allocate their capital optimally first by category, then by company.
- **killer app.** An application with broad horizontal appeal that catapults a category into the tornado phase of the technology-adoption life cycle.
- **king.** See *market-share hierarchies*. A market-share leader whose position is sustained primarily by execution. Compared to gorillas,

kings typically have equally high GAPs but, because they can be more readily swapped out, significantly shorter CAPs, resulting in lower shareholder value.

- **line-extension innovation.** See *innovation types.* An innovation type in the customer intimacy zone that creates a new subcategory to engage a new customer or reengage an old one by targeting their unique preferences.

- **Main Street.** See *technology-adoption life cycle.* The last stage of the technology adoption life cycle, coming at the end of the tornado, it signals a rise in the strategic importance of the conservative customer.

- **managing for shareholder value.** A management discipline that uses long-term investor valuation criteria to prioritize strategic initiatives. An analytical tool that analyzes market capitalization as a function of GAP times CAP.

- **market.** An aggregation of economic activity, organized either by customer or by product segmentation, which sets the context for market-share metrics from which market power is inferred.

- **marketing innovation.** See *innovation types.* An innovation type in the customer intimacy zone that differentiates a mature-market position through novel go-to-market programs affecting interaction with the prospective customer, typically in marketing communications and distribution channels.

- **market power.** See *hierarchy of powers.* Competitive advantage gained by virtue of a company's market-share status in a given customer segment or niche specialty, typically used to offset the company power of a market-share leader.

- **market-share hierarchies.** A model for describing the pecking order in marketplace power among the market leader, a close challenger, and an also-ran. In proprietary-technology-enabled markets with high switching costs, the roles are gorilla, chimp, and monkey. In commoditized markets with low switching costs, the corresponding roles are king, prince, and serf.

- **mature market.** See *category maturity life cycle.* A period in the development of a market when, setting aside cyclical fluctuations, growth rates are modest, typically of less than 10 percent. Strategically, a time when profits take precedence over revenues and market share.

- **monkey.** See *market-share hierarchies*. A company with little to no market share in a category dominated by a gorilla, its strategy is to reproduce the gorilla's in-market offering as best it can and sell it at a substantial discount.
- **mission critical.** Material to outcomes that are central to the fate of a company. Shortfalls in mission-critical activities jeopardize market valuation, among other things.
- **mission-critical context.** See *core/context analysis*. Mission-critical context consists of activities that must be executed to market expectations else dire consequences ensue; however, doing these activities better than others yields no increased differentiation and profit. Strategically, an area where resources are overallocated leading to an underallocation for next-generation initiatives.
- **natural selection.** The outcome of competitions for scarce resources in which winners are more fully represented in the next round and losers are marginalized. Strategically, it drives an evolution in differentiation in search of greater competitive advantage.
- **nine-point checklist.** A product-marketing tool for describing the key variables that make up a market-development strategy. The nine points are: 1) target customer, 2) compelling reason to buy, 3) whole product, 4) partners and allies, 5) distribution, 6) pricing, 7) competition, 8) positioning, and 9) next target customer.
- **offer power.** See *hierarchy of powers*. Competitive advantage gained by virtue of fielding a product or service that has superior features, performance, or price relative to a reference competitor in a target market.
- **off-shoring.** Procuring a given product or service from a company located in another country, whether to exploit a cost advantage, tap into a talent pool, or establish a point of entry into a foreign market.

- **operational excellence.** See *value disciplines.* One of three value disciplines, it invests heavily in processes and systems to differentiate offerings by lower cost, higher quality, or faster time to market.
- **optimization zone.** See *resource recycling.* The right two quadrants in the core/context analysis model that share the attribute of being context, the zone most scrutinized by productivity analysts and value investors. The natural zone in which to recycle optimizers.
- **optimizers.** See *resource recycling.* People who excel at extracting resources from mission-critical context to repurpose for core, optimizers are key to funding the next wave of innovation and deconstructing the organizations that would create inertial resistance to it.
- **organic renewal innovation.** See *innovation types.* An innovation type in the category renewal zone that differentiates a declining market position by migrating resources from a declining category to a growth one, typically through in-house R&D.
- **outsourcing.** Procuring a given product or service from another company rather than staffing it in-house, whether to take advantage of that company's specialization advantages or to focus in-house resources on core.
- **out-tasking.** Procuring a portion of given product or service from another company while retaining a portion in-house, whether to mitigate mission-critical risk or to retain an option on using it to create future core.
- **platform innovation.** See *innovation types.* An innovation type in the product-leadership zone that differentiates a growth market position by consolidating the interface to a legacy environment in service to a next generation of emerging offerings.
- **positioning.** Strategically, influencing the category that a product or company occupies inside a buyer's mind, thereby establishing its reference competitors. Tactically, comparing and contrasting an offer relative to its reference competitors.
- **pragmatist.** See *technology-adoption life cycle.* An adoption strategy

that embraces new technologies when its proponents see others like them adopting them, a follow-the-herd approach that is particularly sensitive to word-of-mouth references.

- **prince.** See *market-share hierarchies.* A market-share challenger whose position is sustained primarily by execution as opposed to proprietary technology with high switching costs. Compared to chimps, princes have far more volatile CAPs because they have the opportunity to displace kings as the market leader but also the vulnerability of being displaced by some another would-be prince.

- **process innovation.** See *innovation types.* An innovation type in the operational excellence zone that differentiates a mature market position by reengineering fundamental processes to create exceptional gains in cost reduction, quality, or time to market.

- **product innovation.** See *innovation types.* An innovation type in the product leadership zone that differentiates a growth market position by R&D to improve features, performance, or market price in an established product category.

- **product leadership.** See *value disciplines.* One of three value disciplines, it invests heavily in R&D to differentiate offerings by more desirable features, better performance, or lower market price.

- **program power.** See *hierarchy of powers.* Competitive advantage gained by virtue of fielding superior go-to-market programs relative to a reference competitor in a target market.

- **reputation.** The mental associations aroused by naming a company or product, in a complex-systems market. A superior term to *brand* when analyzing returns on marketing investments in a complex-systems enterprise.

- **resource recycling.** A human capital management strategy that recycles a workforce to optimize an individual's contributions in one of three zones: invention, deployment, or optimization. A work-management strategy that deconstructs inertia-bearing legacy in order to fuel and accelerate the adoption of next-generation innovations.

- **sectoring.** In contrast to *segmentation,* a scheme that imposes zones on a market to organize territory coverage and sales channel management.

- **segmentation.** Within contrast to *sectoring*, a scheme that infers zones in a market from customers self-organizing into communities of interest. Used to focus market share gains and intensify word-of-mouth references.

- **serf.** See *market-share* hierarchies. A market-share also-ran in a market with low switching costs, serfs enter and exit product categories opportunistically based on short-lived offer power advantages. They are the ultimate commoditizing force. Compared to monkeys, serfs have lower barriers to entry as there is no proprietary technology to clone.

- **skeptic.** See *technology-adoption life cycle*. An adoption strategy that resists the adoption of technologies to the end, believing that the law of unintended consequences will undermine whatever gains they purport to offer.

- **technology-adoption life cycle.** A model that describes how communities react to the introduction of a discontinuous technology, consisting of a progression through five adoption strategies: technology enthusiast, visionary, pragmatist, conservative, and skeptic.

- **technology enthusiast.** See *technology-adoption life cycle*. An adoption strategy that embraces discontinuous technologies on a personal basis as an opportunity to learn and to participate in the leading edge of technology innovation.

- **tornado.** See *technology-adoption life cycle*. A stage in the technology-adoption life cycle during which pragmatist customers, spurred by the appearance of a killer app, enter the market in droves, driving demand to exceed supply, creating a frenzy of expansion and a meteoric rise in equity valuations.

- **value chain.** A progression of processes and providers required to take a product or service from creation through to customer delivery and eventually to disposal.

- **value-chain discontinuity.** One of two forms of disruptive innovation, a value-chain discontinuity destabilizes the value chain in an existing market by challenging the business model of the incumbent. It does not, however, initiate a new technology-adoption life cycle.

- **value disciplines.** A strategy-development model championed by Michael Treacy and Fred Wiersema in *The Value Disciplines of Market Leaders* that focuses value creation on one of three areas: product leadership, customer intimacy, or operational excellence.

- **value-engineering innovation.** See *innovation types.* An innovation type in the operational excellence zone that differentiates a mature-market position by extracting costs from an established product or process design.

- **value-migration innovation.** See *innovation types.* An innovation type in the operational excellence zone that differentiates a mature-market position by transferring focus from a value-losing element in a value chain to a value-gaining one. Two classic value-chain migrations seen in maturing markets are the shifts from product to consumables and from products to services.

- **vertical marketing.** Marketing focused on gaining dominant market share in an industry segment, thereby creating a the market-power position "gorilla in the niche."

- **visionary.** See *technology-adoption life cycle.* An adoption strategy that works with technology enthusiasts to sponsor first-mover adoption of discontinuous technologies in order to gain a dramatic competitive advantage.

- **volume-operations model.** One of two business architectures, optimized for business-to-consumer commerce with individual customers making buying decisions at the point of purchase. More generally, a business model with a high proportion of standardization in the development, distribution, and service of each customer's offer.

- **whole product.** The minimum set of products and services needed to fulfill a target customer's compelling reason to buy, especially important during the bowling-alley phase of the technology-adoption life cycle.

INDEX